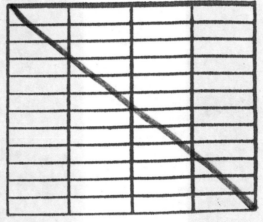

DISTANCE EDUCATION

John R. Verduin, Jr.
Thomas A. Clark

DISTANCE EDUCATION

The Foundations
of Effective Practice

Jossey-Bass Publishers

San Francisco • Oxford • 1991

DISTANCE EDUCATION
The Foundations of Effective Practice
by John R. Verduin, Jr., and Thomas A. Clark

Library of Congress Cataloging-in-Publication Data

Verduin, John R.
    Distance education: the foundations of effective practice / John
R. Verduin, Jr., Thomas A. Clark
        p.   cm.—(The Jossey-Bass higher and adult education series)
    Includes bibliographical references (p.) and index.
    ISBN 1-55542-306-X
    1. Distance education.   I. Clark, Thomas A., date.
II. Title.   III. Series.
    LC5800.V47   1991
    374—dc20   90-46107

Manufactured in the United States of America

The paper in this book meets the guidelines for
permanence and durability of the Committee on
Production Guidelines for Book Longevity of the
Council on Library Resources.

Two taxonomies are reprinted here:
From TAXONOMY OF EDUCATIONAL OBJECTIVES: The
Classification of Educational Goals: Handbook I; COGNITIVE
DOMAIN, by Benjamin S. Bloom et al. Copyright © 1956 by
Longman Publishing Group.
From TAXONOMY OF EDUCATIONAL OBJECTIVES: HANDBOOK
II; AFFECTIVE DOMAIN, by David R. Krathwohl et al. Copyright © 1964
by Longman Publishing Group. Reprinted by permission of Longman
Publishing Group.

JACKET DESIGN BY WILLI BAUM

FIRST EDITION

Code 9107

The Jossey-Bass
Higher and Adult Education Series

Consulting Editor
Adult and Continuing Education

Alan B. Knox
University of Wisconsin, Madison

Contents

Preface

Distance education, although a popular and effective concept in other countries, is still something of an unknown quantity in the United States and, with the possible exception of correspondence courses and telecourses, has until now had little impact here. Why has it not caught on to a greater extent in the United States? In light of its efficacy, it certainly warrants more careful consideration. Perhaps one reason is the relative accessibility of more traditional modes of educational delivery for adults, through the vast networks of community colleges, other colleges and universities, adult learning centers, proprietary schools, and schools associated with business, industry, the military, and other agencies and organizations. These delivery systems serve some fifty million adults, an impressive number indeed.

Yet another reason for the limited availability of distance education—one of the principal ones, we believe—is American postsecondary educators' lack of awareness about just what distance education is, how it operates, and what it can do for adult learning. It is to address this point that we have written *Distance Education*. We have briefly discussed the effectiveness and potential use of distance education in an earlier piece of writing (see Clark and Verduin, 1989) but felt that further research and elaboration were needed.

It is increasingly important for adult educators to give careful consideration to distance education as a means of education. More adults than ever before are entering the educational system, and this phenomenon will continue for some time to come, in part because of the proliferating demands of our technological society and in part because the complexities of modern life—the constant pressure and the juggling of time and responsibilities—make it necessary for adults to seek forms of learning other than the traditional ones.

Although adults learn constantly on their own, much of that learning lacks the guidance and structure a formal educational system can provide. Distance education offers such a framework, as well as advice and feedback from an instructor, while retaining many of the advantages of self-directed, self-planned learning.

This book will serve as a general introduction to distance education for students of adult education and postsecondary educators who lack familiarity with its history, potential, and current status. However, in addition to introducing distance education, we develop guidelines, theories, models, and structures—a knowledge base for incorporating distance education into the U.S. adult education system. Because the guidelines and models presented in the chapters to follow are general in nature, educators must adapt them to the situations at their institutions in ways that meet the needs and goals of individual adult students.

Audience

While teachers at postsecondary institutions, especially institutions of higher education, will profit most directly from the ideas and processes we present, these concepts are also applicable and relevant to other agencies and organizations involved in adult education, such as business, industry, and the military. These organizations have, in fact, made some use of distance education but might be encouraged to intensify their use of it if they were aware of the opportunities that newer delivery modes offer for reaching greater numbers of potential adult learners.

Overview of the Contents

Distance Education is divided into three parts. Part One provides an introduction to the concept of distance education. Chapter

One offers definitions and a historical overview, and Chapter Two a brief description of adults' need and desire for learning.

In Part Two, we undertake an extensive review of current ideas and findings about distance education. Chapter Three identifies six major distance education models for higher education. Chapter Four discusses in detail the current modes of delivery for distance education, and Chapter Five offers an overall appraisal of distance education and compares its effectiveness to that of more traditional modes of education.

Building on that analysis, in Part Three we offer suggestions for implementing distance education. Chapter Six presents theoretical constructs about distance education that build on Moore's theory of transactional distance. In this chapter, we develop the concepts of dialogue and support, structure and specialized competence, and general competence and self-directedness. We propose a foundation for the entire distance education process. Chapter Seven contains a teaching model that takes into account entering behavior, specification of objectives, learning unit design, communication and interaction, and student assessment. The model is tied into a theory of learning that is based on the perceptions of adult learners. Chapter Eight, in which we discuss the organization and administration of distance education, includes guidelines on communication and program evaluation. In the concluding chapter, Chapter Nine, we explore potential directions that distance education may take in the United States in the future. We examine social phenomena such as demographic changes, greater involvement of women and minorities in the work force, and the growing need for technological skills, all of which will increase the need for adult learning through distance education. We review trends and predictions and proffer suggestions about what might be done to make distance education a more viable and worthwhile delivery system for adult education. As a corollary to the discussion in Chapter Five on the effectiveness of distance education as a mode of delivery, the Resource at the end of the book contains an extensive annotated bibliography of research in the field, which allows the reader to see at a glance what comparative studies have been done.

It is our hope that this book will show the way for new opportunities in distance education that will enable more adults to take up learning challenges they might otherwise not have tackled—or to pursue their education with less disruption to their lives than they could through traditional education.

Acknowledgments

We would like to acknowledge the tremendous assistance offered by Patricia Cochran and Patricia Glover as they did the word processing on numerous drafts of this manuscript. Their help was invaluable.

Above all, we appreciate the continued support and encouragement of our family members—Janet, John, and Susan Verduin, and Charlotte Clark and Elmer Clark.

Carbondale, Illinois   John R. Verduin, Jr.
December 1990   Thomas A. Clark

The Authors

John R. Verduin, Jr., is professor in the Department of Educational Administration and Higher Education at Southern Illinois University, Carbondale. He received his B.S. degree in biology and chemistry from the University of Albuquerque (1954), his M.A. degree in educational administration from Michigan State University (1959), and his Ph.D. degree in curriculum, with a cognate in sociology, also from Michigan State University (1962).

His early research interests focused on curriculum process and teacher education, but more recently he has turned to the field of adult and continuing education. He has also published in the field of education for the gifted. His experience includes public school teaching, college and university teaching, and administration in college and in adult education projects. Verduin's books include *Adults Teaching Adults: Principles and Strategies* (1977, with others), *The Adult Educator: A Handbook for Staff Development* (1979, with H. Miller), *Curriculum Building for Adult Learning* (1980), *Adults and Their Leisure: The Need for Lifelong Learning* (1984, with D. McEwen), and *The Lifelong Learning Experience: An Introduction* (1986, with others). He has contributed several chapters in books and has published in numerous journals, including *Lifelong Learning: An Omnibus of Practice and Research* and *Setting the Pace*, the Illinois Adult and Continuing Education Association journal.

Thomas A. Clark is a doctoral fellow in the Department of Educational Administration and Higher Education at Southern

xv

Illinois University, Carbondale. He received his B.S. degree in radio and television (1982) and his M.S. degree in adult education (1987), both from Southern Illinois University, Carbondale. He coauthored *Selected Bibliography of Higher Education* (1984 with D. Tolle), has written about education for the gifted, and has published an article in *Lifelong Learning: An Omnibus of Practice and Research*. He has had developmental experience in distance education at Southern Illinois University, Carbondale—for example, in external degree program building and committee work on exploring alternative modes of educational delivery.

Part One

Distance Education and Lifelong Learning

1

The Idea and Evolution of Distance Education

In New Jersey, Tanya Jackson is finishing an associate degree in human services through Center for Corporate Partnerships of Thomas A. Edison College. Tanya's work as a file clerk at the New Jersey Department of State provides the opportunity for a practicum. She has already fulfilled most of the degree requirements through Thomas A. Edison College Equivalency Program (TECEP) exams, guided study courses, and home video courses as well as through approved correspondence courses and classes taken at a community college located in her region.

In Nevada, Alberto Alvarez has recently completed a major applied research project at the technical college where he works as an assistant administrator. The nearest accredited administration program was 285 miles away, and Alberto found the higher education program of Nova University, with headquarters in Florida, to be the best alternative. Through guided study, a practicum, and gatherings of Nova students in his region for formal education through intensive seminars, Alberto has been able to continue his education without disrupting his work or family life.

In Pennsylvania, microbiology major Gail Takemoto is enrolled in a biotechnology course that is being taught, without travel, by a member of the medical faculty of a Pennsylvania State University campus 100 miles away. Through two-way compressed video, teacher and class can both see and hear each other practically as well as in a conventional class. Gail is taking her other courses in the traditional face-to-face manner, but she believes this videoconference course compares favorably with most of her prior classroom experiences.

In Wisconsin, emergency medical technician (EMT) Diane Whitaker is taking part in a spirited discussion of proper procedure in acute emergency cases with a panel of experts and other EMTs through the Educational Telephone Network (ETN) audioconferencing network of the University of Wisconsin-Extension (UWEX). Several times a year, Diane meets other EMTs at the county courthouse to take noncredit continuing education courses she needs for recertification as an emergency medical technician.

What do all of these adults have in common? They are engaging in distance education—that is, education in which teacher and learner are separate during a majority of instruction. While formal distance education has been around at least since the early nineteenth century, the development in recent years of new telecommunications and information technologies has led to a growing interest in learning at a distance on the part of adults and continuing educators.

Distance education may be characterized as a form of adult education, although it is also used in K–12 instruction. Adult education characteristics of distance education include:

1. *Time and place.* The choice of time and location in distance education appeals to working adults. If time and location are fixed in distance education, they generally reflect the preferences of a majority of potential students, usually adults who prefer evening or weekend study.
2. *Traditional affiliation.* Distance education has traditionally been offered through the continuing education and extension units of colleges and universities as a part of the outreach programs of these institutions. These off-campus units generally provide services for adults, not children. Most students of proprietary schools who learn at a distance are adults as well.
3. *Literature.* Articles, books, and other documents about distance education largely concern programs in which adults are the principal market.

4. *Learner traits.* Successful study at a distance requires certain traits that are more typical of adult than of pre-adult learners. The ability to be self-directed and internally motivated can affect a learner's satisfaction and likelihood of completing a program. However, children may possess these traits as well, and adults preferring pedagogical teaching may adapt to distance education.

Every adult is an adult learner in one way or another. Adults learn continuously as they function in everyday life, particularly in their work, family, and community roles. Most of this learning is of a practical nature, consisting of new knowledge or skills that are applied in personally relevant situations. This practical learning is often planned and directed by the adult without the influence of a formal or informal educational institution or teacher.

Adult Education

A substantial part of adult learning falls into the category of *adult education,* which might be defined as the teaching of adults according to any organized formal or informal plan of education. Adult education activities are considerably narrower in scope than adult learning because they must include the direct involvement of educators in teaching and evaluation. Adult education and adult learning in general help adults better their occupational opportunities and quality of life. Adult, or lifelong, education "can occur in many different places and can involve a variety of emphases in terms of programs. It can be sponsored by and housed in numerous organizations and institutions, both private and public. It can offer learning experiences to the highly educated adult and those who may be perceived as functionally illiterate. It can be designed for those who are economically disadvantaged and for those who may be quite affluent. It is designed basically to meet the needs of adults and, in many cases, the needs of an organization and society in general" (Verduin, Miller, and Greer, 1986, p. 3).

As the population has aged and nontraditional attendance in college has become more common, higher education has become a larger factor in adult education. Students twenty-five years old or older made up 38 percent of college enrollment in 1977 and 42 percent in 1987. They are expected to account for more than 45 percent of college enrollment by 1997 (National Center for Education Statistics, 1988b). Vocational and continuing education programs enroll about 66 percent of all adult postsecondary education students (National Center for Education Statistics, 1988a). Adults enrolled in higher education are much more likely to study part time than full time, and this has contributed to the growth of part-time enrollment in higher education as a whole. Over 50 percent of all vocational students and 80 percent of continuing education students are adults (twenty-five years old or older). Academic institutions, business and industry, and the military are significant suppliers of adult education. Agencies and organizations as diverse as prisons, proprietary schools, churches, hospitals, and rest homes provide formal and informal learning programs for adults. Indeed, government statistics, which show about twenty-three million adults enrolled in over forty-three million courses in 1984, do not reflect much of the enrollment in such primarily noneducational institutions (National Center for Education Statistics, 1986b).

Most of the people who participate in adult education take part in one of three major kinds of programs (Verduin, Miller, and Greer, 1986). The first broad grouping of programs, *adult basic education* (ABE), is aimed at those adults who have not acquired the basic educational skills they need to function in a changing, increasingly technology-based society. Estimates of functional illiteracy in the United States vary greatly, largely because different standards are used in assessing ability. But enrollment in adult basic and secondary education rose 25 percent between 1980 and 1984, increasing from about 2 million adults enrolled to over 2.5 million, indicating the growing demand for this kind of education (National Center for Education Statistics, 1988a). Adult basic and secondary education students accounted for about 11 percent of adults enrolled in 1984. About 8 percent of the courses adults took in 1984 were general education courses. Of course, many ABE students may be studying for job-related reasons. Besides gaining necessary academic skills, adult basic learners may take citizenship classes, earn a high school diploma or its equivalent, or attain other credentials that will help them compete more successfully in society. General Educational Development (GED) preparatory courses have been offered at a distance in several states (Mellon, 1983; Kimmel and Lucas, 1984; Rio Salada, 1985).

The second major type of adult education, *career education,* involves helping adults to prepare for a vocation or profession or to upgrade their job-related skills. About 66 percent of adults gave job-related reasons for taking adult education courses in 1984, making career education the largest of the three major types of adult education in terms of numbers of people served (National Center for Education Statistics, 1988a). Often adults must enroll in courses continuously or recurrently because of the ever-increasing pace of change in the workplace. Career education may involve anything from the training of an unskilled adult in the most basic elements of a specific job to the continuous education of a highly trained professional. Most proprietary education at a distance, and much of the postsecondary distance study that takes place through colleges and universities, is undertaken by adults to prepare for, upgrade, or change careers.

In the third type of adult education, *leisure and enrichment education,* adults are offered learning experiences intended to help them enrich their lives and the lives of others and develop feelings of self-esteem and well-being. As society has become more complex, the personal problems of adults and their concerns about the quality of life have multiplied. If leisure and enrichment education is defined as education undertaken for personal satisfaction or enrichment, about 25 percent of adult education enrollment falls into this category. But if a narrower definition is adopted, counting only courses specifically about leisure, less than 6 percent of enrollment is leisure related (National Center for Education Statistics, 1988a). Therefore, leisure education may be seen as the second most popular or the least popular type of adult education, depending on how one defines it. Regardless, leisure and enrichment education is widely used by adults and is just as important to its participants as adult basic education or career education is to adults participating in these types of educational activities. A significant percentage of nonleisure subject matter, including vocational training, is studied at a distance by adults who merely have a personal interest in learning more about something, and who may pursue it as a hobby or leisure-time activity rather than as a job.

To fill the needs of millions of adult learners, numerous agencies and organizations offer a wide variety of educational experiences. Classes may take place on or off campus, at night, during the day, or on the weekend and may involve anything from computer conferencing to traditional classroom learning. One key to successfully delivering learning experiences to adults is to offer classes at a time and place at which adults are most ready to respond and learn. This is no easy task, but through innovative methods of delivery, many of which might be considered forms of distance education, high-quality education may become more available to adults.

Distance Education Defined

The term *distance education* may have first appeared in the 1892 catalogue of the University of Wisconsin (Rumble, 1986) and was reportedly used by the director of the University of Wisconsin-Extension, William Lighty, in 1906 (Moore, 1987b). Subsequently, the term was popularized in German (*Fernunterricht*) by the German educator Otto Peters in the 1960s and 1970s (Peters, 1968), and was employed as a title for distance teaching institutions in France (*télé-enseignement;* Moore, 1987b). The English term, *distance education,* was probably reintroduced in America by Bjorn Holmberg and Michael Moore at a meeting of the International Council for Correspondence Education (Moore, 1987b). A short definition of distance education might be "any formal approach to learning in which a majority of the instruction occurs while educator and learner are at a distance from one another." This definition is quite similar to the central element of a definition offered by Garrison and Shale (1987).

Printed and written correspondence by mail was the only mode of delivery utilized in most early distance education. Since print materials constituted the vast majority of items exchanged by teacher and learner in correspondence study, print study and correspondence study came to be regarded as synonymous. Actually, any packageable, mailable item can be part of correspondence study.

Early distance educators may have sent phonograph records to learners. Today's educators may mail computer software or interactive videodiscs to their students, to be returned with electronically recorded answers. Indeed, correspondence study can be conducted entirely without the use of the written word through the exchange of audiocassettes or more sophisticated media.

As time went by, educators used other methods of instructional delivery besides correspondence study. The telephone, along with other media conduits such as radio and television broadcasting and computers, came to play a significant role in distance education programs. Because the term *correspondence study* was associated with the written and printed word and did not describe distance education utilizing nonpostal modes of delivery, educators using print, radio, television, and other media at a distance often did not see themselves as working in the same field as educators using written material.

This created a problem for educators attempting to gain acceptance of distance education methods. Distance educators did not share a large body of knowledge, theory, or philosophy. It was natural for them to borrow from related fields such as educational television or continuing education. Literature describing examples of education at a distance was most likely to focus on delivery method or sponsoring institution in the absence of a recognized field based on separation of teacher and learner. The Educational Resources Information Center (ERIC) did not begin to use *distance education* as a descriptor until 1983.

Many items have been proposed to describe learning not based on classroom study. Wedemeyer (1983) states that "five terms are used to include all the types of programs that are non-classroom-based: distance education, non-traditional learning, independent study, out-of-school learning, and external studies" (p. 54). None of these terms, except *distance education* implies all of the elements necessary to describe learning at a distance without adding or deleting methods of study. *Nontraditional learning* may include classroom study in most definitions. *Independent study* appears to exclude group-based distance education while including self-instructional methods, such as the Personalized System of Instruction (PSI), that are often not conducted at a distance. *Out-of-school learning* may include any teacher-learner meetings for learning purposes outside of regularly scheduled classes. *External studies* may refer to education without a residency requirement or to a combination of off-campus and distance study. None of these terms precisely and solely defines learning in which the teacher is at a distance from the learner a majority of the time.

In 1986, Keegan refined his 1980 descriptive definition of distance education, proposing five criteria:

1. The quasi-permanent separation of teacher and learner throughout the length of the learning process: This distinguishes it from conventional face-to-face instruction.
2. The influence of an educational organization both in planning and preparation of learning materials and in the provision of student support services: This distinguishes it from private study and teach-yourself programs.
3. The use of technical media, print, audio, video, or computer, to unite teacher and learner and carry the content of the course.
4. The provision of two-way communication so that the student may benefit from or even initiate dialogue: This distinguishes it from other uses of technology in education.
5. The quasi-permanent separation of the learning group throughout the length of the learning process so that people are usually taught as individuals and not in groups, with the possibility of occasional meetings for both didactic and socialization purposes [p.37].

Comparing Keegan's 1980 and 1986 definitions, one sees an evolution in his thinking. *Separation* of teacher and learner in the 1980 definition becomes *quasi-separation* in the 1986 version, in recognition of the fact that face-to-face teaching is a part of many distance programs. The second element, the influence of an educational organization, is elaborated on in the 1986 version to make clear that distance education is different from what in this book is called *distance learning* or the use of instructional materials or media for self-instructional purposes in the absence of two-way communication with and evaluation by an educational organization.

Keegan moves from an emphasis on the use of print in the 1980 definition to acknowledgment in 1986 that computers and a wide array of audio and video technologies may also serve to unite teacher and learner and convey content. The fourth element of his definition is unchanged, except that Keegan notes that two-way communication distinguishes distance education from other uses of technology in education. Similarly, Keegan retains his previous version of the fifth element of the definition, which allows for the possibility of occasional face-to-face meetings of learners, but he adds that there is a "quasi-permanent absence of the learning group" so that the emphasis is clearly on solitary study. The last element of his 1980 definition, in which Keegan characterizes distance education as an industrialized form of education, was dropped from his 1986 definition because it did not apply to all distance teaching institutions.

A revised definition based on Keegan's two versions and upon further analysis is now presented. Four defining elements of distance education are:

1. The separation of teacher and learner during at least a majority of the instructional process
2. The influence of an educational organization, including the provision of student evaluation
3. The use of educational media to unite teacher and learner and carry course content
4. The provision of two-way communication between teacher, tutor, or educational agency and learner

The first element is more specific than Keegan's use of the term *quasi-permanent*, and characterizes a broader range of applications. If less than half of instruction or, say, less than twenty-four of the forty-eight contact-hours in a college course are completed through face-to-face instruction and all the other criteria for distance study are met, the course could be considered an example of distance education.

The second element of the definition now contains what seems to be the only truly indispensable part of the influence of an educational organization, evaluation, and omits mention of the others. The third element is essentially unchanged, although the more widely understood and widely applicable term *educational media* is used. The fourth element contains tacit recognition that in some industrialized forms of distance education, the student may have contact with different representatives of the educational organization for different purposes. The fifth element in both the 1980 and 1986 Keegan definitions and the sixth element of his 1980 version are omitted in this shorter version. There are many distance education systems in the United States and elsewhere, such as University of Wisconsin-Extension's Educational Telephone Network (ETN), that employ group study at a distance. No restrictions should be placed on group-based study in defining distance education.

This is a minimalist definition. It is not meant to describe typical applications of distance education but rather to describe attributes common to all distance programs. Garrison and Shale (1987) arrived at a similar definition with the principal differences being the use of the term *educational communication* rather than *instructional process* in the first element and the lack of an element referring to the influence of an educational organization and student evaluation in their definition. Of course, without knowledge of whether learning is being formally evaluated and of whether a recognized educational institution is involved in the process, it may be difficult to determine with any certitude whether formal education is occurring. Garrison and Shale may have accepted this element as a given.

Confusion About Distance Education

With so many definitions available, it is still easy to be confused about what is and is not distance education, especially when new educational media such as computers are involved. Some authors appear to define distance education as any instruction using electronic media or individualized learning materials (see, for example, Feasley, 1982). American academics often tend to equate distance education with correspondence study or with the Open University of the United Kingdom (OUUK), a large-scale distance teaching university (DTU) that uses an instructionally designed multimedia approach.

Many questions about the definition of distance education can cause confusion. For instance, if students are requested to read the opinions of distant experts from textbooks while the teacher leaves the room, are they engaging in distance education when they do so? If educators stopped counting contact-hours and instead focused on the total amount of time students spent working on a given course, would schoolwork performed in the absence of the teacher, such as homework, actually be a form of distance education? Is some of what is now classified as conventional education actually distance education? The definition of distance education can quickly become as fuzzy as the definition of open learning or nontraditional education. Of course, all definitions in education are arbitrary categorizations of reality. But some are more useful than others. Once again, distance education can be defined as formal instruction in which a majority of the teaching function occurs while educator and learner are at a distance from one another.

Some people may feel that this definition is too specific, but only a specific definition is of any real help to the academic confused about whether or not a course or program is an example of distance education. Distance education occurs when more than half of the formal instruction, or teaching, is done at a distance. *Teaching* here means contact-hours, by whatever medium, and not self-instructional work performed as an adjunct to in-class work. If the learner participates in the planning of the teaching function and then executes it, as may be done with learning contracts or independent study, this participation can be seen as counting towards contact-hours.

Program Classifications

Distance education programs have been classified in a number of ways. Keegan classified distance study schemes as autonomous—schools or open universities exclusively teaching through correspondence—or mixed/hybrid—distance teaching at a conventional educational institution through independent divisions, seminar and home study, or integrated internal and external teaching (Rumble and Harry, 1982). Similarly, Willen (1981) classified institutions teaching at a distance according to whether they were large-scale centralized operations (which usually teach exclusively at a distance) or more small-scale decentralized models such as are common in Sweden, Australia, and the United States. Holmberg (1981) offered highly similar categories, calling large-scale operations "industrial," and characterizing small-scale approaches as "parallelism" because they parallel residential study on campus.

The number of ways that distance education programs can be offered is practically infinite, and writers have provided many possible models. Here is a synthesis of Kaunda's (1970) and Rumble and Harry's (1982) typologies of distance study in conventional universities.

1. A university offers external exams for credit or credentials, for example, the University of London.
2. A single department offers distance study in its discipline. This occurred at the inception of the University of Waterloo's program.
3. External tuition occurs through extramural or extension departments. This is most common in the United States, usually through continuing education units.
4. Distance teaching units or departments duplicate the work of teaching departments. The University of Wisconsin-Extension fits here, although it is somewhat autonomous and only duplicates some of the on-campus teaching functions.
5. A distance teaching department facilitates rather than duplicates the work of teaching departments, which may be required to accept external students. Found in commonwealth nations where some governing boards mandate this system.

This typology progresses from the model offering the least student support services (in general) to the distance learner to that offering the most. The last model mentioned is used by the highly successful external studies program at the University of New Eng-

land in Australia. Greater explication of the various systems occurs in Chapter Three.

Methods of distance study can also be classified. Edstrom (1970) recognized three types of study practice in distance education: individual study, which is the most common; group study, in which learners meet as a group at a distance from the teacher; and supervised study, in which someone other than a teacher enforces a learning period.

Historical Overview

A brief review of the history of distance education may help the reader put present-day American practices into context. If one considers correspondence for instructional purposes between a tutor and a pupil to be formal education, then distance education almost certainly originated in ancient civilization. The combination of a written alphabet, a rudimentary postal system, and an educated elite must have led on occasion to distance education as royal family members traveled. Similar arrangements probably occurred throughout history down to the present day.

The date of the first publicly announced provision of distance education is in dispute. Battenberg (1971) describes an advertisement in the March 20, 1728, Boston *Gazette* for shorthand lessons by mail. Bratt (1977) cites an 1833 advertisement in a Swedish newspaper offering postal tuition in composition. Neither of these early advertisements mentioned two-way communication or grading.

Isaac Pitman is generally recognized to be the first modern distance educator. By profession a phonographer, he began teaching shorthand by correspondence in Bath, England, in 1840. This method of study appealed to adults who needed new methods of learning that would not conflict with their workdays. Students were instructed to copy brief Bible passages in shorthand and return them to Pitman for grading, using the new penny post system (Dinsdale, 1953). Within a few years Pitman had a staff to take care of the grading.

The University of London, established in 1836 to conduct examinations and confer degrees, was an important factor in the

founding of private correspondence colleges such as Skerry's College and University Correspondence College, which, beginning in the 1880s, prepared students to take examinations for post-secondary-level degrees (Curzon, 1977).

Charles Toussaint and Gustav Langenscheidt founded a modern language correspondence school in Berlin, Germany, in 1856, which still publishes instructional materials under Langenscheidt's name. In 1894, the Rustinches Fernlehrinstitut, which helped prepare students for university entrance examinations, was established in the same city (Noffsinger, 1926). In Sweden, H. S. Hermod founded his namesake institution (now Hermods-NKI Skolan) in 1898. Hermod built on his own experiments with postal tuition in developing his school.

Distance university study in America began in 1874 at Illinois Wesleyan University, where both graduate and undergraduate degrees could be pursued in absentia (Encyclopaedia Britannica, 1970; Rumble, 1986). The Illinois Wesleyan program was discontinued in 1910 (Encyclopaedia Britannica, 1970). The Correspondence University, founded in Ithaca, New York, in 1883, suffered the same fate ("The Correspondence University," 1883; Mackenzie and Christensen, 1971).

Formal American distance study can be traced back to the Society to Encourage Study at Home. This organization was founded in 1873 by Anna Eliot Ticknor, the "mother of American correspondence study," who originated the exchange of comments as well as grades with students (Aggasiz, 1971).

In 1878, John Vincent created a home reading circle for adults. Vincent became one of the founders of the Chautauqua movement, a popular education society based on the idea of expanding access to education to all Americans. He recognized early the potential of correspondence study (Lighty, [1915] 1971). Moore (1989) calls Chautauqua "the first significant distance education effort in America" (p. 223). In 1882, the "father of American correspondence study," William Rainey Harper, induced Chautauqua educators to allow him to start a correspondence study program for his residential summer school students. After Chautauqua became an accredited university in New York state, Harper headed the College of Liberal Arts, which came to emphasize distance study tech-

niques. In 1892, he became the first president of the University of Chicago and founded the first university-level correspondence study division in America, largely using principles and ideas he had learned through his work at Chautauqua (Goodspeed, 1928).

American elementary schooling by correspondence began in 1906 with the enrollment of the first students by the Calvert School of Baltimore, Maryland (Hart, 1947). One of the preeminent American distance teaching units, the University of Wisconsin-Extension, was founded in 1906 (Wedemeyer, 1983). In 1919, University of Wisconsin professors started an amateur wireless station that three years later became WHA, the first federally licensed radio station devoted to educational broadcasting (Engel, 1936). Educational television broadcasting originated at the University of Iowa's W9XK between 1932 and 1937 (Koenig and Hill, 1967).

In 1891, a Pennsylvania newspaper editor, Thomas J. Foster, began teaching mining methods and safety by correspondence. As he added more courses, International Correspondence Schools of Scranton, Pennsylvania, was born. The teaching of technical and vocational skills at a distance became quite common in the United States, bringing with it the problems of assuring quality and ethical business practices. The National Home Study Council (NHSC) was created in 1926 as an accrediting body intended to address such problems (Rumble, 1986). Accreditation of college and university distance programs was similarly performed by the National University Extension Association (NUEA), which held its initial conference at the University of Wisconsin, Madison, in 1915 (Moulton, 1915).

Distance Education Today

Distance education for college credit is a worldwide phenomenon. Kaye (1988) states that the International Council for Distance Education (ICDE) estimates that about ten million people study at a distance worldwide every year. Perry (1984), in a survey of fifty-two countries, found 142 associate or bachelor's degree programs and 61 postgraduate degree programs offered through distance education. Such programs were found in every region of the world except Eastern Europe, from which questionnaires were not re-

turned, but which is known to have developed distance college programs based on the Soviet model (Subramanian, 1971).

A decade after its initial operations in 1971, the Open University of the United Kingdom enrolled 60,000 to 70,000 undergraduates a year (Smith, 1988) and was a model for distance education programs around the world (Keegan and Rumble, 1982). More than 69,000 students had earned a bachelor's degree from the OUUK by 1984 (Rumble, 1986). In America, three universities—the University of Houston, the University of Maryland, and Rutgers University—made available OUUK courses in their original forms. This involved combining the original high-quality text and videotape materials with weekly tutorial sessions (Hartnett and others, 1974). At the University of Maryland, which has offered such courses since 1972, enrollment in the program was about 2,600 in 1982, even though classes were two to three times the normal three-credit length (Lewis, 1983).

The University of Mid-America, founded in 1974, seemed a logical means of coordinating the distance education efforts of large universities in seven midwestern states. In creating courses for use by the consortium, the University of Mid-America adopted the OUUK course team approach. Although it had served over 20,000 students since its founding and its courses were recognized for their high quality, this American experiment ended in 1982, a victim of intraorganizational politics and poor planning (Zigerell, 1984; Lewis, 1983). Although this attempt to emulate the OUUK was not successful, other consortia have survived and prospered in the United States, as can be seen by the high enrollments in the programs offered by television-based consortia.

Over a million adult learners enrolled in the Adult Learning Service (ALS) telecourses of the Public Broadcasting Service (PBS) between the inception of the ALS in 1981 and 1988 (Public Broadcasting Services, 1989). Earlier estimates were that over 100,000 Americans signed up for higher education telecourses each year (Brock, 1985), and another 100,000 took part in telecourses, telelectures, or videoconferences for college credit through television consortia (Niemeyer, 1985). More than 90 percent of distance education enrollment in the United States occurs through postsecondary institutions other than colleges or universities. About four million

proprietary students are enrolled at any given time in schools that the National Home Study Council accredits (Ludlow, 1987). International Correspondence Schools, which is both the first and the largest home study proprietary school, enrolled 70,000 to 100,000 persons a year in 1984 (Young, 1984), and has enrolled over nine million students since 1890 (International Correspondence Schools, 1990). Almost 700,000 members of the armed forces participate in postsecondary courses every year according to figures used in NHSC research (U.S. Department of Defense, 1987). Holbrook (1982) estimates yearly enrollment of 600,000 in these same military correspondence schools.

In addition to the 4 million or so students engaged in correspondence study through NHSC proprietary institutions, over 300,000 people study each year by correspondence at the secondary and postsecondary level through colleges and universities affiliated with the National University Continuing Education Association (Feasley, 1989). A majority of these students study for college credit.

Summary

Adult education is multifaceted and serves many adults who are undereducated or career oriented, or who desire some learning activities of a leisure nature. This formal, conventional type of educational delivery meets the needs of many adults, but perhaps another form of delivery, distance education, could likewise serve many adults in a less traditional manner. Distance education has, to this point, worked with and helped many adults in the three areas mentioned above.

Although distance education and its definition have caused some confusion over time, it can be seen as formal instruction in which a majority of the teaching occurs while educator and learner are at a distance from one another. Distance education is carried out by an organization that develops educational media to unite teacher and learner and provides appropriate evaluation of the learning. In doing so, two-way communication missing in other forms of nonconventional adult learning is provided.

Institutions offering postsecondary distance education fall into a number of classifications and range from universities that offer credit or credentials solely through examination, to autonomous distance teaching universities, to universities offering credit via extension or continuing education unit, to institutions in which external studies departments duplicate the work of on-campus departments.

Although probably started in Europe, distance education in the United States has some early roots. With early leaders like Ticknor, Vincent, and Harper and organizations like Chautauqua, Illinois Wesleyan, the University of Wisconsin, and International Correspondence Schools, distance education has grown to a point here in the United States at which it is ready to serve greater numbers of adult learners.

2

How Distance Education
Serves Adult Learners

As a form of nontraditional, part-time education, distance education serves mainly adult learners (Moore, 1985). Before any propositions or designs can be advanced for effective distance education, recent research on what is known about adults, their learning styles, their motivations, and other related qualities needs to be reviewed and analyzed.

Research on Adult Learners

First and foremost, adults are individuals possessing unique needs, values, attitudes, goals, beliefs, motivations, and self-concepts (Combs, 1959). This individuality certainly complicates the process of education; with such diversity in individual needs, goals, and motivations, where does the distance educator begin? The individuality of the distance learner must be recognized before distance education programs can be designed.

The individuality of adults is reflected in the life roles that they play in society. A change in these roles—whether the roles are related to occupation, family, or the community—has a strong impact on the need for additional or different learning (Cross, 1981).

A recent nationwide study provides new data on adults studying for college credit (Aslanian and Brickell, 1988). The authors of the study conducted a telephone survey of 1,000 adults, twenty-five years or older who had taken a college credit course in the previous two years. Aslanian and Brickell found that, in general, adults taking college credit courses are married (61 percent), female (58 percent), part-time students (80 percent), employed full time (71 percent), and paying for their own schooling (60 percent). Seventy-five percent of adult learners surveyed were between twenty-five and forty-four years old. Their participation in classes declined rapidly as they aged, and it declined sharply after they reached age fifty-five, although Aslanian and Brickell believe that the tendency of older adults to enroll in noncredit courses helped account for this trend. They attributed the high participation of younger adults to life transitions such as career changes that grow less frequent with age. Nearly 90 percent of the adult learners surveyed were white; only 7 percent were black. Not surprisingly, those surveyed were above average in education and income. Most were urbanites or suburbanites, and a majority lived in cities with 10,000–50,000 residents.

A fairly similar profile of adult education participants can be found in reports by the National Center for Education Statistics (NCES), which defines part-time learners as those students seventeen years old or older taking courses reported as adult education by education providers (National Center for Education Statistics, 1988a). Course enrollment more than doubled between 1969 and 1984, according to the NCES, as women came to constitute the majority of adult learners and for-credit enrollment fell from a majority to only 33 percent of the total enrollment. In 1984, most adult learners were employed (80 percent) and had an above-average income and level of education. Forty-seven percent paid for their own courses. Whites constituted 81 percent of the population surveyed. This figure, which is higher than that found by Aslanian and Brickell (1988), may be due to the inclusion of noncredit enrollment. Older adults, blacks, and Hispanics are more likely to participate in noncredit and noncollegiate adult education than in college credit offerings.

Aslanian and Brickell reported a considerably higher number of college credit students, 6.2 million in 1988, than did the NCES in 1985, when it gave an estimate of 5.1 million (Aslanian and Brickell, 1988). They believe that the NCES may be underreporting the overall number of adult learners by taking a "snapshot" of enrollment through telephone surveys every October.

The demographic characteristics of adults studying on campus for college credit can be compared with those of adults studying at a distance for college credit. Apt and Ebert (1983) compiled student characteristics at six identical open learning programs located at midwestern universities participating in a consortium. More men than women enrolled in every program. Otherwise, learner characteristics were very similar to those found in the Aslanian and Brickell (1988) study.

Considerable research in recent years has documented student characteristics of adults studying through telecourses. The Annenberg/CPB Project funded a 1984 study, documented in 1984 by Brey and Grigsby, in which 8,000 telecourse students studying forty-two telecourses were surveyed. According to the resulting data, most students were women (68 percent), white (84 percent), employed (80 percent), and married (54 percent) and had levels of education similar to those reported by Aslanian and Brickell (1988).

Distance from home to school, surprisingly, does not differ very much between conventional students and distance education students. Fifty percent of the adults studying for credit surveyed by Aslanian and Brickell (1988) commuted to class in twenty minutes or less, and nearly 90 percent lived within a forty-five-minute drive of their classrooms. Seventy percent gave convenient location as a prime reason for selecting a college. Aslanian and Brickell note: "The image of the busy adult emerges once again from these data. Rationing too little time among too many demands, adults have little time for class, less time for study, and no time to waste simply getting to class. The best college for an adult may not be the nearest, but it will be the best of the nearest" (p. 82).

Of the telecourse students surveyed by Brey and Grigsby (1984) 60 percent lived within a thirty-minute drive of a college campus, and only 7 percent lived an hour's drive away from a campus. But the majority of telecourse students also said that no travel time and no conflict with their work schedule were motivations for enrolling. This is not surprising if one considers that nearly 66 percent of these telecourse students were also enrolled in on-campus classes. In some rural areas, distance education may be the only real alternative for higher education for a significant proportion of the adult population.

Adult education, whether at a distance or on campus, should be considered in an international context. Van Enckevort, Harry, Morin, and Schultze (1987) found that the age, sex, and marital and employment status of students at four European distance teaching universities in 1984 (the OOUK, the Open University of the Netherlands, the Distance University of Germany, and Universidád Nacional de Educación a Distancia [UNED] of Spain) matched up fairly well with the characteristics of American conventional and distance learners. Incidentally, the United States ranked seventh in the proportion of adults twenty-five years and older enrolled in higher education in 1981.

Learning and Adult Motivation

Learning is signified by a change in behavior or a movement from one state of behavior to another through the acquisition of new knowledge or skills for personal use. Learning takes place as adults interact with objects, people, and events in their environment in order to gain new relevant information that may be useful in some way (Verduin, Miller, and Greer, 1977). This new information is available for use whenever the adult sees fit and may be stored for later use.

From the learner's viewpoint, learning is a conscious effort to acquire the new knowledge and skills that lead to a personal goal of some sort. The distance educator's mission is to provide a learning environment that allows individual adults to interact with appropriate objects, people, and events in order to acquire relevant new behaviors (knowledge and skills); gives adults an opportunity to practice the new behaviors if necessary; and helps adults learn how to apply these behaviors in meaningful situations. As adults acquire new knowledge and skills, or cognitive and psychomotor behaviors, and achieve personal goals, they are also responding in some fashion to the value of the information being learned. This affective dimension must come into play whenever adults attempt to gain new cognitive information or psychomotor skills. The motivations of adult students are strongly tied to the value they place on an educational experience, so the affective characteristics and responses of students must be important to distance educators, just as they are to conventional adult educators.

The importance of the three domains—cognitive, psychomotor, and affective—lies in the fact that they have an impact on the performance of adults and the proficiencies that they possess. Knox (1980) suggests that much of adults' intentional learning activity is motivated by adults' desire to move from their current proficiency level to a new proficiency level. Discrepancies between an adult's current level and desired proficiency level directly affect motivation and achievement in both learning activities and life roles. Proficiency, or the capability to perform effectively if given the opportunity, usually depends on some combination of knowledge, skills, and attitudes that the adult possesses (Knox, 1980). The cognitive, psychomotor, and affective domains actually define the behavioral "package" that each adult possesses. If distance educators are in the business to help adults gain new proficiencies, then these domains must be given constant attention.

Educating adults at a distance would appear to be a big task, but adults actually are continuous learners in an informal way as they adjust to the various role changes that confront them in life. Further, adults are motivated learners; they take classes at a given point to learn more about a topic. They are fairly pragmatic learners who emphasize the practical utility of the information learned, usually as it relates to their economic status.

Learning is a very individual effort, particularly in distance education. Adults vary greatly in their learning abilities and disabilities. Obviously, educators should emphasize the abilities and minimize the disabilities, although weak study skills should be improved whenever possible. Adults' different rates of learning suggest a self-pacing strategy, which can be a major feature in distance education. Although difficult, distance educators should tap the experiences and knowledge that adults already possess through diagnostic and planning procedures to ensure better learning.

Adults like hands-on learning experiences and can learn from a variety of resources. Like other adults, distance students want feedback on how they are doing and do not want to waste their time. Even though a uniform three-day turnaround was reported in a

1983 survey of proprietary schools accredited by the National Home Study Council, students still cited lack of an immediate response as a disadvantage of correspondence study (National Home Study Council, 1983). Students can easily quit a correspondence course if the course loses meaning for them or they do not make satisfactory progress. The completion rate of distance education can be boosted significantly by proper recruitment, counseling, and support of distance learners (Moore, 1989).

Realistic goals, challenges, and reasonable learning speed for the adult are factors that can help adults learn. Chacon-Duque (1987) conducted a study of twenty-nine courses offered through the Independent Living Program at Pennsylvania State University (Penn State) in 1983. He found that completion and pass rates and grade averages of course groups could be explained to a significant extent by a model in which students were less likely to complete and pass a course if it was too difficult or too easy for them. But distance educators must remember that almost any adult can learn any subject if given enough time and attention (Knox, 1986), and that despite the high attrition rate, there is a place for distance education that allows learners to set their own pace.

As might be expected, the motivations of adult learners are very diverse, ranging from the pragmatic to those of an intrinsic nature; however, over time most adults have been highly pragmatic learners (Peterson and Associates, 1979). About 66 percent of adult learners gave job-related reasons for enrollment in 1984; job advancement, getting a new job, and entering a new occupation are strong motivators for adults seeking education (National Center for Education Statistics, 1986b). Adults less frequently gave reasons not related to work such as personal or social reasons, a desire for general education, and study related to volunteer work or societal goals. Adults may also seek additional learning for social relationships, stimulation, and knowledge for knowledge's sake (Houle, 1961; Morstain and Smart, 1974). Denton (1982), in his synthesis of the literature, suggests that the major orientations or motivations of adults for continued learning are preparing for an occupational change or advancement, seeking social relationships, learning for learning's sake, escaping boredom and seeking stimulation, and using knowledge to help some sector of society.

In general, young adults appear to seek education, generally job-relevant in nature, to prepare for their future, middle-aged adults engage in career advancement and transition activities, and older adults are likely to take courses for personal satisfaction, stimulation, and leisure. It is interesting to note that adults with more recent educational experiences tend to do better than those who have not had those experiences.

Students enroll in distance education for several reasons. The most important reason given by students in the Annenberg/CPB study (Brey and Grigsby, 1984) for enrolling in a telecourse was that on-campus classes conflicted with work (41 percent) or with leisure time (12 percent). Twelve percent of students surveyed gave preference for learning at home as their most important reason. Asked why they chose a telecourse instead of an on-campus class, 51 percent of the students cited minimized travel and 12 percent said they wanted to try a new learning method (Crane, 1985—analysis of same Annenberg/CPB data). In a 1987 study by Schrader of 124 students studying medical terminology by correspondence, 64 percent of students surveyed gave the lack of a conflict with their work schedule as a reason for enrolling in a correspondence course, and almost 60 percent cited no travel to class. A bare majority indicated interest in course content as their primary reason for enrolling, and over 40 percent mentioned a preference to study at home.

Distance education can be more convenient and adaptable than classroom teaching for the active adult. Annenberg/CPB telecourse students surveyed noted that they found it easier to work at times that were personally convenient than they would if they were attending a formal class. However, students studying at home without access to a videocassette recorder often did not feel that the telecourse was at a convenient time (Crane, 1985).

Preferring to study at home must mean, to some extent, preferring to learn at one's own pace rather than in class with other adults. Even if the telecourse is broadcast at a fixed time, most of the work in a telecourse involves separate study of the printed word, with the videocassette segment playing the role of a pacing or overview device. Distance education offers students an opportunity to study and learn in a peer-free environment, when and if they prefer it. In some forms, distance education offers the same opportunities for freedom of pace and individual study as does self-directed, self-planned learning, while also providing the guidance, planning, and feedback during the learning experience that is necessary for continued student motivation and completion of the course.

Barriers to Participation

Perceived barriers to participation or retention in distance education have been the subject of several studies in the literature linking retention with student support (such as Murgatroyd, 1982; Woodley and Parlett, 1983) or with learning styles (such as Coggins, 1988; Taylor and Kaye, 1986; Thompson and Knox, 1987). Many of the barriers facing distance learners are the same as those for all adult learners. Cross (1981) found that the barriers most commonly cited by adult learners are cost and lack of time. Cross groups barriers as situational, dispositional, and institutional. Cost of courses and work or family life often become situational barriers since a majority of distance learners pay for their own education. Institutional barriers such as prerequisites, lack of support and informational services, and red tape can discourage participation. Most adults prefer learning in conventional classes, and this and other dispositional barriers related to the unconventionality of distance education seem most likely to lessen adult participation.

Differences Between Adults and Children

Differences between adults and children have been the source of a great deal of controversy in adult education in recent years. *Andragogy,* a theory and philosophy of adult teaching and learning that is widely accepted by adult educators, posits differences between adults and children in terms of self-directedness, experience, developmental readiness, and problem orientation (Knowles, 1980). The most empirically defensible of these differences are based on an accumulation of experience (Brookfield, 1986). Adults have accumulated many experiences that are a great resource for learning.

Another theory of adult learning, based on situational and personal characteristics, is Cross's Characteristics of Adults as Learners (CAL). In this theory, the ways in which adults differ from children according to the research, such as in their positions on lifespan physical, psychological, and sociocultural continuums and their usually part-time, voluntary attendance in classes, are used to create a framework for adult learning (Cross, 1981). Clearly, differences exist between adults and children whatever theory is used. Adults and children are unique individuals with personal goals, motivated by personal interest in a topic and preferring to learn at their own pace, but it seems likely that differences based on experience, developmental stage motivations, voluntary learning status, and self-directedness are to some extent real and are reflected in the attitudes and perceptions of adults. These qualities can make adults quite different from children and even different from one another. Recognizing these differences may be critical for educators to provide successful learning experiences to adults.

Learning Styles

Learning styles have implications for teaching styles. Smith (1982) suggests that certain tendencies and preferences of adults influence their learning styles and the way they would like to acquire new learning. Some adults are inclined toward teacher-centered instruction, and some may opt for self-oriented or self-directed instruction. Some may prefer reading to gather new information, and others may desire a multimedia presentation for acquiring the same information. These learning styles complicate the distance educator's job but must be considered during early planning activities.

Canfield (1983) has developed a learning style inventory that conceptualizes learning style as composed of preferred conditions, content, mode, and expectancy score. An examination of these four dimensions could shed some light on the learning preferences of adults.

The *conditions* of learning consist of eight factors: peer work (working in teams), organization (logical and organized course work), goal setting (setting one's own objective), competition (wanting a comparison with others), instructor (having a good rapport with the instructor), detail (wanting specific information on assignments and requirements), independence (wishing to work alone and independently), and authority (desiring classroom discipline and maintenance of order). Since some of these conditions deal primarily with the classroom, they may not have that much direct meaning to distance education.

Content refers to a student's preference to work in one of four areas: numeric (working with numbers), qualitative (working with words and language), inanimate (working with things), and people (working with people). *Mode* identifies four strategies preferred by adults for acquiring new information. Some adults prefer: listening (listening through lectures and tapes), reading (reading or examining the written word in books and pamphlets), iconic methods (viewing illustrations, slides, movies, and videocassettes) or direct experience (handling things, performing activities, and taking field trips).

The final category in Canfield's inventory deals with *expectancy score*, which is the level of performance students predict for themselves in a learning situation. Students can actually predict whether they will perform at an outstanding level, an average or good level, an average or satisfactory level, or a below-average or unsatisfactory level.

Some parts of Canfield's inventory could be useful to the distance educator in planning courses. The first section, conditions, could establish what kind of learner the adult really is and what kind of environment is best for the learner. As might be expected, learners may range from those who wish high teacher control of the learning direction to those on the other end of the continuum who desire high learner control. Some information on the students' preferred content area would be useful if the learner has a choice regarding course content. Finally, the mode of learning preferred by the learner could be helpful to distance educators when designing the learning experiences. If the student prefers reading, then printed materials could be used. If the student prefers iconic methods, videotapes, slides and other visual materials could be used. Of course, the distance educator often does not have the time or resources to individualize courses, but understanding how individual learners approach learning may make it possible for the distance educator to see patterns of learning styles and plan or adjust course presentations accordingly. Adult learners may or may not learn more easily when the way in which a course is conducted matches their learning style, but they are more likely to be satisfied with the course.

It should also be noted that students entering a learning situation differ in maturity. Hersey and Blanchard (1974) have referred to this type of maturity as "the level of achievement-motivation, willingness and ability to take responsibility, and task relevant education and experience of the individual or group" (p. 28). Generally, nontraditional students who are older can enter a learning situation with more motivation and more relevant experience. Nontraditional students are thus more likely to desire to set their own direction for the learning experience—a learner-centered approach that requires less leadership on the part of the instructor.

Conti and Welborn (1987) suggest that traditional students can be viewed as less mature than nontraditional students in determining their leadership needs or directions for learning. Therefore, maturity, regardless of age, determines the kind of leadership that should be given to a group or individual. As maturity declines, the leadership or direction-giving by instructors needs to be increased, and with increased maturity, less leadership and greater interpersonal activity is appropriate. It follows then that nontraditional students do better under the learner-centered approach and traditional students seem to need more teacher-centered experiences. Although adults are generally more self-directed and may want to set their own direction in the learning experience, they may be highly motivated in other-directed courses that support their personal interests such as job-related education. Distance educators should remember that age is not a factor in this maturity level but that life roles influencing adults to seek further education are factors.

Summary

Every adult possesses unique goals, needs, values, attitudes, motivations, and self-concept. Roles in the family, occupation, and society add further to adults' individual requirements and desire for further education.

More married adults, women, and part-time workers, many with generally good jobs and educations, now attend adult college credit and other adult education courses than ever before. Adults' motivations for seeking additional education vary but tend to be heavily oriented toward occupation or vocation.

Because work schedules or leisure time activities often conflict with on-campus class participation, adults often find distance education more viable. Learning at home also allows for studying and learning at their own pace and obviates unnecessary travel.

Since increasing proficiency brings new knowledge, skills, and attitudes, distance educators need to take account of the cognitive, affective, and psychomotor domains of learning. Adults are generally applied and motivated learners, and their motives are usually practical in nature: What they want to learn has direct application to daily life, often to economic status.

Adults like hands-on learning experiences, and they want feedback on how they are progressing—factors that complicate the distance education process. Adults can, however, learn most subjects if given enough time and attention, despite the differences in their learning rates and capacities. Hindrances to effective adult learning include situational barriers, such as work or family obligations or the cost of schooling, and institutional barriers, such as red tape or unfulfilled prerequisites.

Adults and children should be educated in ways that take into account the differences in their experience, developmental stages, motivations, voluntary learning status, and self-directedness. Those designing distance education should moreover pay attention to differences among adults—in individual learning styles, preferences for acquiring new knowledge and skills, and levels of maturity or ways of responding to new learning situations (for example, to the need for direction and assistance).

Facilitating adult learning at a distance is a highly complex process, which calls for a variety of methods, materials, and designs, as well as for individualized treatment of learners, but the rewards of learner-centered instruction are many.

Strengths and Limitations of Current Practice

3

Key Approaches
to Distance Education

A wide variety of educational systems currently deliver distance education to adult learners. In this chapter, a classification of distance education is presented in which six commonly recurring distance education models are identified and examples of each type of model are given.

Type I

Type I institutions are postsecondary educational institutions offering college degrees to students whom they have not directly taught. There are several Type I institutions and organizations in the United States that offer degrees through combinations of comprehensive course or proficiency examinations; credit for equivalent academic work and experiential learning; and portfolio evaluations of prior learning, life, and work experiences. Descriptions of some Type I institutions follow.

Regents College Degrees. It is easy to confuse Regents College with Empire State College, which is also located in New York state. Regents College is part of the University of the State of New York (USNY), the umbrella educational agency that governs all public and private educational institutions in New York state, while Empire State College (ESC) is part of the State University of

New York (SUNY), which is the public system of higher education in the state. SUNY is part of USNY, and Regents College is named after the board of regents that governs USNY.

In 1970, the board of regents created the Regents External Degree Program, later called Regents College Degrees. This program has no campus, resident faculty, or student body in the traditional sense. Unlike Empire State College, Regents College awards a degree to anyone who can meet its requirements, without requiring that a faculty mentor guide the student in the design and execution of an academic program (Hall and Hassenger, 1982). In essence, the Regents College program is a purer example of Type I distance education than the Empire State College program (which is presented last in this section).

The Regents program offers associate and bachelor's degrees in liberal arts studies, business, and nursing. In the decade after its founding in 1972, more than 35,000 people enrolled, of whom about 21,000 were still enrolled on a continuous basis in 1982 (*Regents External Degrees*, 1982). By 1990, more than 46,000 students had graduated and over 8,000 enrolled each year (Peinovich, personal communication, 1990).

The Regents program grew out of New York State's College Proficiency Program, which first awarded credit by examination in 1963. The College Proficiency Program, later renamed Regents College Examinations (RCE), exists parallel to the Regents College Degrees program and offers tests in over fifty-four college subject areas (Whitney and Malizio, 1987). In 1976, RCE contracted with the American College Testing Program to make its examinations available outside New York State under the name ACT/PEP (American College Testing/Proficiency Examination Program). Today, ACT/PEP exams are offered through more than 200 testing centers nationwide and through DANTES at military bases around the world (Whitney and Malizio, 1987).

The central idea behind the Regents program is that people with knowledge equivalent to that denoted by a college degree should be able to earn a degree by demonstrating that knowledge regardless of how it was acquired. A number of alternative methods of demonstrating knowledge for credit may be used singly or in combination by Regents College students:

- College courses, taken for credit, offered by any regionally accredited college or university
- Proficiency examinations, including Regents College examinations in more than forty subjects offered by the University of the State of New York
- Military service school courses and occupational specialties evaluated and recommended for credit by the American Council on Education (ACE)
- Special assessment of college-level knowledge gained through independent study or other means for which existing proficiency examinations are not appropriate, offered by Regents College Degrees and Examinations
- Noncollegiate-sponsored instruction, such as courses offered by business, industry, government agencies, or volunteer organizations that have been evaluated for college credit by the New York National or ACE Programs on Noncollegiate-Sponsored Instruction
- Federal Aviation Administration (formerly Civil Aeronautics Administration) Airman Certificates
- A combination of these ways of earning credit (New York State Education Department, 1987, p. 46)

Regents and College proficiency exams are prepared by over 500 college and university faculty members from state institutions acting as consultants to USNY. Graduate-level credit is available to individuals who can pass proficiency exams designed to test the skills of teachers working with students with learning disabilities. However, most exams are intended to test introductory and advanced-level undergraduate knowledge. Questions may be multiple choice, short answer, essay, or case study based. The consultant faculty grade the exams as well as prepare them. Program advisers based in Albany are available to all students via telephone or mail, and volunteer advisers based in public libraries and colleges throughout the state are also available to students and potential students. The Regents program is not funded by the state. Exam costs range from $25 to $500 and averaged $35 in 1982. Other sources of funding have included the federal government and private corporations (Regents College Degrees, 1986).

The quality of Regents College graduates may be indicated by the fact that about half of Regents associate degree holders go on to baccalaureate study, a majority of them at conventional institutions, while Regents bachelor's degree recipients progress to graduate or professional programs at about the same rate (Regents College Degrees, 1986). Regents College recently created the Institute for Distance Learning to research distance delivery methods.

Thomas A. Edison College. An arrangement with the New Jersey Board of Higher Education in 1972 allowed the Regents College Degrees and College Proficiency programs of the state of New York to cut duplication and costs by sharing exams and faculty with the newly created Thomas A. Edison College in New Jersey. Thomas A. Edison, like the Regents College, is an examining institution that does not teach students and that has no full-time faculty. About 5,300 students have graduated since the college was founded in 1972. Currently 7,200 students are enrolled, taught by over 200 part-time faculty. Edison students are on average thirty-nine years old; 96 percent are over twenty-five. They reside in every state in the nation and in more than twenty-five foreign countries (J. Ice, personal communication, 1990). Thomas Edison offers six associate and five bachelor's degree programs. Bachelor's degrees are available in liberal arts, business administration, applied science and technology, human services, and nursing.

A major philosophical premise of this college and other nontraditional institutions and programs is that credit should be given for demonstrable knowledge or skills, regardless of where, when, or how they were obtained. Although it has its own guided study curriculum, Edison is largely a certifying and examining body. A great deal of its energy and resources are used in evaluating outside sources of learning that may be granted credit equivalency. Transfer of credit, equivalency exams, assessment of prior learning, and independent learning courses may be used in completing an Edison College degree. No limits are placed on how credit is earned or the number of credits transferred, except that courses must fit degree requirements. Edison's national prominence and leadership are evidenced by the replication at numerous higher education institutions of programs and methods pioneered at the college (J. Ice, personal communication, July 1990).

The college has its own proficiency examination program, the Thomas A. Edison College Equivalency Program (TECEP), that parallels its guided study coursework and also administers American College Testing/Proficiency Examination Program (ACT/PEP), College Level Examination Program (CLEP), and Defense Activity for Non-Traditional Education Support (DANTES) exams. It evaluates the results of these exams administered elsewhere as well as the results of exams administered by the U.S. Armed Forces Institute (USAFI), the forerunner of DANTES (see next section). Students can also earn credits by passing exams based on twenty-seven telecourses on videocassette that can be obtained from a private company, the College Video Company. TECEP and other equivalency tests are given at Edison State College in Trenton and at eight regional test sites around New Jersey. Out-of-state students may take TECEP exams at selected colleges and universities, and military personnel stationed abroad may take them at military base testing offices under the supervision of a proctor. Individuals who possess certain health care, aviation, and business license certificates or who attain certain army and navy ratings are entitled to Edison credit.

Up to twelve hours of credit can be earned by demonstrating mastery of one of twenty-one languages through proficiency tests developed by New York University. Independent study through Ohio University; Penn State; University of Nebraska, Lincoln; and Indiana University is recommended by Edison College as a method of fulfilling requirements in addition to use of the college's own guided study independent learning courses and other independent study methods. Edison College offers workshops to state residents on portfolio development, study skills, and career counseling. It evaluates the training programs of organizations in the state through the Program on Noncollegiate Sponsored Instruction (PONSI) and provides on-site academic services for more than sixty corporations through the Center for Corporate and Public Partnerships (Thomas A. Edison State College, 1989). Working with the New Jersey Department of State and its Nontraditional Education Program, Edison State enrolled thirty-six full-time civil service employees of the department in its associate and baccalaureate programs in 1985. Students preferring direct classroom instruction were allowed to earn credits through three colleges—Trenton State, Burlington, and Mercer County Community Colleges (Eveslage, 1986).

Defense Activity for Non-Traditional Education Support (DANTES). The military furnishes another good example of a Type I institution. Members of the United States armed forces receive support in their voluntary educational efforts through the Defense Activity for Non-Traditional Education Support. DANTES replaced the U.S. Armed Forces Institute in many of its functions when the USAFI was discontinued in 1974. Exams for credit in about fifty academic and vocational/technical fields are available through DANTES. Using evaluative and credit recommendations from the American Council on Education, DANTES sets requirements for military specialties and ratings and awards students two to six hours of postsecondary credit for each test passed. DANTES also administers the Scholastic Aptitude Test (SAT), ACT, GED, the Graduate Record Examination (GRE), the Graduate Management Admissions Test (GMAT), and the National Teacher Examination (NTE) and tests to military personnel. It cooperates with stateside postsecondary institutions in the awarding and transfer of high school and college level credit, including credit for experiential learning. Through its *Independent Study Catalog* and *Guide to External Degree Programs,* DANTES facilitates distance and external degree enrollment in American high schools and postsecondary institutions.

The War Department created USAFI in 1941 (renamed in 1974 by the Department of Defense). Later, the Department of Defense created DANTES to guarantee that the testing of learning was standardized throughout the military ("USAFI . . . ," 1966). The overall goal of DANTES is to guarantee that the separate and unique educational systems of the branches of the military all meet the same minimal standards of quality (U.S. Navy, 1985).

Empire State College. Founded in 1971 as part of SUNY, Empire State College has graduated 15,000 students and currently enrolls about 6,400 students annually at over forty locations throughout New York (Empire State College, 1988). The college has about 113 full-time and 225 part-time faculty members. Each ESC learning site is served by eighteen to twenty faculty, who present the full complement of ESC learning areas to 500 or more students. ESC was the first public nontraditional institution of higher education to receive regional accreditation by the Middle States Association of Colleges and Universities ("CAEL . . . ," 1988). ESC's original mission included:

• Creation of alternative structures and programs to increase access for those unable or unwilling to study on campus
• Development of academic content responsive to individual purposes and emerging social needs
• Devising of educational methods that can serve diverse students with widely varied needs
• Ensuring of program quality at reasonable cost

Like Regents College, Empire State has no campus or permanent faculty. Undergraduates may begin or end their studies at any time of the year. But unlike at Regents, each student works with a faculty member, called a mentor, who is permanently affiliated with another postsecondary institution (Empire State College, 1987). The mentors help plan and coordinate modes of study, instruct in their own field, contract for tutors in other fields as needed, and also generally guide and assess the academic work of the students (Worth, 1982).

ESC operates like a hybrid between Type II consortium-based and University-Without-Walls programs and Type I institutions that grant degrees without directly undertaking instruction. ESC remains a Type I school because it contracts out practically all of its services.

By its very nature, Empire State is learner centered rather than institution centered. It does most of its recruitment by word of mouth (Gallien, 1986). Students begin their study at ESC by planning an individual degree program that takes into account prior learning by awarding credit for it. Each individualized degree program plan is reviewed by ESC's Assessment Office, Faculty Assessment Committee, and the Office of Program Review and

Assessment before it receives final approval. Empire State is the only SUNY college that offers both two- and four-year undergraduate degrees. Both associate and bachelor's degrees are offered in business, management, economics, interdisciplinary studies, and community human services. Bachelor's degrees are also available in fire service administration (Empire State College, 1987).

Graduate study is also possible at ESC. Empire State offers a master of arts degree in policy studies, with concentrations in business, labor, or culture. An interinstitutional graduate council appointed by the president of SUNY administers this master's degree program.

The primary mode of education at ESC is the learning contract (Bear, 1988). A learning contract is a "specific, negotiated plan of study, covering a particular period of time, yielding a fixed number of credits, and including specification of resources and an agreed mode of evaluation" (Worth, 1982, p. 11). The widely publicized and successful use of learning contracts at Empire State may have encouraged the establishment of American University-Without-Walls programs in much the same manner as the successful use of multimedia distance education at the Open University of the United Kingdom has encouraged the creation of distance teaching universities in many other nations.

However, while learning contracts are the predominant mode of study at ESC, registration in courses at other institutions, residency programs, interdisciplinary studies, professional and liberal arts programs offered through state government units, and structured distance courses available through the Center for Distance Learning (CDL) can also be used by students working toward a degree (Worth, 1982).

The CDL is an option offered by ESC to students who wish to study independently at a distance but who prefer more structure than is offered by contract learning. The CDL has made great use of modified Open University of the United Kingdom course materials in developing its academic offerings. In recent years, it has experimented in the delivery of courses on line through computer conferencing and electronic mail (Roberts, 1987).

One of ESC's residency programs, called FORUM, features three weekend residencies in Syracuse, New York, during each twenty-four-week term. Working adults interested in management careers take part in seminars, lectures, panel discussions, films, and special workshops and meet individually with mentors during FORUM weekends. Most of the coursework needed by FORUM students to complete their bachelor's degree programs is obtained through independent study.

ESC has agreements with twenty-five New York community colleges that enable graduates of these colleges to earn up to sixty-four hours of credit toward an Empire State bachelor's degree before transferring (Empire State College, 1987). A minority transition program designed to improve the completion rates of minority students at ESC was, in fact, conducted in conjunction with eight of these community colleges (Worth, 1982). ESC has collaborative agreements with eight two-year colleges that give their students access to an individualized four-year program (Empire State College, 1988).

ESC has gathered a considerable amount of information on its students and their educational outcomes. The Students Biographical Inventory, administered to over 5,000 ESC students between 1974 and 1982, led researchers to conclude that the average student is a white, married female, thirty-seven years old, who holds a professional position and studies part time. Students reported on the inventory that they chose ESC because of the independence and individualized attention it offered. They reported that their work at ESC helped them develop independence, improve their research and study skills, and enhance their personal development (Empire State College, 1987).

ESC research on graduates also showed that about 50 percent sought an advanced degree and that more than 75 percent of those applying were accepted by the graduate school of their choice. Most who were accepted felt that their preparation at ESC was good. Of the ESC graduates surveyed, 50 percent said their employment circumstances had improved as a direct result of their degree. They noted increased professional status, higher pay, and more job responsibilities and satisfaction. More than 25 percent reported receiving a job promotion or getting a new job because of their study at Empire State (Empire State College, 1987; Worth, 1982).

Type II

Type II institutions are postsecondary educational institutions offering degrees to students whom they have already taught. Degree requirements can be met through a combination of credit for prior learning, life and work experiences, credit by examination, distance education, and experiential learning.

Type II universities, colleges, or programs might be said to be examples of both external and distance study. External degrees can be defined as those in which half or more of the credits needed for a degree may be earned or awarded for work external to the traditional on-campus programs of the institution. Assessment for prior learning often plays a large role in these programs.

While those external degree programs that have a significant distance education component are of most interest here, the only truly accurate way to classify external degree programs as being mostly distance or mostly conventional in nature is to look at the records and coursework of individual students. If more credit is given for distance study or by examination than for classroom study, not including experiential and portfolio credit, the program might be called a distance education program. But this definition is very complicated and not of much use in describing many programs overall. The flexibility of learning options available in many programs allows one student to follow a program that is mainly conventional while another uses mostly distance education methods. Certainly, if an external degree program is structured around face-to-face classroom study, whether on or off campus, then the program is a conventional one.

The number of external degree programs grew quickly during the 1970s. In 1971, the Ford Foundation gave $800,000 to the Union for Experimenting Colleges and Universities, a consortium, to develop the University-Without-Walls program (UWW) of flexible and individualized learning on each of its members' twenty-five campuses (Losty and Gardiner, 1978).

Stephens College Without Walls Program. The Stephens College Without Walls Program (SCWW) was one of the original twenty-five University-Without-Walls programs founded in 1971.

SCWW requires 120 semester hours of credit for the bachelor of arts degree, at least twenty-one of which must be completed with Stephens faculty following successful completion of a liberal studies seminar. Students can work with the SCWW faculty through independent study, intensive or conventional classes, and weekend seminars.

Early graduates of SCWW reported that the degree contributed significantly to their effectiveness at work. Almost 50 percent had gone on to advanced studies, and only about 14 percent encountered difficulty in being accepted to further study because of their external degree (Losty and Gardiner, 1978).

University-Without-Walls programs are very diverse, but their students' overall characteristics are similar. Most students at the seven UWW's surveyed by Stetson (1979) were thirty to forty-nine years old, 75 percent were white, 66 percent were employed full-time, and over 66 percent had completed two or more years of college. UWW faculty and staff viewed their program and graduates as good or better than the conventional ones but also felt that on-campus faculty and staff viewed the UWW program as inferior (Stetson, 1979). Sharp and Sosdian (1979) surveyed 1,486 graduates of thirty-two external degree programs and found similar demographics, although the nonwhite graduate population was higher in University-Without-Walls programs.

Nova University. This Type II institution has a national reputation among educators, as do Empire State College and Regents College. Nova University, which has its headquarters in Fort Lauderdale, Florida, has been a leader in program innovation since its founding in 1964. It provides traditional on-campus classroom-based education in many fields but is best known for its highly successful field-based master's and doctoral programs. These postgraduate programs developed in accordance with Nova's mission, which is to serve not only the educational needs of traditional students but also those of employed professionals, regardless of their schedules or distance from the central campus (Manburg, 1983). To fulfill this mission, Nova offers regionally accredited, field-based graduate programs for continuously employed professionals seeking master's, specialist, or doctoral degrees in disciplines such as

higher education, educational administration, child care administration, adult education, business, accounting, psychology, and
information science (personal communication, O. C. Lewis, vice-
president for academic affairs, Nova University, July 1990).

Nova's field-based programs operate in twenty-four states
and in three foreign countries. Delivery formats vary somewhat
from program to program. Students in Nova programs are generally
assigned to groups called clusters, once enough have enrolled in a
given geographic area. A professional in the field of study is then
assigned to coordinate the academic and business affairs of each
cluster and to serve as a liaison between the students, the university,
and the faculty. Students usually attend mandatory weekend classes
or seminars and may be required to attend week-long summer sessions, as well, in some programs (personal communication, O. C.
Lewis, July 1990; Manburg, 1983).

Nova offers field-based postgraduate education through the
Center for the Advancement of Education (CAE), the Friedt School
of Business and Entrepreneurship, the Center for Computer and
Information Science, and the School of Psychology. One fairly representative program is the higher education Ed.D. doctoral program
offered through CAE. Students in this program must attend seven
modules, each of which includes three seminars. After completing
practicums for five of the seven modules they have chosen, students
must sit for a comprehensive exam and finish a major applied research project (MARP).

Through the practicums, students gain experience in applying the theory they have learned in the seminars to actual problems
or projects within the institution at which they are employed.
Students' completion of the MARP, a much more ambitious and
rigorous type of practicum than the others, constitutes a final demonstration of the applied research skills they have acquired through
the program. Students work on the MARP independently, with the
help of a three-person committee composed of an adviser, a local
reader, and a representative of Nova's central campus (personal
communication, O. C. Lewis, July 1990).

Students are expected to keep pace with the other members
of their cluster, and they must remain employed in their field of
specialization. When they meet with faculty members at seminars,

Nova students make learning contracts similar to those used at Empire State, setting forth learning objectives to be completed through independent study. Students may join clusters at three times of the year and must finish their seminar work at a rate of one seminar every three months during the first two years of the program.

More than 10,000 letters written by local educators who have observed the practicums of more than 3,000 Nova students, judging them to have had a positive and substantial effect on the field, attest to the quality of Nova's field-based programs. Nova graduates have also been frequently evaluated by state-selected consultants as part of program assessment. Most of these consultants have felt that the expertise of those performing the practicums met or exceeded the summative objectives set for Nova programs. Several systematic studies of the educational administration doctoral program have reached similar conclusions. These surveys have shown among other things, that about 33 percent of graduates have held leadership positions in professional organizations, more than 50 percent have served as consultants outside their school systems, and almost 90 percent have helped initiate change intended to improve local schools or school systems (Sroufe, 1982). The superintendents of five of the nation's largest school districts are graduates of Nova programs (personal communication, O. C. Lewis, July 1990). Nova University offers a postgraduate paradigm for field-based seminar and independent study that has been emulated by many other graduate-level nontraditional programs.

Type III

Type III institutions are conventional universities that offer distance education through extension, independent study, or continuing education units. Most academic distance education providers in the United States fall into this category. There are many ways of further subdividing institutions that mix modes of delivery (see Rumble, 1986; Keegan, 1986; and Holmberg, 1986 for examples).

Because so much college level instruction at a distance occurs through correspondence or independent study, a look at the distance education enrollment of top Type III higher education providers in 1987–1988 as presented by Feasley and others (1989) is of interest (see Table 1.)

College credit enrollments are the most important for the purposes of this discussion. The enrollments of the top five institutions in college credit instruction, Indiana University, Brigham Young, Pennsylvania State University, the University of Minnesota, and Ohio University, are quite substantial. Thomas A. Edison College prints the correspondence study curricula of Indiana, Pennsylvania State, and Ohio University in its catalog for the convenience of its students, although the independent study courses of certain other universities that Edison has also evaluated may be used in fulfilling its degree requirements.

Pennsylvania State leads in overall enrollment. Of its nearly 22,000 enrollees, almost 14,000 are enrolled in noncredit courses and only 185 are enrolled in high school programs (Feasley, 1989). In contrast, Indiana, Missouri, and Nebraska, the third, fourth, and fifth largest providers overall, have no more than a few hundred noncredit students each. Missouri and Nebraska are first and second in high school enrollment, with over 12,000 enrollees each, but Indiana emphasizes college enrollment. None of the top fourteen programs in terms of overall enrollment specializes in only one of these three areas. Ohio University (number fifteen) exclusively serves college credit students, and Purdue (number nineteen) limits its services to noncredit offerings. Their exclusivity puts both in the top five in their respective areas of concentration. Some individual programs are discussed below to illustrate the nature and general activities of Type III institutions.

Department of Independent Learning, Pennsylvania State University. The development of distance education at the twenty-two campuses of the Pennsylvania State University (PSU) system has taken a different path from that taken by the University of Wisconsin and its extension program. PSU's College of Continuing Education and Extension has concentrated mostly on the creation of a class-based university extension service at 250 locations that utilizes regular and part-time faculty for instruction. This extended campus system is supplemented by correspondence study, educational television, and other educational media (Laverty, 1984).

Table 1. Distance Education Enrollment at Higher Education Institutions.

A. *Total Enrollment*		B. *College Credit Enrollment*	
1. Pennsylvania State University	21,971	1. Indiana University	10,890
2. Brigham Young University	19,073	2. Brigham Young University	10,508
3. University of Missouri	18,086	3. Pennsylvania State University	7,832
4. Indiana University	16,735	4. University of Minnesota	7,696
5. University of Nebraska	15,589	5. Ohio University	6,223

C. *High School Credit Enrollment*		D. *Noncredit Enrollment*	
1. University of Missouri	12,779	1. Pennsylvania State University	13,954
2. University of Nebraska	12,383	2. California State University, Sacramento	6,181
3. Texas Tech University	9,017	3. Purdue University	5,367
4. University of Texas, Austin	8,414	4. University of Florida	2,826
5. Brigham Young University	8,262	5. University of Wisconsin	2,712

Source: Derived from Feasley and others, 1989.

Pennsylvania State's Department of Independent Learning (DIL) has been offering independent study courses since the early 1900s. The DIL provides both on- and off-campus audiovisual services to conventional students and independent study opportunities to students who are unwilling or unable to attend on- or off-campus classes. Enrollment in independent study courses fluctuated between 9,000 and 13,000 students per year from 1975 through 1983. In 1981–82, 12,761 distance students were enrolled, about 50 percent in college credit courses and 50 percent in noncredit courses (Laverty, 1984). By 1987–88, enrollment had risen to 21,971, with about a 60/40 percent breakdown between noncredit and college credit students (Feasley and others, 1989). It is possible to complete a bachelor's degree at Penn State entirely by independent study, but the mission of the independent study program at the school is still mainly to supplement residential instruction. Experiments began at the school in 1965 to determine the efficacy of television as a teaching medium. Today, open broadcasts over educational television stations and cable broadcasts over the Pennsylvania Learning Network (PENNARAMA) are important forms of delivery of independent study courses.

PENNARAMA, or the Pennsylvania Learning Network, is the result of a consortium between Pennsylvania State University and the state of Pennsylvania's Education Communication Systems. PENNARAMA uses thirty-one cable television outlets to reach the homes of over 700,000 cable television subscribers. Courses are presented three times a week and repeated six times a day so that students can watch at times convenient for them. Most students are in their thirties or forties. Assignments and texts are exchanged by mail, and midterm and final examinations are administered at local sites using area educators as proctors. Associate degrees may be earned entirely via PENNARAMA if a single on-campus class in public speaking is successfully completed (Stern, 1987).

The use of compressed video for instruction was pioneered at Penn State in 1985. By greatly reducing the size of the signal needed for transmission, compressed video technology will allow Penn State to lease most of the bandwidth for data communication and voice channels, giving instructional signals a "free ride." Penn State's Strategic Plan for Telecommunications envisions video connection of classrooms on all twenty-two campuses in this manner (Phillips, 1987). This innovative use of technology supports the College of Continuing Education's mission of supplementing residential instruction since it will be used essentially to expand the use of current classroom teaching. On-campus experiments with electronic mail and computer conferencing point toward possible new directions in independent study, and a satellite link makes it possible for Penn State to beam what is largely "residential instruction" to interested parties around the world (Phillips and Santoro, 1989).

Brigham Young University. Brigham Young, while vying seriously for top enrollment with Penn State, is somewhat handicapped in out-of-state enrollments by its ties with the Church Educational System of the predominantly Mormon state of Utah. Brigham Young offers about 300 college level credit courses through the Independent Study program of the Division of Continuing Education. The mission of the Division of Continuing Education is not only to reach off-campus and part-time students but also to assist regular daytime students. Two associate degrees are available by independent study, but only about a year's worth of independent study can be counted toward an on-campus bachelor's degree. The university offers a church-oriented bachelor of independent studies degree intended to provide an extensive general education to working adults (Brigham Young University, 1989).

The University of Minnesota. The University of Minnesota's Department of Independent Study (DIS) is part of the College of Continuing Education and Extension. About 8,600 students were enrolled in the Independent Study Program in 1987–88, 95 percent of whom were taking college credit courses. Enrollment is open and may occur at any time of the year. Students may opt for a learning contract instead of structured course assignments, demonstrating their mastery of course content on the final. They also may take course exams after preparing independently, as in the Regents and Edison College programs.

As at Penn State, the university has no prohibition against completing a bachelor's degree through independent study. But although there are nearly 400 courses offered via independent study, not enough courses in any one discipline are offered to make it possible to finish a degree using the university's independent learning materials alone. The DIS does offer eleven certificates, four of which can be completed entirely by independent study and seven others that can be partially finished at a distance.

As has happened at many other campuses, the University of Minnesota developed a facilitating agency—the University Without Walls—whose task was to help students locate the resources they needed to create an individualized degree program. Now called the Program for Individualized Learning, this program makes it possible for students to earn a degree through a combination of credit for prior learning, credit by examination, on-campus study, courses from various independent study programs, and independent study projects. Degree requirements include an approved area of concentration, a strong grounding in the liberal arts, and proficiency in written English (Bear, 1988).

The DIS offers two programs—Courses by Independent

Study and Courses by Radio and Television. In both cases, the courses are for residential credit, and all instructors are approved by resident departments. About 385 courses, of which only 10 are non-credit and about 50 are high school credit, are offered via independent study. In 1981–82, 7,845 students took college level courses through the DIS (Laverty, 1984). By 1987–88, college credit enrollment had declined to 7,696 students (Feasley and others; 1989).

Wide-ranging certificate programs for teachers, health care professionals, and people involved in business and industry may be completed through independent study, usually in combination with extension classes, day classes, or summer session classes. Most independent study instructors are drawn from university faculty, although some are from other colleges or universities as well as business or the professions (Laverty, 1984).

Both DIS programs—Courses by Independent Study and Courses by Radio and Television—rely heavily on print materials. Television- and radio-assisted courses are delivered not only via open broadcast but also by cable TV and audiocassettes or video-cassettes at libraries and learning resource centers across the state. In both DIS programs, instructional designers or editors assist instructors in the development of their course materials for media delivery (Lewis, 1983; Laverty, 1984). Like the University of Wisconsin-Extension and Penn State, the University of Minnesota has used diverse methods and media in the delivery of its off-campus programs.

New York Institute of Technology. The American Open University of the New York Institute of Technology (NYIT) offers three degree programs through a combination of computer conferencing and correspondence study. Course learning packages, including textbook, outlines, and assignments are mailed to students. The NYIT Computer Teleconferencing System can be used by students with microcomputers and modems for dialogue with faculty who teach and advise the students. NYIT offers bachelor of science degrees in general studies, business administration, and behavioral sciences, with five possible concentrations in the behavioral sciences degree programs (New York Institute of Technology, 1988). NYIT has developed computer courseware packages as well, such as a ten-unit program for introductory psychology called Psychware, which include a faculty manual and student workbook. The software provides a series of interactive simulations, experiments, and tutorials that illustrate selected course topics (Slotnick, 1988). The computer-centered courses of NYIT represent another method that can be used by conventional institutions to make college credit and degrees more available to nontraditional learners.

Type IV

Model Type IV involves consortia of education-related institutions formed to provide distance courses in common or over a wide geographic area. A 1981 survey located seventy-one active television consortia in the United States, and a count of all educational consortia, large and small, could easily reach into the thousands. Consortia have played a large part in the development of postsecondary distance education in the United States. A consortium can be defined as a "formal organization of two or more member institutions, administered by a director, with tangible evidence of member support" (Niemeyer, 1985, p. 55). Since educational programming is so expensive, whether it is purchased or produced, educational institutions form consortia to share the costs and the risks of failure. Consortia members grant the same credit for participation, bringing a degree of consistency to their distance education practices (Niemeyer, 1985).

University of Mid-America. The University of Mid-America (UMA) was a large-scale television consortium patterned after the Open University of the United Kingdom that operated in the American Midwest from 1974 through 1982. UMA grew out of the University of Nebraska's SUN project and eventually involved eleven universities in seven states.

UMA granted neither credit nor degrees since its curriculum consisted of courses offered by member schools. It started with an emphasis on television but gradually came to rely heavily on print and other media. Tensions developed between various factions and institutions in UMA since, unlike the Open University of the United Kingdom, UMA sought to develop an open-university-style consortium in a nation with a highly accessible and well-developed educational infrastructure. UMA was dissolved due to lack of funding in 1983 just as attempts were underway to make it a national external-degree-granting institution to be called the American Open University. This name was subsequently used by the New York Institute of Technology in its baccalaureate via computer program, described earlier.

The National Technological University. The National Technological University (NTU) is a nonprofit consortium of twenty-four engineering schools formed in 1984. It broadcasts about 5,500 hours of credit and noncredit courses to over 100 industrial and corporate sites around the nation each year (Fields, 1987; Mays and Lumsden, 1988). Like other strictly facilitating institutions, it has no faculty or campus. Its headquarters at Colorado State University coordinates the distribution via a satellite network of courses produced at member institutions. Master's degrees in five programs can be earned totally through NTU: computer engineering, computer science, electrical engineering, engineering management, and manufacturing-systems engineering. Curricula are designed by interinstitutional faculty committees and are subject to review by educators from colleges and universities not belonging to NTU.

NTU began by videotaping classes and mailing copies to participating institutions, but in 1985 it acquired a transponder and began satellite broadcasts from some member schools to other member schools. Only about one-third of NTU students report watching live satellite broadcasts at their site since videotapes of the broadcast are available to watch at a more convenient time (Mays and Lumsden, 1988). NTU shares its satellite network with another engineering consortium, the Association for Media-Based Continuing Education for Engineers, which offers noncredit courses and seminars to those already working in the field. NTU evolved out of this association over the course of a decade as some members of the association's board conceived of and began an institution that would offer credit courses by satellite (Mays and Lumsden, 1988). Corporate sponsors of NTU include AT&T, IBM, Hewlett-Packard, and many other large technical companies.

The Electronic University. The Electronic University is a for-profit institution owned by TeleLearning System. It acts as a central clearinghouse for computer courses offered by a shifting group of participating colleges and universities. Some courses are sent by floppy disc, while others are on line. Faculty and students converse via electronic mail and computer conferencing. Students can earn bachelor's degrees from Regents College and Empire State, among others, through the Electronic University. On-line libraries and information data bases can be used by students who, needless to say, must be fairly wealthy to participate in this kind of study (Bear, 1988; Turner, 1983).

Type V

Type V institutions are autonomous institutions established specifically for the teaching of distance students. Type V schools might be called distance teaching institutions since they include schools at all levels—elementary, secondary, vocational/technical, and college. Distance teaching universities have been opened around the globe in nations where the educational infrastructure is not well developed or where access to higher education is highly restricted. Many DTU planners have used the Open University of the United Kingdom as a model. Because of the high quality of its publications and the many laudatory articles written about it, the OUUK is probably the only distance education unit that is positively viewed by American academics in general. No DTUs exist in United States; however, there are DTUs on the North American continent, and distance teaching institutes (such as the International Correspondence Schools) offering postsecondary but noncollegiate study are very common in the United States.

Two Canadian DTUs, Athabasca University in Alberta province, Canada, and Télé-Université (T-U) in Quebec, have achieved considerable success. Athabasca University was originally established as a conventional campus-based undergraduate-degree-granting institution in the late 1960s. In 1975 it was rechartered on a five-year trial basis as an open distance teaching university. It was given permanent status as a university in 1978.

At Athabasca University, baccalaureate degrees in liberal

studies and administrative science can be finished completely at a distance. A bachelor of general studies degree is also offered that can be partially or completely earned through the accrediting of university-level coursework completed elsewhere (Abrioux, 1984). A telephone tutor may be consulted about problems related to study by calling a toll-free number. Athabasca University enrolls about 10,000 students, which is about the minimum enrollment economically feasible for a DTU utilizing instructional design and course team approaches. Only about 38 percent of enrolled students complete courses, a very low figure even for distance institutions (Shale, 1984). Athabasca University has been the site of a large amount of research concerning the effectiveness of various methods of presenting components of distance education (Shale, 1984).

Télé-Université in Quebec was created in 1972 at least partly in response to the creation of the Open University of the United Kingdom. T-U was given permanent, autonomous status in 1974 and grew rapidly between 1977 and 1981. It was reorganized in 1981 so that its management would better fit its functions as a DTU.

T-U offers credit certificates for thirty credit hours and bachelor's degrees for ninety credit hours. It does not compete with the other provincial universities since it does not have specializations in any discipline. T-U follows a liberal arts approach and encourages students to study in many disciplines. Students may choose a sociocultural science and technology or labor-management emphasis in their programs.

Télé-Université relies heavily on print media. About 80 percent of learning materials are print based. As at Athabasca University, students who call toll-free numbers can contact tutors. Audiocassettes are an important component of many courses and videocassettes and open and cable television broadcasts are used to some extent. The average T-U student is a thirty-five-year-old woman with a university degree. Of the students enrolled, 60 percent are women and 60 percent live in areas of Quebec province not served by conventional universities. T-U has enrolled over 50,000 students since 1974, nearly 90,000 if repeat registrations are counted (Lamy and Henri, 1983).

Type VI

Model Type VI involves educational media developed by recognized educational or informational organizations used without the assistance of an educational organization by informal distance learners. This is certainly the biggest category of all, for it includes not only self-instructional materials of all kinds, including media intended for conventional education such as textbooks, but also educational uses of distance media by incidental learners and indeed use of all media that might be considered educational or informational when used by someone engaged in incidental or self-planned learning. The point of offering this category is not to impress readers by adding up how many hundreds of millions of times each year Americans engage in individual "distance learning," but rather to point out that learning at a distance is an integral, even essential, part of the lives of most Americans today. Looking at their own distance learning activities might give people a more accurate idea of what distance education is rather than the traditional views of it as "matchbook education."

Summary

Numerous postsecondary institutions and organizations currently offer distance education to adult learners. The offerings range from awarding degrees without direct instruction to simply providing media to distance learners. The form of education delivered varies according to the nature of the institution and its mission.

Some institutions offer degrees through various combinations of course or proficiency examinations, as well as credit for experiential learning and life and work experiences. These Type I institutions offer degrees and course credit to students whom they have not taught directly.

Type II institutions offer degrees to students whom they have taught in some measure; and degree requirements can be met through a combination of prior learning, life and work experiences, examinations, and distance education coursework. These institutions offer both external and distance study in their programs.

Conventional universities can offer distance education degrees and coursework through extension, independent study, and continuing education, while still maintaining their regular programs on campus. These Type III institutions offer considerable correspondence and independent study in their programs. They are the major academic providers of distance education in the United States.

The consortia of institutions are seen as Type IV providers of distance education. They have played a large part in the development of distance education in the United States and were developed to share costs, materials, and programs and to provide consistency in distance education practices.

Type V institutions are those that have been established specifically for teaching at a distance. These distance teaching universities or institutions are popular in foreign countries but, with the exception of the vocational-technical proprietary schools, have not developed in the United States.

Educational and informational organizations that develop educational media used by informal distance learners fall into the Type VI category. These organizations prepare media for people engaged in incidental or self-planned learning but do not offer any assistance with the process.

Most distance instruction is provided by institutions of Types III, IV, and V—institutions or consortia devoting part or all of their resources to distance education for adults. Distance educators, after reviewing these systems, should determine which one, or possibly which combinations or modifications of systems, would be most useful for their distance education needs. All can be effective in meeting selected goals, as defined by institutions and their adult clients.

4

Delivering Programs
to Learners

A variety of modes and systems can be used to deliver distance education. Many of these can be combined into multimedia packages that appeal to students with different learning styles. A discussion of the major modes and systems of delivery and their strengths and weaknesses follows.

Audiocassette

The audiocassette may be the most overlooked distance medium. Bates (1982) claims, "The greatest media development during the twelve years of its existence has been the humble audiocassette" (Yule, 1985, p. 318). Many people have cassette players, even in less-developed regions. Six of nine DTUs surveyed by Rumble and Harry (1982) used audiocassettes, as did five of twelve DTUs surveyed by Bates (1982).

The phonograph record was the first form of recorded audio. Although record use is flexible, records are bulky and easy to damage and require considerable manipulation. Learners can easily find a particular passage on a record, but the disadvantages of records tend to outweigh the advantages, especially if the expense of record players versus radios or tape players is considered. Although open-reel tape recorders gained in popularity after World War II, the introduction of the audiocassette in 1970 led to the near disappearance of open-reel tapes in nonprofessional settings and substantially cut into the market of phonograph records.

Despite a large increase in audiocassette use by consumers, use of this medium for educational purposes by formal institutions is lower than might be expected, according to Takemoto (1987). She gives three reasons for the limited acceptance of audiocassette: the bias against audiovisual media among instructors, their preference for videocassettes, and the insufficient inventory of audiocassettes in the national market (less than fifty) created for formal educational uses. Her conclusions are somewhat contradicted by Lewis (1985), who reported on a survey by the Western Interstate Commission on Higher Education (WICHE) to which 344 of the 575 public and private postsecondary institutions located in the thirteen western states that belong to WICHE responded. Audiocassettes were used by 29 percent of the institutions for off-campus instruction and 66 percent for on-campus instruction. Audiocassette was the most popular form of audio technology for instructional purposes, more popular than radio, teleconferencing, and telephone (Lewis, 1985).

The Open University of the United Kingdom has made widespread use of audiocassettes. OUUK administrators cite low cost as a reason for using them, and academics say audiocassettes give them control of courses. Students indicate that they like the convenience and informality audiocassettes offer them (Yule, 1983). A graduate-level management course offered on audiocassette to master of business administration students by an American university was as effective in terms of achievement as the on-campus classroom version of the course, and students using the audiocassette program highly recommended it (Hales and Felt, 1986). The Annenberg/CPB Project offers nine college-credit courses on audiocassette, each consisting of twelve to eighteen lessons about topics such as American history, sociology, and psychology ("CAEL . . . ," 1988).

Advantages and Disadvantages: The audiocassette is essentially a scaled-down version of open-reel tape, enclosed in a box. It requires considerably less manipulation to use than phonograph records or open-reel tapes and can be taken along in a pocket or purse and listened to while driving or exercising outdoors. As with any prerecorded, learner-controlled media, audiocassettes allow students to control the time of day and week in which they study and the speed with which they progress. Flexibility and ease of manipulation may make students feel that they are in control of their learning. Variable numbers of cassettes can be produced, while the cost of broadcasting operations remains the same whether there are many students or few. Audiocassette programs can be the actual length of the presentation, but radio programs may need to be made to fit a time slot. Since audiocassettes allow one to stop and review material, programs on audiocassettes can have a higher level of complexity than radio broadcasts.

Audiocassette and print together are a powerful teaching tool (Bates, 1982). Obviously, when audiocassettes are intended to accompany a visual source, the visual source must match the audiocassette in degree of learner control. Audiocassette, which can be used repeatedly and wound back and forth to match corresponding jumps from one place to another in the text, match easily with pictures and diagrams.

Some disadvantages of audiocassette, however, include the need for playback equipment and the need for a production and distribution system. Audiocassette can be used for interaction between teacher and learner, but it is difficult for students to find places in a lesson on the tape or to break monologues up into important points that need to be answered. Rapid movement from one section of the audiocassette to another and indepth didactic conversation are difficult to achieve on audiocassette. The telephone appears to be the best medium for this kind of interaction.

Telephone

Although the telephone has been available since 1876, its use for distance education is relatively recent. The invention of loudspeaker telephones in the United States in the late 1950s increased the growth of group study at a distance (Pinches, 1975). A variety of teleconferencing possibilities have been created since then by the development of electronic switching devices for uses in telephony (Brown and Brown, 1984).

The telephone transmits more than just voices. Indeed, the nation's telephone channels may be looked at as being similar to the mail delivery system. Just as correspondence study is a delivery method that may carry modes of communication such as audio-cassette, videocassette, or printed written and visual materials, distance education via telephone wire or channel may involve signals enabling one-way communication visually by electronic blackboard or by audio through lectures or tapes in addition to two-way communication or interaction through single or multiple telephone conversations and by computer.

Perry (1984) surveyed 304 institutions offering 468 programs at a distance in over eighty nations and found the telephone used at all educational levels. The telephone was employed more in developed regions such as Europe and North America, where institutions surveyed used the telephone at a 29 percent and 43 percent rate, respectively. Only 5 percent of Asian programs and no African programs used it. Overall use of the telephone was about 22 percent. Rumble and Harry (1982) found that six of nine DTUs they surveyed used telephone tuition. The three universities that do not use the telephone are located in three developing nations—Venezuela, Pakistan, and the People's Republic of China.

The WICHE survey of higher education in thirteen western states found that 17 percent of the institutions surveyed used audio conferencing for instruction on campus, and 10 percent used it off campus. Regular telephone service, or tutoring, was part of instruction on campus in 15 percent and off campus in 12 percent of the schools (Lewis, 1985).

Telephone communication includes single- and multiple-user systems. Monologues, or one-way recorded messages, may be accessed by telephone. Dialogues between teacher and student for tutorial, feedback, or other purposes are the most traditional uses of the telephone in distance education. Students may also communicate with other students. Group use of telephony, involving scattered individuals or people gathered at a particular location, has greatly expanded the interactive possibilities of telephone learning.

Teleconferencing combines broadcast lectures, recorded audio materials, telephone conversations with the teacher and other students, and, sometimes, visuals on electronic blackboards or slow-scan television sent over another telephone line. Takemoto (1987) believes that this format "embodies all of the potential requirements of an effective educational medium—accessibility, quality, integration, control, and interactivity" (p. 26). Rio Salada Community College in Phoenix, Arizona, uses teleconferencing with its radio courses to deliver orientation, feedback, and course review (Takemoto, 1987). Teleconferencing has been successfully employed in the continuing education of pharmacists (Roeder, 1983), piano teachers (Hugdahl, 1980), social workers in remote parts of Alaska (Kleinkauf and Robinson, 1987), and foster parents and social workers in Montana (Deaton and Clark, 1987). It has even been used to provide short courses to nursing home patients for community college credit (Stanley-Muchow and Poe, 1988).

The most extensive telephone network for educational purposes in the United States is Wisconsin's Education Telephone Network which enrolled over 32,000 students in 1980. In that year, ETN connected over 200 meeting sites in 100 towns and cities via twenty telephone companies and over 5,000 miles of voice channel (Feasley, 1982). ETN was formed in 1966 by the University of Wisconsin-Extension as a way of furthering its mission to extend the boundaries of the university to the boundaries of the state. ETN began with medical staff education and grew to serve the continuing education needs of many professions. A second telephone network, the Statewide Extension Network, which offered slow-scan television, enrolled over 2,100 learners in 1980, five years after its creation. The twenty-three SEEN centers featured *electrowriters,* which allowed exchange of still images via telephone lines before slow-scan TV was installed (Feasley, 1982).

Technical breakthroughs and adjustments to technical limitations greatly facilitated SEEN's growth. Teleconferencing using the regular telephone system was abandoned after a year of variable service, and four-wire lines to study centers were rented instead. SEEN obtained better telephone service this way but lost the flexibility of regular teleconferencing. Subsequent minimization of transmission noise levels further improved the quality of service (Reid and Champness, 1983).

The cost to the supplier to transmit telephone conversations by satellite does not vary significantly no matter how distant the parties in a telephone conversation are. International teleconferencing is not prohibitively expensive and should be a growth area as international academic boundaries continue to diminish.

Advantages and Disadvantages: The telephone has several advantages as a medium for distance teaching. It is flexible and relatively inexpensive and is an interactive, not a one-way, method of communication. It can be used to provide individual attention, diagnose the learner's problems, and reduce the learner's sense of isolation. Through teleconferencing, it can be used to reach specialized groups or individuals over a wide geographic area (Bates, 1982).

Although almost all Americans have access to a telephone and most can get to study centers for group teleconferencing, telephone access is not so widespread in developing nations and service is often unreliable. While the cost of telephone study may seem reasonable to Americans, it is more expensive than the use of audiocassettes in countries where distance education efforts must use only the bare essentials. The lack of visual stimuli in instruction by telephone and the expense of some forms of telephone-based distance study systems suggest that the telephone should be combined with other media in most cases (Bates, 1982). The telephone may be linked to other media at a reasonable cost. Equipping meeting sites for video origination and providing hardware for distribution of the video signal to other meeting sites is very expensive. The percentage of videoconference sites in the United States that can be expected to originate the video portion of programming is, therefore, small, so the use of the telephone for return information from the video receiving sites to the video sending sites is likely to continue. This may be changed somewhat by developments in video transmission allowing small-scale telephone videoconferencing, which might be used with small groups of students.

Radio

Radio was invented at the turn of the century. The explosive growth in the number of radio stations in the 1920s and 1930s led to the establishment of the Federal Communications Commission (FCC) in 1934. The commission allocated AM radio channels to educational uses beginning in 1940. FM radio, invented in 1935, came to replace AM educational broadcasting starting in the 1950s.

FM radio has less noise and less variability in signal strength than AM radio. It also uses more bands, some of which can be used to broadcast programs to special receivers located in nearby areas. About fifty stations in the United States were broadcasting on unused bands in 1979. By 1982, programs included special reading services for the visually impaired in about twenty-five cities (Feasley, 1982).

Public FM radio was used for on-campus instruction by 11 percent of institutions responding to the WICHE survey and for off-campus instruction by 7 percent of the institutions (Lewis, 1985). It is usually used as part of a multimedia mix. Community colleges appear to make greater use of this delivery method than do four-year institutions. At Milwaukee Area Technical College, faculty develop "Technical School of the Air" radio and television segments that are broadcast twice weekly by Wisconsin public broadcasting stations. Ninety miles away, the University of Wisconsin prepares "University of the Air" radio courses broadcast by WHA Madison, and statewide in conjunction with correspondence study components (Lewis, 1983). However, most public radio stations in America do not participate in formal higher education programs. "Radio has played a relatively quiet but steady role in U.S. formal education" (Takemoto, 1987, p. 22).

Radio is used for adult education in many nations and is still a fast-growing phenomenon in some developing nations. Five of seven multimedia adult basic education projects in Europe that were the subjects of case studies by Kaye and Harry (1982) used radio broadcasting.

In nations with low literacy rates, radio is an important adult education medium because it can to some extent replace print. While most people have individual access to a radio in developed nations, thirty or forty people, on average, listen to each radio in the developing world, which has only about seventy-five million radios. Radios are cheap, costing $20.00 or less in developing nations. Postal delivery is often highly unreliable in these countries, as is telephone service, making radio an obvious alternative. Even individuals who do not formally sign up for radio courses may engage in distance learning by listening to them for free. As Rumble (1986) notes: "In Latin America, radio broadcasting organizations were among the pioneers of distance education, and this is reflected in the structure of many current systems where there is less emphasis on print and individual correspondence tuition, and more on locally organized listening groups" (p. 9).

Advantages and Disadvantages: Radio's advantages include easy access, relatively low cost, immediate availability, and the possibility of changing content quickly if necessary (Perraton, 1982). But radio has drawbacks, too, especially when compared with the other media generally available. Some people simply do not learn well by radio. It is difficult to concentrate on a radio program and ten or fifteen minutes seems to be the optimum length for effective listening and learning. If the words are not simple and the pronunciation clear, many listeners may lose the train of thought. Concrete programs featuring a few points using simple words and dramatization appear to work, but this is probably not the form in which most educators would want to use radio (Perraton, 1982). Radio listeners must listen at a fixed time to programs that they cannot pace. The widespread availability of audiocassette technology allows learners with both a radio and a cassette player, or a radio-cassette player, to tape programs for later listening.

The lack of a visual component and the noninteractive nature of radio are also major disadvantages. Of course, interactive radio does exist. In Australia, learners engage in conversation with their teachers by two-way radio. Two-way FM radio can be used to provide an interactive element in videoconferencing, much like telephone, but the lack of visual information and noninteractive nature of one-way radio are more commonly overcome through combination with other media.

Just as audiocassette is the most cost-effective audio technology for one-way communication with small groups, radio broadcasting is the most cost-effective technology for reaching mass audiences. For groups of 500 students or fewer, audiocassette is cheaper than radio, but for larger groups, distance teachers should consider using radio as part of their media mix.

Other Audio Media

Besides audiocassette, telephone, and radio, several other forms of audio technology deserve mention. Although phonograph records, like open-reel tape, have been largely displaced by audiocassette, over 11,000 books are available through the Talking Books Program on records that require special players. Fifty-six regional libraries and the Library of Congress make these books available to the public (Heinich, Molenda, and Russell, 1985). Compact disc is an exciting new technology whose main educational use is as a data base (see the discussion of computers later in this chapter). Microcassette, a scaled-down version of audiocassette, is easy to carry and good for taking notes but has poor sound quality, which makes it undesirable as a means of educational delivery.

Television

Television is a video medium with great potential as a distance delivery mode. It is used in a bewildering variety of ways, both in distance and conventional education. Visual media can be traced back to still pictures, the oldest form of recorded media. For many, many years, still pictures have been combined with print in texts. With the invention of photography in the early nineteenth century, illustrations in text gained accuracy and realism. The development of motion pictures in 1884 and of talkies in 1926 led to the widespread use of film in education after World War II. Television, invented in 1926, also blossomed as an educational medium during the postwar era.

Broadcast Television. In broadcast television, the signal is beamed through the air to TV receivers without the use of wires or cables. Most educational television in the United States is transmitted by open broadcast. Even the regional programming of Community Antenna Television (CATV) systems is picked up on open broadcast signals and then sent through coaxial cables to customers. Practically every American household—99 percent—has a television set (U.S. Department of Education, 1989). In Lewis's 1985 survey of 344 WICHE member institutions, 36 percent reported off-campus use of broadcast TV for instruction. The Corporation for Public Broadcasting (CPB) reported a slightly lower figure, 32 percent, in a nationwide survey (Whittington, 1987).

Educational television broadcasting requires the existence of a network of educational stations. Noncommercial educational television stations increased in number and gained larger operating budgets following the adoption of the Public Broadcasting Act of 1967, which authorized the establishment of the CPB. The CPB in turn authorized the Public Broadcasting Service and National Public Radio (NPR) as distribution networks for educational programs to noncommercial stations. The 1967 act also provided for federal support and financing of educational broadcasting. In 1966, 126 educational television stations were on the air, with total budgets of $51 million and $7 million in federal support. By 1972, 233 educational television stations were broadcasting, with combined budgets of $158 million and $31 million in federal aid (Carnegie Commission, 1979).

The 1972 FCC rule requiring the inclusion of educational stations in the programming of CATV systems also increased the audiences of PBS stations, and put these stations on an equal footing with the more popular commercial stations (Federal Communications Commission, 1972). Television delivery of college credit courses—once largely limited to over-the-air broadcast by PBS stations, which did not have full coverage of the nation—now included the retransmission of broadcasts via CATV. With the development of the one-half-inch home videocassette in the late 1970s, three forms of television delivery could be used in the home for educational purposes: open broadcast, CATV, and videocassette.

Of course, more delivery methods are involved if the origin of the program broadcast by the local PBS station is also counted. It is still common to use point-to-point microwave to relay live or prerecorded national programs or to mail prerecorded three-quarter-inch videocassettes to the local station. Many PBS stations now get their "feeds" from program sources around the country via satellite and store them on videocassette for later airing. Satellite delivery of programs provides more reliable service at a reduced cost.

Cable Television. In 1952, the first CATV, or cable television, system was built in the United States. By 1964, over a thousand cable TV systems were in operation in the country. Educational cable TV was facilitated by a 1972 FCC rule requiring twenty-channel capability by cable operators. Four kinds of access were to be provided to the public by cable systems: public, educational, governmental, and leased (Federal Communications Commission, 1972). As they travel through coaxial cable to the homes of subscribers, CATV signals must be boosted and rebooted, which increases not only the signal power but also the noise in the signal. At some point, there is too much noise in the transmission for the signal to be considered of acceptable quality. This gives cable TV systems an effective operating limit of ten or twenty miles.

Interactive cable television would allow individuals to access programs and talk with the instructor as do groups in central sites. Interactive cable already exists since phone-in shows allow local residents to talk with on-air personalities. Some interactive systems such as QUBE, first activated in Columbus, Ohio, in 1977, allow viewers to respond to questions by use of a special keypad. Instant feedback on the correctness of answers is provided. This test-oriented communication takes place on a much greater scale than does two-way audio communication between learners (Baldwin and McVoy, 1983). About 17 percent of WICHE institutions surveyed in 1985 used one-way cable off campus but only around 2 percent employed interactive cable TV for off-campus teaching (Lewis, 1985).

Telecourses. The popularity of telecourses, which combine video, text, and other sources, was increased by the creation of the PBS Adult Learner Service in 1981. In the same year, the publisher Walter Annenberg made a long-term grant of $150 million to the Corporation for Public Broadcasting for the funding of projects using television and other telecommunications or information media to enhance the quality and availability of higher education for working adults (Stern, 1987). The Adult Learning Service works with public television, colleges, and independent producers to develop new courses. PBS expected about 20,000 adult learners to sign up for its initial 1981–82 academic year. Instead, 53,000 students nationwide enrolled for college credit telecourses at 555 colleges and universities working in cooperation with 237 public television stations. By the end of 1988, over 1,500 colleges and 300 PBS stations had teamed up to register over a million enrollments in ALS-distributed telecourses (Public Broadcasting Service, 1989). For the 1989–90 season, thirty-seven telecourses were offered by an extension of the Adult Learning Service which uses satellites to feed programming to member stations. Over 200 colleges have become Adult Learning Satellite Service members, and about 1,100 utilize some of its programming (Public Broadcasting Service, 1989).

Niemeyer (1985) located seventy-one postsecondary television consortia enrolling 100,000 students in 1982. In its first six years of operation (1974–1980), the Dallas County Community College District enrolled 39,194 telecourse students. Other major producers and distributors of telecourses include Coast Community College (California) and Miami-Dade Community College District (Florida).

Early telecourses on television usually were poorly produced and followed a talking-head format that probably reduced potential viewership. But by the late 1970s, this had changed. For example, Kentucky Educational Television's GED series was praised for its high production values and good instructional design (Cervero and Cunningham, 1976). An important influence on American educational television was the British Broadcasting Company (BBC), which has always been a significant source of educational television programming. BBC telecourses and documentaries, which reflected the BBC's subsidized status and stability, set a standard for American and other telecourse developers to follow (Mareth, 1986).

Microwave Broadcasting. Similar in range to CATV but able to reach nonwired viewing sites, instructional television–fixed service uses lower-power microwave broadcasts to serve sites up to twenty-five miles from the studio. Another use of microwave broadcasting is for point-to-point TV transmissions, commonly used by TV networks and stations, CATV systems, and educational institutions to relay TV signals for rebroadcast or introduction into closed-circuit systems. Microwave relay transmission is used in large-scale educational television systems such as the Indiana Higher Education Telecommunication System (IHETS) and PENNARAMA in Pennsylvania. IHETS connects the major institutions of higher education in Indiana through a microwave relay system. PENNARAMA is a statewide system linking cable television systems in thirty-one Pennsylvania cities via a microwave trunk route (Stern, 1987). Pennsylvania State is now using microwave for two-way compressed video transmissions between its campuses and learning centers. Instructional Television-Fixed Service or point-to-point microwave was used by about 11 percent of institutions off campus in the 1985 Lewis survey.

Compressed Video. Pennsylvania State, Ohio State, and some other universities are beginning to use digitized TV signals, which, being "compressed," take up less room in a signal, allowing the carrying of additional audio and data signals that may pay the cost of the video portion. Two-way video transmission via closed-circuit methods may be more affordable in the long run using such compressed signals, although start-up costs are high. Acker and Albarran (1988) predict that integrated services digital networks, including compressed video, will supplant current analog telecommunications networks.

Aerial Broadcasting. An unusual method of transmission was used in a 1960s experiment in educational television broadcasting. The Midwest Program on Airborne Television Instruction used an airplane circling at 23,000 feet to transmit instructional television programs to students at schools in six states (Danna, 1984). The experiment clashed with the interests of commercial TV broadcasters, who feared it would encourage for-profit "stratocasters" to broadcast from high in the atmosphere. What came next—open broadcasting from space—makes these fears seem almost ludicrous today.

Satellite Broadcasting. The creation of geosynchronous satellites in the 1960s has led to the routine use in American education of TV transmissions relayed by telecommunications satellites. Most satellites involved in educational broadcasting transmit to receivers with ten-foot dishes, usually serving customers such as cable TV companies, stockbrokers, and libraries. The satellite beam is focused into a region-sized "footprint" that keeps the cost of receivers and the satellite power requirements within reason. Cost tends to dictate group viewing sites when such multipoint-distribution services are used for educational purposes.

Individual reception of television from space, or direct broadcast satellite (DBS), has long been a dream of educational visionaries. Several nations in Europe and Asia have been able to develop education-oriented DBS systems using small (one-meter) dishes, but the United States has been slow to develop such systems. Power, frequency, and other technical limitations of DBS systems are likely to keep the price of transmissions to individual households prohibitively high when compared with the cost of other sources of postsecondary education in America (Heinich, Molenda, and Russell, 1985).

Consortia that engage in satellite videoconferencing, such as the National University Teleconferencing Network (NUTN) and the National Technological University (NTU), were discussed at some length in Chapter Three. These consortia distribute college level instruction via satellite to learners at specially equipped receiver sites. But these video consortia do not utilize satellite alone. Most grew out of videotape-based engineering programs and other graduate programs. Some member institutions, lacking receiver equipment, still receive their programming on videotape or via microwave, and many students watch a videotape of the live satellite broadcast at a time that is convenient to them. Besides using the telephone, which adds a semblance of interactivity, students use print materials such as syllabi, assignments, and class notes that are provided for them, depending on the number of students and teaching sites. NTU has sent print materials via computer to students with the necessary equipment since 1988. But satellite video is an important component of the media mix. It has greatly increased the geographical range of program distribution of video consortia (Mays and Lumsden, 1988). In Lewis's 1985 survey of media usage at 344 WICHE member institutions, 9 percent of the schools reported on-campus instructional delivery via videoconferences utilizing one-way video and two-way audio, and 3 percent reported off-campus use. Two-way video use on campus was reported by only 2 percent of schools and off campus by 3 percent.

Videocassette. Videocassette and videocassette recorders have added a new dimension to the development, distribution, and use of educational television programming. Any program developed for one-way broadcast can also be put on videocassette, and many telecourses are. Telecourses on videocassette may be provided to adult learners or the learners may create their own educational cassettes by taping telecourses as they are broadcast. This allows educators in areas where most people own videocassette recorders to broadcast telecourses at times when live viewership is unlikely, such as early morning. Telecourse viewership has almost certainly been increased by the use of home videocassettes, although this may not be reflected in the numbers, because videocassette course enrollment is usually counted as independent or correspondence study rather than telecourse study. A nationwide survey by the Corporation for Public Broadcasting found that 32 percent of responding colleges offered telecourses via videocassette (Brey, 1988).

In Idaho, master's degree programs in engineering and computer science, as well as continuing education courses and credit courses, are offered through the University of Idaho's Video Outreach Graduate Program. Off-campus students watch videotapes of on-campus classes and take comprehensive examinations upon completion of their coursework (Rigas, 1982). Videotape consortia, such as the Northern Illinois Learning Resources Cooperative, a consortium of Illinois colleges, offer courses by videocassette through learning centers and public libraries (Zigerell, 1986). Much of this activity may go unnoticed, since college telecourse study via videocassette is generally counted as a form of correspondence study and is not yet included in PBS/ALS statistics on viewership.

Videocassette use in adult and higher education is not limited to college credit telecourses. Brush and Brush (1986) report that about 8,500 for-profit and nonprofit organizations in the United States spent $2.3 billion in 1985 to prepare videocassettes for use in training, communication, and promotion. Over 1,100 postsecondary-level video courses are available (Weisner, 1987).

Videocassette was used on campus by 85 percent and off campus by 32 percent of the 344 western colleges and universities surveyed by Lewis (1985), making it the most commonly used of the nonprint instructional technologies surveyed. Just as audiocassettes are convenient to use and flexible when compared with radio broadcasts, videocassettes have similar advantages when compared with television broadcasts. Videocassettes are also much easier to manipulate than film, just as audiocassettes are simpler to use than open-reel tape.

As was noted earlier, audiocassette production is cheaper than radio broadcasting up to a certain size of learner market, at which point radio use becomes more cost efficient. The same can be said of videocassette production, which may be an efficient means of providing telecourses in areas where educators believe there is not sufficient learner interest to justify television broadcasting.

Advantages and Disadvantages. The production, distribution, and transmission of television programming can be such a complex project that more can go wrong, resulting in poor or disrupted service, than with any other medium. Except for computer use, television broadcasting has the highest start-up costs and overhead. Television's greatest limitation, requiring that it be supplemented by interactive media, is that, basically, it is a one-way method of communication. But because it can be delivered in so many ways and because it so closely approximates the appearance of face-to-face instruction, which many teachers and students prefer, television has great potential as a distance education medium.

Computers

Computers can be used to present educational material and to perform many other functions in the process of instruction. Computers may be the size of a typewriter (microcomputer), a desk (minicomputer), or a room (mainframe). Most computer applications in distance education can be classified as computer-assisted instruction (CAI), computer-managed instruction (CMI), or computer conferencing (CC). Elements of both CAI and CMI are found in computer-based instruction (CBI).

Computer-Assisted Instruction. CAI involves the use of the computer as a teaching machine. An instructional unit is presented through the computer to the student, and as the student interacts with the instructional presentation, learning occurs.

Heinich, Molenda, and Russell (1985) list six modes of computer-assisted instruction: drill and practice, tutorial, gaming, simulation, discovery, and problem solving. Drill and practice and tutorial modes are basically question-and-answer formats. Tutorials simulate the basic responses of a human tutor through "branching" answers to learner behavior. A branching program allows the computer to follow through on different learner responses with different sequences or levels of instruction. Computer games related to an educational topic may be incorporated into instruction. Simulations take a real-world situation and reduce it to its essential elements, creating a system whose behavior varies in response to different conditions created by the learner's responses. Discovery learning requires the student to use inductive logic to empirically develop rules or procedures that explain evidence in a data base. Problem solving with a computer involves the student's defining the problem and then manipulating variables or otherwise searching for a solution using the computer for calculation and arrangement of data (Heinich, Molenda, and Russell, 1985).

Some educators question the applicability of CAI to adult education. The English educators Bostock and Seifert (1985) state that question-and-answer instruction, the most frequently used computer format, is of little use to adult educators except for remedial instruction or skills training since most adult education is andragogical and devoted to teaching high-level liberal arts and humanities courses. They see considerable use for simulations and modeling and for more "intelligent" CAI systems, if these systems ever are developed. Bostock and Seifert's observations seem less applicable in the United States where most adult education falls outside of the liberal arts area.

The first instructional use of computers occurred at the University of Illinois in 1960. The university was the birthplace of Programmed Logic for Automatic Teaching Operations (PLATO), a versatile CAI system in which student terminals are connected by telephone lines to a large mainframe computer. The speed and power of the mainframe computer allow many users to access the computer at the same time. PLATO terminals can be connected to peripherals such as videodisc players, slide projectors, and speech synthesizers that may then be activated at the appropriate time in instructional sessions by the central computer. This allows students to combine media without additional effort and at the proper pace.

Rachal (1984) reviewed studies in which PLATO was used in

correctional or military settings or basic skills centers to provide ABE/GED instruction. Most of the studies showed students using PLATO outperforming students using conventional learning methods, but Rachal cautions against seeing PLATO as a panacea in these settings. Further, the cost of large-scale CAI systems like PLATO is much higher than that of conventional instruction. Twelve adult education administrators interviewed by Kasworm and Anderson (1982) all indicated that cost and time considerations were their largest concern in considering the use of CAI.

Most CAI systems probably involve the use of software programs in personal computers. Indeed, PLATO software is available on disc. Control Data, a longtime PLATO user, bought the software for its 1,100 computers (Heinich, Molenda, and Russell, 1985).

The New York Institute of Technology has developed a CAI package called Psychware. Psychware is designed for use in introductory psychology courses and offers users simulations, tutorials, and games (Slotnick, 1988).

Computer-Managed Instruction. Computer-Managed Instruction (CMI) includes a variety of applications of computers in the administration of individualized instruction in which there is no direct learner interaction with the computer (Heinich, Molenda, and Russell, 1985). Conventional colleges and universities make large-scale use of computers in the management of instruction that is not individualized. Computer-generated mail informs students of grades, class schedules, and registration and other deadlines, and relays student information to faculty members. Faculty members often use computers for CMI as well. Computer workstations connected to the central mainframe can be used for testing and monitoring students' progress. Some colleges and universities, such as Clarkson College and Drexel University, require entering students to purchase a personal computer, which, when connected to the mainframe with a modem, increases the potential for CMI as well as for other computer applications in conventional education settings ("Computer Chronicles," 1990).

CMI is more important in distance than in conventional education because in distance education the student may not have access to any of the formal or informal on-campus means by which students are notified of important information. TEL TEST, a CMI system developed by International Correspondence Schools of Scranton, Pennsylvania, is an alternative method of testing. Students with touch-tone telephones can use their keypads like computer keyboards to phone in their answers to criterion-referenced test questions. Using a computer-generated voice, TEL TEST provides immediate feedback on the student's test score and gives page numbers for rereading in response to incorrect answers. Scores are automatically recorded in the student's records, and in some cases the shipment of additional learning materials is triggered (Valore, 1984).

A CMI system called Computer-Assisted Distance Education (CADE) was first used by Hermods Correspondence School of Sweden in 1970. Through the use of CADE, computer-generated comments, rather than comments by a human tutor, could be mailed to students along with test results. Computer comments were programmed responses to particular mistakes in test answers. The computer, being tireless, gave each student 300 printed words of comment, on average, as compared to the 20 to 50 written words given by human tutors (Baath and Manson, 1977, in Feasley, 1982).

Computer-mediated-education (CME), a subset of CBI, refers to computer applications that facilitate rather than provide instruction. CME uses computer conferencing, electronic mail, networks, facsimile, teletex and videotex and other electronic delivery systems to facilitate learning. Computer conferencing permits two-way transfer of information between computer users. A number of colleges and universities now use computer conferencing to allow real-time dialogue between teachers and learners. Computer conferencing has been used at Rochester Institute of Technology in New York to provide dialogue between teacher and telecourse students (Coombs, 1989). At the American Open University of the New York Institute of Technology, computer conferencing is used in independent study courses to supplement print material delivered via electronic mail to home computers (Hailes, 1986). People appear to be more willing to discuss things of an emotional or personal nature on the computer than they are in person. New students indicated that interest in the computer-mediated communication process was itself the main reason for enrolling in courses using computer conferencing (Phillips and Pease, 1987).

Electronic mail has been called electronic correspondence study because of its widespread use for the distribution of documents via home computers. The Annenberg/CPB foundation funded an electronic text consortium that developed and tested a number of experimental uses of the medium (Carey and Dozier, 1985).

Computer networks allow multiple users to share resources and instructional programming. Networks can be formed at a number of different levels and with different purposes, from national data bases to local discussion groups. Many networks provide library support to off-campus students, solving a perennial problem. Students of Telelearning System's Electronic University have access to more than eighty data bases, including large libraries (Bear, 1988). Eastern Oregon State College developed an Online Reference and Document Delivery Service Library Network to provide computer searches and telefacsimile of documents to learners in a ten-county region. Microcomputers located in libraries are used for public access (Cutright and Edvalson, 1988).

Teletex is the one-way display of text and graphics generated by a computer on a modified TV set. Videotex refers to TV displays of computer data base information that can be controlled by the learner through a keypad or keyboard. Teletex allows students to view preselected pages of information, and videotex allows students to conduct data base searches and even receive CAI using the central computer rather than a home personal computer or workstation (Heinich, Molenda, and Russell, 1985).

Advantages and Disadvantages. Computers facilitate self-paced, individualized learning. In the CAI mode, they can give students immediate positive reinforcement and feedback. Graphics, electronic print, and sometimes sound can be utilized in a learning situation, making the computer, in a sense, multimedia. Microcomputer systems using software on disks allow learners great control over time and length of study as well as a degree of interactivity during instruction and quick access to particular sections of instruction. Computer simulations, like videodisc simulations, can be used to train and evaluate learners when real-life experimentation is inadvisable or expensive—in medicine, aviation, and engineering, for instance. The CAI capabilities of systems such as PLATO make large-scale individualized learning possible. The problem is cost. Further disadvantages of CAI include the lack of instructional software, especially for adults; the computer's reinforcement of program designers' tendency to use lower-level cognitive objectives when developing instructional materials; and the large amount of time and effort required to design materials that cannot be purchased elsewhere (Heinich, Molenda, and Russell, 1985).

CMI facilitates large-scale individualized instruction. But as in other computer applications, courseware lags behind and must be chosen carefully to fit the needs of a given institution. CMI abilities may be in short supply, too, except in certain mainframe programs like PLATO Learning Management, which build on CAI courseware. Replacing the human tutor with CMI may be more efficient, but the affective and social growth students may lose is not reflected in test scores.

Computer conferencing, electronic mail, and other means of electronic delivery used in CBI allow people with home computers to gain access to a variety of degree programs and on-line information and library resources. The rapid or instantaneous turnaround possible with computer communication makes dialogue easier. Cost is once again a problem. Unless public access is provided, only the relatively affluent will be able to afford computer-based distance education.

Computer networking is flexible enough to allow on-line data base access at the national level and for small computer groups locally. User agreement on how to go about networking and cost are potential difficulties.

The educational use of teletex is extremely limited because the learner cannot communicate with the central computer (Heinich, Molenda, and Russell, 1985). Teletex may be used for announcements on educational CATV systems. Videotex systems have high start-up costs and, therefore, require high rates of participation and high user fees that may be difficult to generate. For learners unable or unwilling to buy a home computer, videotex might be used for computer-assisted distance education.

A number of factors may limit the use of computers in adult distance education. CAI, the predominant mode of computer use in distance education, may not be appropriate for higher levels of learning since it does not facilitate teacher-learner communication or promote learner autonomy as do computer conferencing, electronic mail, and on-line data base use (Kaye and Harry, 1982; Bates, 1986). Access to computers by adults is limited, although over half have access when workplace computers are considered (U.S. Bureau of the Census, 1989). Home computer users must be motivated and proficient enough to do without the physical presence of a tutor, which tends to narrow the market of potential users even further.

Interactive Videodisc

Videodiscs hold about 54,000 frames per side, enough room for about an hour of color visuals with sound or several thousand pages of text (Heinich, Molenda, and Russell, 1985). Different levels of interactivity are possible with videodisc:

Level 1. A videodisc player and monitor are combined for simple functions (play, stop, rewind, and others) commonly performed with videocassettes in educational settings.

Level 2. A simple microprocessing unit is included in the videodisc player, which makes simple branching possible in the instruction.

Level 3. An external computer interfaces with the videodisc player, making flexible prescriptive branching based on user input possible.

Level 4. Levels 1-3 are the commonly described levels, but a fourth level is possible. Level 4 would include data downloading from videodisc into computer, modification of program, and return to an erasable videodisc as well as compressed digital storage of video and audio signals to increase capacity.

Attainment of this fourth level, perhaps by the year 2000,

should greatly increase videodisc use in distance education, since making master discs would be less expensive (Miller, 1987).

Advantages and Disadvantages: Interactive videodisc permits individualized, self-paced learning. It requires learner interaction, presents branching instruction, and is more convenient to use than videotape. The quality of its freeze-frames and slow-motion ability are higher than videotape's as is student access to particular frames. As a result, students using videodiscs learn faster and retain their learning longer, although their level of achievement probably does not differ from that of students using videocassettes (Heinich, Molenda, and Russell, 1985). Videodisc lasts indefinitely with proper care and can be used for keeping records and gathering research data during instruction.

The main drawback of videodisc is cost. Making master discs is very expensive, so many copies must be made to bring unit cost to an acceptable level. The videodisc players and computer systems needed to use this medium also add to the initial cost of videodisc use.

Print

Print has always been the dominant medium in distance education and will continue to be the most-used form of delivery in the foreseeable future. Worldwide surveys of distance education show that print is by far the most used medium and is considered the most important medium in the presentation of learning materials by distance educators (Lewis, 1985; Holmberg, 1989).

Considerable confusion surrounds the term *correspondence study,* which originally referred to written instruction through the mails. Later the term was used inclusively to denote not just print study at a distance but also the use of telephone tutoring as well as audiocassettes, phonograph records, and other mailable instructional materials delivered along with textbooks and study guides. To call everything delivered or exchanged by mail a correspondence study aspect of distance education appears correct, but the components of this correspondence study package need to be clarified. Telephone tutoring or other electronic interaction not achieved via the postal service are alternative modes of distance delivery used in combination with, not as part of, correspondence study.

Bates (1982) notes that print is the most convenient and flexible medium for the presentation of new information and ideas and can be used by students selectively and at their own pace. All twelve distance teaching universities established in recent years use print (Bates, 1982) as do the large majority of distance education programs at all levels surveyed worldwide (Perry, 1984). Most schools that do not use print use radio to reach audiences with low literacy rates.

Advantages and Disadvantages: Print has many advantages as an instructional medium. It is familiar, inexpensive, and portable. Its format allows readers access to any section, in any order, for any length of time. A highly developed postal service makes distribution easy in most countries. It is the only medium that can be utilized without additional equipment, anytime and anywhere that a source of light is available.

One disadvantage of print is that it can give only a vicarious experience of reality, and some parts of reality are not easily conveyed in writing, such as taste and smell. But these are also limitations of audiovisual media. Most audio and visual experiences can be described in print by reducing a large number of stimuli to a few essential observations. But this can be a double-edged sword if the author lacks good writing skills or cannot discriminate between important and unimportant information. If the readers do not have the necessary experiences to comprehend concrete illustrations or reality-based arguments offered by the author, they may have difficulty learning. If their proficiency in written language is low, they may find learning by print difficult if not impossible. In fact, print-only correspondence study appears to have considerably higher dropout rates than telecourse study using both television and print. In telecourses, as in most distance education, print delivers most of the instructional content (Weisner, 1983). The television might be considered a pacing device, a motivator, or a medium appealing to learning styles different from those reached best by print (Zigerell, 1984).

The speed of interaction is another difficulty with print instruction at a distance. Adults want to know how they are doing in their studies, but by the time they receive feedback in a print-only format, they may already have lost interest in the answer, as they move on to another topic or drop the course entirely. The use of the telephone as a feedback and tutorial device allows near-instantaneous interaction between teacher and learners and substantially lessens the argument against print-based instruction.

All of the other media used in distance study may be employed in combination with print to overcome the problems of using print alone. Those aspects of reality not easily conveyed by print or audiovisual media, especially practical aspects of a course of study, require live seminars or other face-to-face teaching methods for effective communication. In some subjects, such live instruction is a necessary part of distance education.

Many of the high-technology media and combinations of media recently developed are presented as solutions to the boredom of print-based instruction, and yet many are electronically print based themselves and others often leave most of the teaching to the print with which they are combined. The computer is a good example. Computers in many ways simulate the text or the physical operations one performs while using a text. The programmer writes a program which is read by the student electronically by punching keys instead of by flipping pages. Through combination with and incorporation into other media, print will probably remain the dominant medium of distance instruction for a long time to come.

Profile of Distance Education Systems Today

Perhaps not surprisingly, surveys of higher education distance programs, both in the United States and internationally, indicate that correspondence study remains the backbone of this type of instruction. Surveying 468 international programs, mostly at secondary and postsecondary levels, Perry (1984) found that over 95 percent used correspondence study. Most programs used a multimedia approach, with audio media (besides telephone) by far the most popular electronic medium. Residential schools, experiential education, study centers, and regional services were each part of the delivery system of about 25 percent of the programs responding. It is interesting to note that in Perry's study only 29 percent of institutions surveyed used correspondence study alone.

Bates (1982) surveyed media use at twelve distance teaching universities and found that broadcast radio and television were being used less and less. Based on criteria such as accessibility, convenience, and availability, media such as print, audiocassettes, and telephone were proving to be better choices (Zigerell, 1984).

Lewis (1985) surveyed the uses of instructional technology at 344 public and private colleges and universities located in thirteen western states. Videocassettes and audiocassettes were the most heavily used media off campus, followed by computer-assisted instruction, telephone, and radio. Lewis found a strong positive relationship between the size of the institution and the likelihood that it used information technologies for instruction. Public institutions made greater use of these technologies than did private ones. Computer tends to be used more in scientific disciplines and audio and video more often in the social sciences and humanities. White-collar professionals were the largest student group served—on campus by 23 percent and off campus by 26 percent of responding institutions. Sixty-six percent of surveyed institutions had created institutional technology task forces or study groups. Nearly 50 percent belonged to consortia, usually computer or telecourse oriented.

The greatest barriers to effective use of information technologies were internal issues, such as failure of the incentive and reward system to encourage faculty participation—named by 83 percent of institutions surveyed—and lack of appropriate courseware—cited by 82 percent. Faculty resistance was greater to audio and video technologies than to computers. Fairly similar conclusions were obtained in a previous (1983) survey by Lewis of seventy colleges and universities nationwide that were chosen in an attempt to provide a representative sample.

Based on these surveys, it appears that instruction through technology is now a permanent part of distance education and conventional education at most institutions of higher education. While separate survey results for other forms of adult education are not available, it appears likely that the use of instructional technology or media is also growing fairly rapidly in them as well.

Summary

A variety of delivery modes can be used to further the learning of adults through distance education. Within the "audio" modes, telephone, radio, phonograph records, and audiotapes are in wide use in distance education. Audiocassettes provide convenient packages of information that can be used practically anytime and anywhere by busy adults. Radio can be used to reach mass audiences of learners, while telephone promotes real-time interaction between teachers and students. The major drawback of audio media is that they lack a visual component.

Video media have also had a great impact on distance education. Television programming can be delivered to learners in ways ranging from open-air broadcasts to cable to satellite reception. Videocassettes and VCRs have made it possible for adults to choose the times and places in which they view video media. As with radio, large numbers of students can be reached through television broadcasting. However, the most commonly broadcast materials, recorded telecourses, cannot be revised quickly, and they do not offer the opportunity for immediate revision that live television does. The cost of video media is high and the production process is very complex compared with that for audio media.

The advent of the computer has given distance education new horizons. Computer-assisted instruction, computer-managed instruction, and computer-managed education all offer ways to enhance adults' learning experiences. Computers afford adults self-paced learning with immediate reinforcement and feedback. The cost of hardware and the scarcity of appropriate software are the major impediments to the use of computers in distance education for adults.

The interactive videodisc shows great promise, because it permits individualized and self-paced learning, but its costs are even more prohibitive than those of computers alone. Until recently, too, local videodisc development has to all effects been impossible.

Printed media are the mainstay of distance education and will probably remain that way for some time. They are convenient, flexible, familiar, relatively inexpensive, and highly portable. The

major drawbacks of print are that it can give only a vicarious experience of reality and that it requires good writing skills on the
part of the educator. It is, however, effective in combination with
other media.

Currently, print media remain the backbone of distance
education and are often used in combination with other media.
Multimedia approaches using audio- and videocassettes, teleconferencing, television, and computers are growing in popularity. All
in all, it appears that instructional media, appropriately used, will
play a crucial role in the future development of distance education.

5

Assessing
Program Quality
and Effectiveness

This chapter presents an overview of factors related to the effectiveness and general quality of distance education in the United States. Distance higher education is growing in importance in the United States, but it is still largely consigned to the continuing education and extension units of colleges and universities. Distance education may become an important part of the efforts of colleges, universities, and other agencies in the United States to provide adults with lifelong education if it can win support of on-campus faculty and administrators, who often view distance education as inferior. Unless their attitudes and perceptions change, it is unlikely that distance education will be accepted and utilized as a mainstream method of delivery in American adult and higher education. The research on distance higher and adult education, and the findings and conclusions based on it, may be useful to people engaged in the current dialogue concerning the effectiveness and quality of this innovative means of delivery in education.

    This chapter attempts to synthesize the approaches to research on distance education and the important findings of such authors as Keegan and Rumble (1982), Rumble (1986), Keegan (1986), and Holmberg (1989). Other findings are also included to provide a wide range of evidence regarding the effectiveness of distance education for adult learning. Major headings for this appraisal are derived from Gooler (1979), whose schemata have often been adopted for use in the assessment of distance education.

Besides the basic criteria offered by Gooler, we have added another one, that of acceptability. With distance education still perceived as being in its embryonic stage in the United States in comparison to other countries and often seen as questionable by many postsecondary educators, acceptability was a necessary category.

More space is devoted to some of the criteria than to others, mainly because of the availability of evidence. In many cases, additional discussion and other ideas for thought are offered along with the available evidence. We hope that this will aid current and future distance educators in the pursuit of their goals.

Learner Outcomes

Learner outcomes in higher education have been researched intensively for many years. All forms of positive learner outcome might be characterized as being the result of development of student talent, whether they are measured solely in terms of outcome or whether the level of development of the entering student is taken into account, as in the value-added approach (see *Affective Skills*, following). Learner outcomes cover a very broad continuum of behavior and have been categorized in a wide variety of ways. In this section of the chapter we will review learner outcomes in three major skill areas—cognitive, psychomotor, and affective—and then discuss the dropout rate in distance education.

Cognitive outcomes of distance education and related topics such as instructional media and adult education have been the subject of considerable research. The following section, combined with the Resource, represents the most comprehensive presentation of the comparative research studies on distance versus conventional adult and higher education and related topics that has been performed to date.

Both mediated versus conventional and distance versus conventional education achievement comparisons are included in this section. Based on past research, most experts in the pedagogical uses of media would agree with Clark (1985a) that although the introduction of a new media system usually brings with it a "novelty effect . . . media are mere vehicles that deliver instruction but do not influence student achievement any more than the truck that delivers our groceries causes changes in nutrition" (p. 445).

Media experts like Clark therefore question the very idea of conducting media comparison studies since they believe none of the differences in student achievement can be related to media differences. Distance education versus conventional education achievement studies have one important difference. They usually compare mediated learning at a distance with traditional classroom study, thereby adding a comparison of separation and face-to-face contact of teacher and learner to media versus classroom teaching achievement comparisons.

Convinced of the fundamental equivalence of distance and conventional modes of delivery, distance educators are likely to cite a few sources and move on. However, a large audience of faculty and administrators in adult and higher education are not so easily convinced of the equivalence of mediated education, at a distance or in classroom, when compared with traditional lecture and discussions led by a teacher. It is primarily for them that this section has been researched and written.

Cognitive Skills. Research will be presented here on the effectiveness of self-instructional methods that are usually offered on campus with some direct instructor contact but that can also be incorporated into distance education schemes through study centers or home study. These methods include audiotutorial, mastery learning, programmed instruction, telecourses, correspondence study, computer, and videodisc.

Audiotutorial is an instructional method in which audiocassette, print, and visual media are combined in self-instructional units. Two meta-analyses of audiotutorial versus conventional education studies both arrived at a similar effect size—.17 (Kulik, Kulik, and Cohen, 1979; Willett, Yamashita, and Anderson, 1983). This means that audiotutorial raised average exam scores from the 50th to the 57th percentile. In other words, the control group scored at the 50th percentile and the audiotutorial learners scored, in comparison, at the 57th. The effect size essentially expresses the degree to which the distribution of scores in the control group and experimental group do not overlap, or the degree to which the null hypothesis, that there is no effect, is wrong (Cohen, 1977). It tells the researcher how much of the difference between two groups cannot be explained by the variability of scores in the two treatments. An effect size of .17 denotes a shift in the average distribution of scores of the experimental group (in this case, audiotutorial learners) .17 of a standard distribution rightward from the average distribution of scores of the control group, which is comprised of conventional classroom learners. Effect sizes are often described in terms of percentiles or even letter grades since many readers find standard distributions rather abstract. A .17 effect size is small but significant, a .27 effect size is moderately significant, and a .47 effect size is very significant and means that experimental learners scored about a full letter grade higher than control learners in a number of studies subjected to meta-analysis.

Mastery learning involves the achievement of behavioral objectives through immediate feedback, remediation, and repeated testing, usually on an individual basis. The two most widely used mastery learning systems are Bloom's group-based Learning for Mastery (LFM) and Keller's Personalized System of Instruction (PSI).

A number of meta-analyses of mastery learning have yielded high effect sizes, denoting high achievement, relative to control groups, for students at college and K–12 levels using both LFM and PSI (Guskey and Gates, 1985; Kulik, 1983; Kulik and Kulik, 1987; Willett, Yamashita, and Anderson, 1983). Although LFM and PSI have proven extremely successful in comparison studies, both require more instructional time than do conventional teaching methods. Higher dropout rates in the mastery learning section than in the control group may raise achievement results in some studies since the remaining mastery learning students may be more motivated than the conventional students. In addition, studies appearing in dissertations often show much smaller gains in achievement than do those in published articles (Kulik and Kulik, 1987).

Mastery learning is a method of designing instruction that may be applied to any medium, but it is usually print based. The detractors of correspondence study should take note that according to higher education studies, these print-based mastery learning systems show the greatest comparative achievement gains of all instructional systems.

What makes mastery learning so effective? Kulik, Jaksa, and Kulik (1978) conducted a comprehensive review of PSI, concluding that four features were mostly responsible for the program's effectiveness: frequent quizzes, immediate feedback, a mastery requirement before progression, and adequate reviews. Any decrease in evaluation lowers student performance in PSI (Kulik, 1983). In a 1982 meta-analysis of ninety-four studies involving students from kindergarten through college, Lysakowski and Walberg found extremely strong mean effect sizes—1.28, .88, and .94 individually and .97 overall—for three educational features, instructional cues, participation, and feedback, that are features of most individualized instruction. It should be noted that some electronic media—most notably, computers—can incorporate instructional design or mastery learning features into software.

In *programmed instruction* students are given immediate reinforcement—the correct answer—after each of a series of small steps. B.F. Skinner originated programmed instruction in 1968, basing it on the principles of behaviorism (Skinner, 1968). Like the reviews of programmed instruction that preceded them, meta-analyses of programmed versus conventional instruction show that students using programmed instruction achieved slightly better test scores than their counterparts using conventional methods.

Several meta-analysts have found a small but significant advantage for programmed over conventional instruction at all levels of instruction (Hartley, 1978; Kulik, Cohen, and Ebeling, 1980; Kulik, Kulik, and Schwalb, 1985). Programmed instruction appears to work much better in social science courses than in mathematics. More recent studies, in which better designed programmed materials may have been used, yielded better results than the many studies undertaken in the 1961–1975 period (Kulik, Schwalb, and Kulik, 1982). However, programmed instruction still yields less impressive results than other print-based instructional systems such as LFM or PSI, even in recent studies.

In a 1984 review of *telecourse* achievement, Zigerell concluded that "while the results of some studies are unreliable because of poor controls, most of the reliable studies . . . confirm the earlier findings that performance does not significantly differ between tele- course and classroom students taking equivalent courses" (p. 51). Purdy (1978), reviewing the effectiveness of telecourses, noted that in studies over the years by the Chicago TV College, the Coast Community College District, the Dallas County Community Col- lege District, and the University of Mid-America "in the few cases where there were significant differences between performance of home TV students and classroom face-to-face students, the differ- ences were more often in favor of the TV students than others" (p. 3). Similarly, Whittington (1987) reviewed over 100 studies of telecourse versus conventional achievement, practically all of which showed equal or superior cognitive outcomes on the part of the telecourse students.

Looking more broadly at television-based instruction, Chu and Schramm (1975) compiled all available studies comparing tele- vision and conventional classroom performance in equivalent courses at all academic levels. They concluded on the basis of their massive review that a wide variety of courses had been taught suc- cessfully using television, in most cases with "no significant differ- ences from standard results of conventional teaching" (p. 31). While many of these studies concerned uses of television in the K–12 class- room, they nevertheless exhibit the effectiveness of the medium as a teaching tool.

A limited collection of studies in which television is clearly used at a distance in higher education, rather than as an adjunct to conventional classroom teaching, are presented in the Resource. In all but one case, distance higher education via television yielded the same or better student achievement than conventional methods.

Formal studies of the academic effectiveness of *correspon- dence study* have been few and far between. Reviews of research are even rarer—only a handful appear in the literature.

Of these reviews, the most comprehensive was performed by Macken (1976). Surveying sixty-seven American studies of the effec- tiveness of correspondence education at the college, technical, and high school level, Macken concluded that there was "no significant difference in learning outcomes between the two methods [corre- spondence and conventional study]" (p. 27).

Childs (1966), quoted in Wakatama (1983), summarized the results of some American studies comparing distance higher education with conventional study. She says, "Studies by Feig, Mallory, Thompson and Ziegel compared grades earned by college correspondence study students with those earned by classroom students in the same courses, and all found differences in favor of the correspondence study group" (p. 26).

As with television study at a distance, available comparative achievement studies involving correspondence education can be found in the Resource. Again, with a single exception, all of the studies found that academic achievement via correspondence study was equal or superior to that achieved through conventional study.

A great number of *computer* versus traditional classroom instruction comparison studies have been done in the last decade. Many reviews and meta-analyses on the subject have recently appeared in the literature.

Niemiec and Walberg (1987) synthesized the results of three reviews and thirteen meta-analyses of computer-assisted instruction from kindergarten through college. They concluded that CAI raised student achievement on examinations from the 50th to the 66th percentile, meaning that on average students in the CAI section scored a full letter grade better than did the control group. The mean effect size of the thirteen meta-analyses, .42, reflected very strong CAI effect sizes in elementary and special populations, but results were not as impressive at the secondary and college levels. For instance, Kulik, Kulik, and Bangert-Drowns (1985) found an effect size of .47 among elementary school students, compared to an effect size of .32 for students in grades 6–12 (Kulik, Bangert, and Williams, 1983) and an even less impressive effect size, .26 for college students (Kulik and Kulik, 1985).

Only one meta-analysis appears to have been done of the effectiveness of CAI in adult education. Kulik, Kulik, and Schwalb (1986) analyzed twenty-four noncollegiate adult education comparisons of computer-based instruction and conventional education and found an average effect size very much like that found for CAI overall by Niemiec and Walberg (1978)—about .42, or an average gain from the 50th to the 66th percentile. Niemiec and Walberg call this effect size "moderately effective" when other factors have been allowed for. But Kulik, Kulik, and Schwalb found a mean effect size of only .29 for CAI studies. The higher effect size of computer-based instruction overall was caused by the inclusion of a few studies of two other types of computer-based instruction, computer-managed instruction and computer-enhanced instruction (CEI), which showed extremely strong effects (.72 and 1.13, respectively). In other words, adult education effect sizes (.29) for CAI fall exactly in between those for secondary (.32) and college (.26) education.

One advantage of computer-based instruction that was considered "dramatic" by the Kuliks and Schwalb was a 30 percent decrease in time needed for instruction. Thus adult educators who are discouraged by the modest (.29) effect size of CAI may still opt for computer use because it may allow for effective training of more learners with the same resources. However, finding software designed for use in adult education is still a problem.

Two reviews of computer-based adult education that are not meta-analyses are the studies by Orlansky and String (1979) and Rachal (1984). Orlansky and String (1979) reviewed forty-eight evaluation studies of computer-based education (CBE; apparently the same as CBI) in military training, finding it significantly superior in fifteen of forty-eight comparisons and inferior in only one. Orlansky and String felt that the overall difference in achievement had no practical significance because no significant difference in achievement was found in thirty-two studies. However, they reported a 30 percent savings in instructional time, just as Kulik, Kulik, and Schwalb (1986) did in their later study.

Rachal (1984) reviewed studies of computer-aided instruction in the ABE and GED classroom. Of the seven studies including comparisons of achievement between CAI and traditional instruction, four showed a strong effect size for CAI and the other three favored the CAI treatment, but not by a significant amount.

The status of computer-based education in a given study as an example of conventional or distance study is often uncertain. The vast majority of studies involve computer use at group locations where the teacher is not explicitly described as being absent during more than half of the instruction. The presence or absence of the teacher is simply not seen as a variable in most of these studies. The handful of studies in which distance teaching methods were definitely used can be found in the Resource.

Videodisc is a fairly recent phenomenon. Although it has been possible for some time to connect various visual media to computers, only with the appearance of videodisc has it been possible to quickly find any part of a visual recording and show still frames perfectly. Thirteen achievement comparison studies on videodisc versus conventional instruction located in the literature date back to the late 1970s. About half of these studies appeared in a small-scale review by DeBloois (1983). Videodisc, like computer-based education, usually yields significantly better student achievement scores than does classroom teaching in comparison studies.

Controversy over Media Comparison Studies. The use of media comparisons in determining the instructional effectiveness of various media is a subject of contention, and many points are arued again and again. The published exchange of views between the Kuliks' research groups and Richard Clark on the efficacy of computer-based education is a good example.

Clark (1985a) points out the apparent novelty effect in a meta-analysis of secondary school computer experiments in which the effect size fell as longer and longer experiments were examined (Kulik, Bangert, and Williams, 1983). Kulik, Kulik, and Bangert-Drowns (1985) respond by stating that, overall, the difference between short-term CAI studies (.46 effect size) and long-term studies (.34 effect size) is not significant. Clark also notes the apparent discrepancy in effect sizes reported in dissertations (.20) and unpublished studies (.30) when compared with those in published studies (.50), charging that editorial gatekeeping is biased in favor of high effect sizes.

Using a 1985 Kulik and Kulik study as an example, Clark (1985b) makes a point about the effect of good controls. In those studies in which the same college instructor taught both sections, and developed the content for both treatments, the effect size was only .13—about the same as in programmed versus conventional instruction studies. Add all the sources of confounding together, Clark concludes, and the effect size is "negligible" (p. 139). Kulik, Kulik, and Schwalb (1985) respond by citing their recent meta-analyses in which same-instructor comparative achievement studies yielded a .24 effect size favoring CBE, while different-instructor studies resulted in a .38 effect size. This difference in effect sizes, they say, is "not significant, [although] the direction of the difference . . . is consistent with Clark's notions" (p. 385). As for the difference in content so often found in studies, the Kuliks feel that research is better if the experimental method does not contaminate the control section (Kulik, Kulik, and Schwalb, 1985).

For those who are not advocates of instructional innovation, it may seem fairly obvious that the most valid studies of mediated instruction are those that are most highly controlled. However, it is interesting that in the meta-analysis cited by Clark, a .13 effect size still remains when content and teacher differences are eliminated.

As was previously noted, computers save students time, 30 percent or so. Here, perhaps is an explanation for why CAI and other CBI methods, as well as videodisc, may still have an advantage over other educational media. If students in both treatments of a CBI study are given an hour to work and if students in the experimental (CBI) section finish, on average, in forty-two minutes, they have more time to review or learn new material. While there may be nothing inherent, besides speed, that distinguishes the computer or videodisc system from other electronic media, much of the confounding that accounts for the larger effect size found in studies of these systems may be attributable to the level of instructional design that is most automatically invested in software. As Clark notes, the center of disagreement between him and the Kuliks is the amount of confounding involved in comparison studies. While the Kulik research groups may believe there is some real difference in effect size left over after subtracting confounding, Clark does not. It seems inevitable that Clark's view will be the more widely accepted one as time goes by. However, strong arguments for new media can be developed on the basis of speed, access, and other factors. It seems likely that the battle between media theorists and media advocates will merely shift to new ground.

It must be remembered that while CAI and other CBI methods yield greater effect sizes than other electronic media (except videodisc) when compared with conventional study, even larger effect sizes have been found for print-based mastery learning methods that typically incorporate instructional design, mastery learning, objectives, feedback, and criterion testing. CBI methods and PSI or LFM have many similarities, and recently, far more CAI studies and projects have been done than PSI or LFM studies and projects. It is simply more acceptable and more funds are available to write computer programs incorporating instructional design than to create similar print-based learning materials.

In the real world, few administrators will devote resources to print-based materials utilizing instructional design. PSI features such as frequent mastery testing, which requires the repeated development of new forms of each test, can become costly or time consuming as time goes on. And of course, computer systems are multifunctional, having applications in administration, classroom management, and other aspects of education. The computer, seen in its practical context is not just an inert carrier, as Clark might say, of new methods or design; rather, it may be the best medium of all for the efficient delivery of instructionally designed learning experiences precisely because of its wide availability.

The practical superiority of the computer gains theoretical strength from the recently created science of nonlinear economics. Like the scientific theory of nonlinear dynamics, or chaos, nonlinear economics holds that slight changes in variables early in the development of a process may make great differences later on because of a kind of snowball effect (Arthur, 1990). As computers were increasingly adopted by American educational institutions in the 1970s for instructional purposes, more and more programs were written. More software meant economies of scale, making instructional designed computer learning materials more available and affordable. The cost of computer hardware dropped even as the power and speed of the typical unit rose. Other factors, such as the multiplicity of use of computer systems in education, combined with the appeal of the available software to encourage large investments in computers in education. This in turn had the effect of precluding a switch to another medium. For similar reasons, the computer market became divided. While IBM-compatible computers came to dominate business markets, Apple-compatible computers became strongly entrenched in K–12 education.

At this point it is difficult to see how any other medium

could receive the support necessary to develop software on a large-scale basis. By choosing the computer early on, American faculty and administrators have chosen it for the foreseeable future, if not forever. Nonlinear economics also has implications for videodisc. Because adoption is on an institution-by-institution basis in our state-based educational system, technologies that require mass production of software to justify production costs, such as videodisc, have so far made little progress outside of government and industry. Videodisc must compete with the computer in many of its functions, such as simulation. If our system of adoption had been differently constituted, videodisc might have been much more important in American education at this point in history.

Psychomotor Skills. People who say one cannot teach skills and practical subjects at a distance often assume that print alone is being used. In addition to the widespread acceptance and use of do-it-yourself books, students often have access to kits, other media, or trips to conventional facilities in combination with distance study (Dodds, 1981). Holmberg (1989) notes, "The training of skills in the so-called psychomotor domain is often seen as more of a problem in distance education than it need be, above all at fairly elementary stages, in developing countries and elsewhere" (p. 26).

Holmberg (1989) thinks it likely that distance education will expand into fields such as surgery, chemistry, and engineering. In these fields, simulation techniques can be effectively used in place of the demonstration of many procedures and techniques requiring psychomotor as well as cognitive and affective skills. For instance, students using interactive videodiscs displayed superior cognitive performance over control groups who received conventional instruction in college physics, chemistry, and biology laboratory work (Stevens, 1984; Smith, Jones, and Waugh, 1986; Bunderson and others, 1984). Interactive videodisc has been used to train mechanics, whose training was subsequently verified by hands-on examinations; to teach airplane equipment troubleshooting and operational procedures; and to teach basic photography skills to college students (Maher, 1988; Peiper, Richardson, Harmon, and Keller, 1984; Abrams, 1986).

Medicine is one area in which the usefulness of distance education has traditionally been called into question. Of course, there is little doubt that continuing medical education, which often contains an independent study component, has been effective in the United States. A 1987 meta-analysis of 254 studies by Beaudry showed that continuing medical education had a very significant effect on physician knowledge and performance and a moderate effect on patient health status. Beaudry found individualization of instruction to be a significant instructional variable. In a related meta-analysis, the effectiveness of visual media instruction in changing or forming attitudes of students studying nursing was found to be significantly better than that of conventional study (Sebermer, 1988). Emergency medical technicians performed well in real emergency situations after being trained by videodisc and even used the videodisc as a reference tool on the way to specific emergency situations. Medical students who undertook independent study at Ohio State achieved scores on the National Board of Medical Examiners test similar to those of students who studied the traditional program and they performed similarly in required clerkships (Sachs and others, 1985).

Some of the aspects of medical education most difficult to convey via text-based independent study, such as medical techniques and procedures, can be demonstrated via interactive videodisc. In addition to the aforementioned use in biology and chemistry lab simulations, videodisc has recently been successfully using in the teaching of cardiopulmonary resuscitation, auscultation of the heart, preparation and administration of intramuscular injections, and complex medical tasks (Lyness, 1987; Branch, Ledford, Robertson, and Robinson, 1987; Ebner and others, 1984; Andrews, 1985). Of course, training via videodisc must be verified through performance of the actual procedure, which is a standard evaluative component of this kind of training.

Affective Skills. The role distance education can play in the socialization and affective growth of the adult learner is often questioned. According to Keegan and Rumble (1982), "Most criticism of distance education focuses on its effectiveness in the affective domain, which is concerned with values, attitudes and beliefs that are 'caught' rather than 'taught.' Many people argue that they can only be 'caught' in a social context, and that this element is not provided in distance teaching systems" (p. 233).

Holmberg (1989) asserts that "experience shows that distance education can be effective in bringing about attitude change" (p. 7). Sparkes (1985) notes that "teaching in the affective domain requires a form of communication with a strong appeal to the emotions" (p. 9). He cites television, radio, novels, and drama as effective means of communicating affectively. The efficacy of media in the affective domain when used by media experts is a widely accepted given, in both advertising and education (Cafferata and Tybout, 1989; Simonson, 1984).

Chickering (1974) and Feldman and Newcomb (1970) found evidence of affective development among residential college students, and Chickering (1974) found that commuter students attending different types of colleges started and stayed behind residential students in terms of affective development. Bloom (1964) found that affective growth tended to decelerate in adulthood. Given these findings, it might be predicted that only "limited affective growth" could be expected of adult nonresidential Empire State College students (Lipsett and Avakian, 1979, p. 213).

Despite these findings, considerable affective growth has been documented among nontraditional students. New students at Empire State College, a nontraditional institution that uses learning contracts to a large extent, were given an instrument intended to measure affective growth in terms of six affective objectives of the school, as were control groups at other colleges who also were nonresidential adult students. When the students were retested ten to eleven months later, the overall growth of the Empire State students was significant, while that of the controls was not (Lipsett and Avakian, 1979).

Insufficient socialization is a common criticism of distance education. This criticism may result partly from the comparison of full-time and part-time students since part-time adult students in general are likely to take a much smaller role in campus life than are residential students. Socialization may be seen in terms of the affective impact of college on students' values, personal goals, and aspirations. Sources of socializing influences are usually thought of as both internal and external to the institution and include student background, the normative influences of the academic and social structure of the college, and the mediating impacts of both parental socialization and noncollege reference groups (Weidman, 1987). This type of framework may be inappropriate for adults, who usually have their own family, job, and a social life. Their involvement in learning in off-campus social situations is an area that deserves study.

Far from leaving students devoid of affective skills, distance higher education may teach important life skills that have strong affective components. In a 1982 study, Valiga analyzed the responses of 12,682 alumni who had taken the American College Testing Alumni Survey between 1980 and 1982. When asked the degree to which their college education contributed to their personal growth in twenty-four possible areas, respondents indicated that learning on their own, working independently, persisting at difficult tasks, and organizing time effectively were the areas in which their most extensive personal growth occurred (Valiga, 1982). These general skills, not related to a job or a school subject, are precisely the kinds of self-directed learner attributes identified with success in distance education (Coldeway, 1986) and precisely the kinds of attributes distance educators seek to impart to their students (Holmberg, 1989). While distance educators and administrators can do much to motivate learners to achieve affective objectives, external factors alone cannot assure affective growth. Students must possess the personal motivation necessary to take advantage of opportunities for growth (Inglio, 1985).

Dropout Rate. Why do distance students drop out? Many theories and models have been advanced recently, focusing on a number of factors that appear to influence dropouts (for example, Kember, 1989; Billings, 1988; Garrison, 1987). Chacon-Duque (1987) concluded on the basis of dropout patterns and surveys that perceived course difficulty and level of learner motivation and persistence were good predictors of student dropout from Pennsylvania State University's Independent Learning courses. According to Bartles (1982, in Holmberg, 1989), agreement between personal interest and course or degree structure is the most decisive factor in the determination of learner success or failure. Holmberg (1989) concludes that older, mature, better-qualified enrollees versus traditional students are most likely to have the strong motivation that is necessary to succeed at a distance.

Many recent international research studies have focused on dropouts in distance education (for example, Garrison, 1987; Herrmann, 1988; Taylor and others, 1986). Since retention of students in distance education is usually lower than retention in equivalent conventional education activities and retention is linked to motivation, learner motivation in the distance section of random-assignment comparative studies of achievement may be higher because only the most motivated students will remain in distance education. This means that dropout rates can affect the validity of comparative distance student versus conventional student academic achievement.

Distance higher education units usually have open admissions policies and serve older part-time students, some of whom stop submitting lessons when they have learned what they want to know (Holmberg, 1989). A dropout rate higher than that in conventional higher education is almost unavoidable. This also holds true for external degree programs, which often have a distance education component. Studying retention at the University of Minnesota's College Program for Individualized Learning, Holm (1988) found that just under half of 1983–84 enrollees were still active in the program or graduated in the fall of 1987. Factors such as proximity of residence, previous postsecondary education, and length of professional experience were correlated with persistence.

The OUUK and other distance teaching universities have managed to hold dropout rates to an acceptable minimum and to graduate many students unqualified for conventional universities through a combination of high-quality learning materials and a comprehensive learner support system (Moore, 1987b; Sewart, 1981). The completion rate can have a strong effect on the efficiency of distance education units because a common rationale for distance education is that it can produce the same kinds of graduates at a lower cost than equivalent conventional education. For example, the average cost per student at the Open University of the United Kingdom was once calculated as 50 percent of the cost at a conventional British university (Wagner, 1977). This argument loses merit if the quality of distance education graduates is good, but the cost per student is inflated by high dropout rates (Rumble, 1986).

Access

Access to education is perhaps the most common rationale for the use of distance education. Practically every distance education or external degree program involves an improvement in access to education at some level in a particular area. Learners may be tied to one area because of weather, remoteness, geography, or all three, as they are in Alaska. But they also may choose distance education because they feel psychologically distant from conventional education or uncomfortable about class participation or because distance education does not conflict as much with their work schedule or leisure time or, perhaps, because the subject is not available conventionally or for many other reasons. Some learners use distance education to take an additional course at the same time that they are enrolled in traditional classroom courses (Brey and Grigsby, 1984).

The need for distance education to give students access to courses is sometimes clear-cut as, for example, in Del Rio, Texas. Located in a region with 100,000 residents along the Mexican border, Del Rio was the site of the area's only health care center. The population was growing, and an acute shortage of registered nurses was exacerbated by the lack of a local nursing program. The problem was solved through a locally based associate degree nursing program in which audioconferencing with an existing nursing school at Big Spring, Texas, and videotapes of Big Spring classes were combined with identical courseware and availability of library materials. Not only was attrition less than half that of the associate degree nursing students attending the Big Spring school, improving cost effectiveness, but there were also no significant differences in course grades or scores on national nursing tests of Del Rio and Big Spring students. This distance education project created employment, training people with critical skills needed to address important social needs (Holdampf, 1983).

But there is another side to the access question. Learner background, telecommunications infrastructure, and, most of all, cost can limit access. High start-up costs of distance education, not only for hardware but also for instructional program development, can be mitigated through sharing of costs in a consortium.

Still, learner access to learning resources is often inequitable (Sullins and others, 1987). On-line bibliographic services offered by private companies or library systems require computer access and literacy use. Programs may focus on serving graduate or professional student populations or using high-technology methods to serve elite populations at home or limited populations at study centers. Inner-city, rural, and minority students studying at low educational levels often cannot pay for their schooling and, therefore, the volume of programs designed to meet their needs is unlikely to be sufficient in an era of less governmental intervention.

At-home access to distance education often depends on the availability of particular media to a given target audience in a given area. The pervasiveness of television, radio, and telephone and the presence or easy affordability of audiocassette players all recommend the use of these media in distance education. Some new media such as computer and videodisc are not easily accessible for most Americans, but 58.1 percent of U.S. households had VCRs in 1988 (U.S. Bureau of the Census, 1989). Clearly, programs that target the relatively small segments of the population owning computers or working as professionals are increasing access for those groups, but access for less affluent citizens is better increased through the provision of programs relying heavily on print, television, telephone, audiocassette, and, especially in rural areas, videocassette.

Distance education has enabled educators to overcome geographical, temporal, or psychological barriers to participation in education. However, the quality and extent of access to education achieved through distance education depend greatly upon economic realities and educational priorities and missions. Whether Americans have the societal will to change these priorities or missions or to allocate funding needed to overcome economic inequalities should become apparent before the turn of the century.

Quality

Quality is not a well-defined topic in education. It is common for people reviewing program quality to be unwilling or unable to define exactly what is to be assessed (George, 1987). Such specificity can destroy the vague consensus around which agreements are often built in academia. Traditionally, the quality of academic institutions has been based on indicators such as entrance standards, famous graduates, reputational rankings, or the presence of illustrious faculty (West, 1984). American higher education has never emphasized the comprehensive examination at the undergraduate level as have European institutions (Freedman, 1987), but learner outcomes were the focus of considerable research in the 1960s and 1970s (Kuh, 1985). Several authors in the 1980s supported the idea that the quality of a college education was best measured in terms of the value added to graduates, measured from entry to outcome in cognitive, personal, and social terms. An important indicator of this added value is the level of involvement of students in academic and extracurricular school activities (Astin, 1987; Kuh, Coomes, and Lundquist, 1984).

Quality and the External Degree. According to Freedman (1987), "The single most important determinant of quality in continuing higher education is its faculty" (p. 170). Encouraging greater faculty participation, hiring adjunct professors where necessary, and training faculty about how to teach in continuing higher education situations improves the quality of nontraditional programs, according to Freedman. He believes that special degree programs should follow review processes "no less rigorous than for other degree curricula, though the criteria for review may not be identical" (p. 171).

The explosive growth of postsecondary educational consortia in the United States is having a favorable effect on the perceived quality of continuing higher education, according to Freedman (1987): "A great deal of adult degree study takes place away from campus, and the resulting problems of quality control are a constant source of discussion among continuing educators. . . . Reviewing bodies are bound to concern themselves with the availability of resources at off-campus sites. . . . One plausible arrangement that can meet this objection is a consortium of institutions" (p. 90).

Freedman (1987) offers several other factors important in the perceived quality of nontraditional higher education programs, including:

1. Widespread use of credit for experiential learning. Credit for experiential learning will continue to create suspicion about quality in the academic community until widely accepted assessment criteria and procedures are instituted.
2. Longer time to completion. However, programs such as the University of Oklahoma's bachelor's degree in liberal studies have shown that "highly motivated adults can complete the requirements for a degree through part-time study taking only about 50 percent longer than full-time students enrolled in traditional programs." The longer time that students take to complete nontraditional programs concerns many educators (p. 93). Completion time is also a concern of European authors such as Keegan and Rumble (1982), who utilize a "response time test" to measure this factor.
3. Accurate assessment of student performance. Some educators may question whether the individual course grades of nontraditional degree students are truly equivalent to the grades of traditional students. Or they may wonder if longer part-time study means that students retain fewer skills and less knowledge at graduation. The comprehensive examination, commonly used in European higher education and in American graduate degree programs, may be an answer. The University of Oklahoma's liberal studies program has made successful use of it.
4. Status of adult degree programs. Graduate and professional part-time programs fare somewhat better, but "on the whole, part-time degree programs suffer from the same marginality that pertains to continuing education in general—partly because their students are different from the traditional students and partly because they contain several nontraditional elements and are assessed and reviewed in nontraditional ways" (p. 94).

Quality and Distance Education. Keegan and Rumble (1982) have used several criteria to measure the quality of distance education. These criteria are quality of learning materials, suitability of distance education to subject taught, provision of education versus instruction, and the intersubjectivity of learning at a distance.

The quality of instructional materials used by distance teaching universities is generally recognized to be high, according to Keegan and Rumble. Moss and Brew (1981) found that most conventional higher education staff at three English universities were familiar with OUUK texts and television programs, although less than 50 percent recommended them. OUUK books are on the reading lists of many conventional universities (Keegan, 1986). Clearly, many American academics might call the Press of the Open University of the United Kingdom one of the top academic presses in the United Kingdom today.

The quality of learning materials in American distance education is certainly more variable. While some materials are produced by consortia with instructional designers and top scholars, others are produced by individual institutions for the use of small audiences. Some of these small programs might be compared to the widely respected external studies department of the University of New England (Australia), whose learning materials are "functional, not gaudy, and frequently reflect their origin in the lecture notes for on-campus students" (Keegan, 1986, p. 260). Those small scale programs that offer increased personal attention to compensate for possible weakness in their learning materials can achieve good outcomes (Holmberg, 1981).

The suitability of distance teaching for certain subjects was covered at considerable length in the previous section on psychomotor skills. The combination of distance education and conventional laboratory sections, as well as the use of technology-based laboratory simulations, greatly extends the effectiveness of distance education in teaching hands-on and "extreme-care" subjects, such as medicine and flight mechanics. The use of high-technology and conventional teaching methods together can greatly diminish the cost advantages of distance study when compared with traditional instructional methods. However, the cost of instruction will still probably be less than that of the cost of conventional instruction in these fields, which can be extremely high.

Some authors have contended that true education, as opposed to instruction in skills, cannot occur at a distance (Escotet,

1980), especially at the university level (Carnoy and Levin, 1975). They emphasize the socialization aspect of a college education, as do such American educators as Astin (1987) who place emphasis on "involvement in learning." A related charge is that distance education does not allow student and teacher to take part in a truly shared experience, precluding the intersubjectivity that is critical at the culminating stages of education (Peters, 1973). Charges such as these are difficult to answer. The importance of socialization is recognized by the OUUK, which offers direct student interaction with tutors at study centers, residential work for some courses, student self-help groups, telephone tutoring, and "even helps to fund the Open University Student's Association, [designed to] provide an environment for socialization without debarring the independent learner" (Keegan and Rumble, 1982, p. 235). Such efforts are, however, limited so as not to undermine the OUUK's cost advantage.

In the United States, similar charges might be successfully brought against proprietary programs, which enroll most postsecondary distance learners. But these programs usually offer instruction in a skill, not education, and those accredited by the National Home Study Council deliver what they promise. In college and university distance education, the question of education versus instruction, socialization, and shared experience seems to be largely focused around the question of direct dialogue. Dialogue is discussed at some length in Chapter Six.

Effectiveness and Efficiency

Rumble (1986) defines effectiveness when he says that an "organization is effective to the extent that it produces outputs that are relevant to the needs and demands of its clients" (p. 211). If effectiveness is the extent to which real outputs match ideal or desired outputs, then efficiency refers to the cost of reaching these effective outputs (Rumble, 1986).

In their appraisal of distance teaching universities, Keegan and Rumble list the following indicators of effectiveness and efficiency: the cost effectiveness of these universities relative to conventional universities; the cost efficiency relative to conventional universities; and the cost benefits of distance and traditional university educations. The OUUK is not cheap, says Keegan (1986), noting its heavy spending on television, student support, and study centers. Still, its cost is perhaps half that of conventional British universities (Wagner, 1977). As Holmberg puts it: "Distance education, as applied to large student bodies, is characterized by very favourable cost-benefit relations provided that the distance-teaching element predominates. It is primarily the arrangements for face-to-face sessions, such as study centres, residential schools, and classes of various kinds, that modify or negate the validity of this statement. . . . It is true that use of sophisticated and costly media and technology also in some cases detract from the favourable cost-benefit relations, but this does not change the overall picture of distance education as economical" (1986, p. 203).

Essentially, efficiency means nothing if desired outputs are not reached. Because quality is difficult to evaluate, cost effectiveness is as well. Keegan and Rumble (1982) suggest measuring not only the quality of the output but the quality or value added to students as a result of their studies. As noted earlier, value-added assessment is currently a topic of interest in the United States and is being investigated by distance and nontraditional education institutions.

The benefits of education are difficult to arrive at or to compare, making cost benefits also difficult to figure. Benefits to OUUK graduates may be less dramatic than benefits to graduates of conventional programs, but graduates of OUUK may be compensated by not losing work time as they study (Wagner, 1977). However, they will have a shorter work life, on average, and usually have less job mobility (Mace, 1978). Determining the cost benefits of U.S. distance education and related programs is also difficult. The benefits to working adults of a college degree are best compared to the benefits received by other adults studying conventionally, rather than the benefits received by traditional-aged students, but research on the employment success of external degree program graduates usually compares adult with traditional-aged graduates (Doyle, 1979).

Impact

The impact of a distance teaching university on the educational system may be long term or short term. Does an institution's success mean it is emulated by others, who adopt its model? Certainly this is the case for the Open University of the United Kingdom or the University of New England (Australia). Does a consortium grow or inspire similar consortia? Do certain innovative delivery systems come into widespread use? There are many examples of the impact of distance higher education in the United States. Much of this impact occurred during the nationwide growth in the 1970s and 1980s of consortia using audioconferencing, videoconferencing, computer conferencing, and telecourse delivery systems, serving primarily higher education audiences.

Perhaps because the development of a consortium is not strongly felt in a single place and often only affects a certain part of a mainly conventional institution's academic programming, the impact of the proliferation of distance education consortia in the United States in the 1980s is less noticeable than, say, the development of the distance teaching universities inspired by the OUUK. Yet the impact of distance education consortia on higher education is impressive. The impact of new technologies such as the computer on all parts of higher education is even more impressive and may help to explain the favorable opinion educators hold of such successful innovations, an opinion that helps to pave the way for application of these technologies in distance education.

Relevance to Needs and Expectations

Relevance to national, local, and individual needs is identified by Gooler as another criterion for the assessment of distance education. American higher educators might be more concerned with national, state, and institutional-service-region employment trends and projected shortfalls and changes; regional and state service needs; and individual needs for personal and career development.

Needs are determined to a large extent by possible markets. What is the student market in the region, the state, the nation? How do occupational markets match up with trained personnel, now and in the future? American businesses and even the nonprofit sector are adopting this marketing orientation. This philosophy requires that a producer of goods or services find out what people want and provide it. The traditional viewpoint in American business, before market survey research made the marketing orientation commonplace, was the production orientation. This viewpoint implied that one should produce the goods or services one thinks are best and then try to get people to buy them.

American higher education faculty have traditionally made choices about curricula based on professional understandings within fields and colleges about what courses and programs were best, citing when necessary their academic freedom to make such decisions without external pressure or coercion. Today most colleges and universities, through faculty committees and administrations largely composed of former faculty members, deliberate the needs filled by a course or program before instituting it, but the pace of change is still slow. Distance education units, being on the periphery of institutional affairs, may find it easier to respond to perceived needs but will often find that their plans cannot be carried out because of their low standing on the financial priority list. For example, in Florida, a survey of the educational needs of AFL-CIO union members led Meinhold (1981) to recommend in a report to the Board of Directors of the Southeast Florida Educational Consortium that a bacculaureate program utilizing on-campus and distance educational delivery methods be instituted, but the program apparently was not instituted.

Realistic planning for needs is important. Hershfield (1986) asserts that the Learn Alaska Network, a statewide telecommunications system designed to reach Alaskans living in remote areas, was poorly planned. The network was too extensive and expensive, and programming was underbudgeted. As a result, Hershfield says, the costs of the program outweighed the benefits. He suggests the use of planning models asking questions, starting with the identification of markets and needs.

The most sophisticated use of market survey and strategic planning techniques in a distance education unit in North America probably occurred at Athabasca University in Canada. For example, a market survey in 1984 concerning a proposed natural resources planning and management external degree program asked potential enrollees to give their opinions on employment prospects, professional development, the degree offered, delivery modes, and programs and curriculum design (Curtis and Bakshi, 1984). A step-by-step model for researching demand for proposed curricula was developed (Curtis, 1985). Administrators at Athabasca engage in strategic planning and marketing, quality assurance, and accountability measures (Murgatroyd and Woudstra, 1989).

Generation of Knowledge

It is the responsibility of colleges, universities, and other educational agencies to generate and share knowledge. Distance educators have helped develop the research literature on "problems, issues, and practices in educational delivery, the nature of the adult learning population, and the use of technology in education" (Gooler, 1979, p. 50). Holmberg (1989) discusses at length the reasons that distance education should be considered an academic discipline. Many of the reasons he lists are linked to generation of knowledge. Distance education has played a significant role in the development and use of many instructional materials and media designs that have had an impact not only on distance education but on other forms of educational delivery for adults and traditional-aged students. However, much of the new knowledge in the United States about the use of distance education is imported from other countries whose distance education systems are more developed than those in the United States. American efforts have not generated much knowledge since distance education is still in its early stages in the United States, but educational thinkers and researchers will undoubtedly begin to generate more information in this area. This is a must for their fellow professionals.

Acceptability

Keegan (1986) refers to the status of learning as the recognition that the learning is accorded. The term *acceptability* used here includes the status or recognition afforded learning based on perceptions of its quality. This broader term, not employed or cited as a criteria by Gooler or the other authors, refers not only to *status,* or perceptions of educational quality on the part of those outside the institution, but also to *attitudes* toward specific distance education applications and toward distance education in general held by students, faculty, and administrators, whether or not they are participants in distance education.

Status. Keegan and Rumble (1982), in appraising the distance teaching universities, list the following indicators of status: acceptance of credits earned at the universities by other educational institutions when students transfer, acceptance of the degrees and diplomas awarded as qualifying students to go on to higher-level studies, recognition of the awards by employers, and esteem for the distance teaching institutions and their awards by the community at large. They note that many DTUs already had credit transfer agreements by 1982. In the United States, most universities are willing to accept some distance education or nontraditional college credit from any accredited institution, although most put limits on the amount of such credit that they will accept (Bear, 1989). Similarly, graduates of the OUUK have applied for and gained entrance to graduate and professional schools in large numbers. In the United States, the graduates of external degree programs in the late 1970s applied at average to above-average rates to institutions offering further study and were just as acceptable to them as students from conventional programs (Sosdian and Sharp, 1978; Beshiri, 1978). This is not really surprising since these students often listed further study as an educational goal (Board of Governors of State Colleges and Universities, 1978).

McIntosh and Rigg (1979) found that about 50 percent of British employers surveyed felt that the OUUK degree was equivalent to that of other British universities. American external degrees were also accepted by most employers and yielded tangible job benefits (Sosdian and Sharp, 1978). Seventy-two percent of Board of Governors graduates surveyed reported that their employers fully accepted the degree as a credential (Board of Governors of State Colleges and Universities, 1978).

The OUUK and its credentials are held in considerable esteem in Britain. Among the reasons are an association in the public mind with the British Broadcasting Corporation and its quality programming, the involvement of top-caliber authors and academics, political sponsorship by Lord Perry, representation on national

educational and governmental committees, receipt of national research awards, and an international reputation (Keegan, 1986).

Attitudes. Attitudes toward distance education play an important role in decisions about who will use it and how and when
it will be used. Lewis and Wall (1988) state that in addition to those
obstacles commonly encountered by people promoting innovative
teaching on campus, distance educators face several other obstacles.
Faculty may be resistant to public exposure, fearing that their
course materials or content or their teaching styles may come under
attack. The resistance of faculty to off-campus learning, which this
chapter is an attempt to address at least in part, is described by
Lewis and Wall (1988) in these terms: "Some instructors are resistant to dealing with students who cannot get to campus, having
little or no sympathy for the student whose life situation does not
permit attending college in the traditional manner. Among these
are teachers who believe they cannot teach if they 'cannot see the
students' faces,' or who are [even] reluctant to try interactive transmission systems that enable instructors to see students in classrooms
located a distance across the campus. Some believe that 'you can't
teach this way,' no matter what" (p. 12). They also note that some
faculty see as unhealthy the narrow focus on serving well-heeled
professional markets, the primary justification for the use of new
technologies off campus. Of course, this may be a reflection of the
priorities presently assigned to professional and other graduate-
level education in college and university missions.

The public image of distance education, both in general and
with regard to specific institutions and programs, must inevitably
affect the adoption and status, internally and externally, of distance-
based innovations in educational delivery. The Open University of
the United Kingdom may have shed its correspondence study image
(Rumble, 1986), but American distance education programs have
not, and, in many cases they do not want to do so. Individuals
working in the correspondence study field, either at colleges and
universities or proprietary schools, would like to see changes in the
public's image of postal study, which they see as mistaken and
stereotypical. In turn, college programs do not want to be stereo-
typed as "mail-order outfits." The director of Ohio University's

independent study division, Richard W. Moffit, notes: "Everybody remembers home-study schools that used matchbooks to advertise their programs. University correspondence study is sometimes equated to the proprietary schools. Many of these schools are very good, but . . . they have a different focus" (Watkins, 1984, pp. 1, 4).

Misperceptions abound even within higher education institutions, according to Von V. Pittman, director of the University of Iowa's Center for Credit programs, who declared at a correspondence study conference, "We all complain about the status of continuing education on our campuses. I would maintain that there is sometimes a caste system even within continuing education—correspondence study sometimes is to continuing education what continuing education is to the university" (Young, 1984, p. 84).

It certainly seems possible that some sort of major rift may occur between those distance higher educators who rely heavily on correspondence study methods and those who also use one-way or two-way electronic dialogue. Computers are probably more acceptable to academics than correspondence study as a means of conveying print, simply because educators and the public in general have assigned an exalted (if sometimes terrifying) image to computers. Even though most of the instructional content and dialogue in telecourse study occurs through correspondence, the exciting, if checkered, image of television still appears to be sufficient to draw viewers.

Distance educators who do not consider themselves correspondence study teachers see the public's equating of distance education with correspondence study as a problem. One way they attempt to change the public's perception is by emphasizing the innovative high-technology aspects of the program—certainly this is a major emphasis in the literature. To the correspondence study educator, on the other hand, this approach is hypocritical and a betrayal of the field's roots. Correspondence educators worry that the call for more dialogue in distance education through electronic methods may not really broaden access since fewer people will have access to such technology than currently have access to print.

Ging and Blackburn (1986) studied the experiences with and attitudes toward telecourse education of 630 faculty and 598 administrators who inquired in a mail survey about the possible use of

Annenberg/CPB telecourses. Usable survey were returned by 107 faculty who subsequently used telecourses and 240 faculty who did not as well as by 167 administrators. Faculty who adopted telecourses usually expressed a belief in the value of instructional television based upon pedagogical conditions, positive impact on enrollments or reputation, or its utility in reaching geographically remote learners. Support of change among top administrators and a history of successful innovation in the institutions were two contextual predictors of adoption. Academic usability was seen as a key consideration of faculty in deciding whether or not to use the telecourses. Ging and Blackburn assert that based on their model they were able to make 90 percent accurate predictions about which faculty and administrators would adopt Annenberg/CPB telecourses.

A study of 418 University of Michigan faculty gauged their receptivity to an external graduate degree program. The respondents were generally favorable to the idea (Johnson, 1984). But faculty are probably more receptive to graduate than undergraduate external degrees.

Faculty working in University-Without-Walls external degree programs at seven institutions tended to rate the academic quality of these programs as being the same or better than that of traditional programs, while nonparticipating faculty usually held the opposite opinion (Stetson, 1979). Medsker and others (1975) surveyed faculty at eighteen California universities across the state with special degree programs and found that participation and experience in the program was linked to a positive attitude about the program.

Attitudes play a large role in status, which in turn can function to make the assumed inferiority of distance education a self-fulfilling prophecy. Scott (1985) reports that in the late 1970s, a survey of external degree program policies and practices at fourteen state institutions of higher education revealed differing levels of program integration into the institution. Although admission and graduation requirements were usually similar in off-campus and on-campus programs and off-campus credit was easily transferred to on-campus programs, most external degree instruction was performed by adjunct professors who were paid less. In the University-Without-Walls programs during the same period, the proportion of senior faculty was higher. Regular faculty who taught in external degree programs often felt they were slighted in terms of professional advancement. Fifty percent of the respondents to a survey by Stetson (1979) felt that their institution did not fund its external degree program on an equal basis with on-campus programs. Clearly, attitudes, status, and program effectiveness are highly interrelated.

Student attitudes toward distance education have also been studied. Like nonparticipating faculty, students who did not take part in University-Without-Walls programs perceived them as inferior to conventional programs, and participating students, like faculty, saw them as being of higher quality than conventional programs (Stetson, 1979). Students taking part in distance higher education generally perceive distance education positively although they may not get exactly what they expected. Crane (1985) notes that "Annenberg CPB telecourse students perceived the courses they took as being as difficult, interesting, and as challenging as on-campus courses. Some first-time users were surprised at the amount of work asked of them" (p. 1). However, most telecourse students were very satisfied with the grade they received and the quality of the course materials. Regardless of age, gender, previous experience with telecourses, or attendance at a two- or four-year college, most students were satisfied with the course overall. One source of discontent was the frequency of on-campus class meetings, which averaged only two to three required and two optional sessions a semester at participating institutions. About 33 percent of the respondents wanted more such meetings, and only about 4 percent wanted fewer (Crane, 1985).

Summary

From the evidence presented in this chapter (and also in the Resource), distance education methodology appears to achieve cognitive outcomes equal to those achieved by the more traditional means of education delivery for adults. In many cases, the scale even tips toward distance education. Distance education can also be effective when considering affective and psychomotor outcomes. All of this information should allay some of the suspicions of current and future postsecondary educators who question this particular mode of delivery for adult learning. The dropout rate, higher than in conventional education, is a continuing problem in distance education. Perceived course difficulty and personal motivation are problems. Better learning materials and support systems are viewed as ways to reduce the high rate.

Besides learner outcomes, the evidence and discussion on the other criteria for distance education offered by Gooler (access, quality, cost effectiveness and efficiency, impact, relevance to needs, and generation of knowledge) seem to favor distance education. Even though the current information is heavily oriented to other countries and their work in distance education, there is little reason to believe that similar evidence cannot be generated in the United States. The limited evidence in this country seems to suggest that success is highly possible when greater implementation occurs.

Wider use of distance education depends in part on its acceptability to practicing professionals in the field. It appears that those educators who have been involved in some phase of distance education feel strongly about its use and potential, while those with little knowledge or use question its viability. The key to greater acceptability, then, is to encourage the educator (and administrator) to become more knowledgeable and move toward some implementation activities.

Part Three

*Strengthening
the Theory and Practice
of Distance Education*

6

Program Foundations

Before any specific designs for a distance education program are offered, it is important to offer some foundation or rationale upon which the program can rest. This foundation should be useful and fit the definition of distance education as expressed earlier. In order to build a foundation, current thinking and ideas in distance education and adult education and in other meaningful areas should be examined. This chapter reviews the various proposals in these areas and offers a summary that can serve as a foundation for the practice of distance education.

Distance Education Theory

Michael Moore's (1973) theory of independent study is widely considered to be one of the better-developed paradigms related to the field of distance education. He began his research with the belief that instruction could be divided into two fields of study: face-to-face, or contiguous study, and separate, or noncontiguous study. The distinguishing characteristic of both independent study and distance education is the separation of teacher and learner that makes the use of media a necessity. Programs designed to encourage independent or self-directed learning, such as do-it-yourself books by experts in a field, result in learning that might be called distance learning. Distance education, on the other hand, requires formal evaluation and two-way communication with an educational agency as well as independent study, based on Keegan's (1986) definition. Because he considers the concept of distance or separation to be crucial, Moore (1973) categorizes independent study and distance programs in terms of *transactional distance,* which is basically an expression of the sense of distance felt by the learner in the educational transaction in question. He defines transactional distance in terms of two factors, dialogue and structure.

Dialogue refers to two-way communication between teacher and learner. Transactional distance is greater when there is little dialogue and smaller when there is more dialogue. By *structure,* Moore means the degree to which objectives, study methods, and evaluation may be adapted to the needs of individual learners. More structure increases transactional distance, while less structure decreases it.

Moore (1973) offers these examples of the categories of transactional distance:

	Example	*Program*
1.	Programs with no dialogue and no structure	Independent readings
2.	Programs with no dialogue but with structure	Radio or telecourses
3.	Programs with structure and dialogue	Correspondence study
4.	Programs with dialogue and no structure	Rogerian tutorials

Because teachers and learners are separate during instruction, says Moore, learners must be emotionally independent, self-motivated, and capable of coping with learning problems on their own—in a word, autonomous. This assumption is substantially borne out by studies of field independence and dependence in distance learners. Moore, therefore, sees autonomy as another important dimension of distance education. He classifies programs in terms of the autonomy learners can exercise in the setting of objectives, choosing of study methods, and making of decisions concerning evaluation. Overall, Moore sees *independent study* as occurring in any program in which teaching and learning take place while teacher and learner are separate and in which the learner's influence in determining objectives, study methods, and decisions about evaluation is at least equal to the teacher's influence (Keegan, 1986).

In emphasizing learner autonomy, Moore takes the same position as have a long line of respected educators, including Knowles, Bruner, Rogers, and many others. Moore, in speaking of the fostering of dependency in the public schools, says that students "need to develop an independent stance in educational transactions" (Moore, 1980, p. 24). "Autonomy is the stated objective of most educators," he says, and "the critical task for adult educators is to restore and support the learner's autonomy" (pp. 25–26). Since adults are most motivated to learn things related to their life problems, Moore says, teachers should help adults focus on problem-related topics that they are motivated to learn. In sum, adults "must be treated by educators as autonomous learners who exercise their autonomy at all stages of the program" (p. 26).

Clearly, Moore's definition of independent study can only be used to describe a minority of distance education programs, some internal independent study programs, and most self-directed learning efforts since it requires that the learner's control of the course be at least equal to the teacher's control. Moore may be defining independent study in a fairly traditional manner, not intending his definition to cover all types of distance education. Perhaps he sees his definition as an ideal.

A Model of Distance Education

However, we were concerned with finding a theory that can be used to explain the phenomenon of distance education both subjectively and objectively and which provides a framework by which distance education can be related to adult and conventional education. We felt it was especially important that this theory be useful in explaining what teaching and learning styles worked and how they worked in different situations. Since no existing theories seemed to fulfill these criteria, we decided to develop a more representative model, building especially on Moore's theory but also considering what research and reason presented as valid in previous theories. We consciously attempted to avoid either-or thinking in formulating this new viewpoint because it leads to one-sided viewpoints that are already too common in educational theory making.

This model owes much to the work of Moore (1973, 1977, 1980). Without the work of Moore and the others mentioned in this chapter, it is unlikely that we would have conceived of this approach. We believe that using many of Moore's concepts to develop a theory that better fits distance education in practice, while tying it to adult and conventional education overall, represents an evolution, not a rejection, of the concepts he advanced.

The present model, like Moore's, begins with the concept critical to distance education, separation of teacher and learner. And it also includes Keegan's (1986) definition of distance education as requiring evaluation and two-way communication in addition to this teacher-learner separation. What Moore calls autonomous learning and we call distance learning covers a much broader variety of situations than does distance education since it consists of any use of media for self-study. This concept of distance learning does not appear to have been fully developed under any name by previous authors. Yet virtually everyone engages in distance learning since it encompasses all intentional use of media such as newspaper, books, television, or radio for the purpose of learning rather than entertainment. Distance education is a subset of distance learning that includes evaluation by distance educators and two-way communication with them and that usually includes the structuring of media content and use by the educator. Distance educators may find the concept of distance learning useful in their attempts to dispel the negative images of distance study prevalent among potential students and conventional educators. By relating distance education to familiar personal experiences with distance learning, proponents of distance education may be able to overcome attitudinal barriers to the use of distance education in the United States.

Moore's categorization of programs in terms of dialogue, structure, and learner autonomy is a good starting point in the development of a theory of distance education, but the way he defines these terms appears to limit their usefulness. Moore's concept of dialogue, or two-way communication, is sound, but it should include the idea of support since the basic reason for dialogue is to provide support of one kind or another to the distance learner.

Field-independent students may only be concerned with dialogue to the extent that they can get answers to questions about content, but field-dependent students are more likely to use dialogue to receive emotional support for their efforts. For this reason, high-dialogue instruction, which is needed when the support required involves more than the supplying of directions, may be necessary to attract and retain field-dependent students. For this reason, the first dimension of the model presented here is called *dialogue/support*.

Our view on structure differs considerably from that of Moore. Moore defines structure in terms of the responsiveness of the program to the objectives, study method, and evaluation of individual learners. The work of Beder (1985), which defines structure as a function of the formality of the subject matter, was used in our model. Some fields of study in distance, adult, and even pre-adult education, in which competence may only be a matter of basic understanding of principles or problems, need only minimal structure. A high level of structure is needed in other fields in which many years of study may be necessary before a learner is competent enough to set objectives and study methods or to take part in evaluation. This competence in a field, or *specialized competence*, is seen as a situational attribute (Pratt, 1988) that may occur among adults or children studying at a distance or conventionally, based largely upon the learner's expertise or lack of it, and that is usually a function of the structure of the subject matter.

But there is another side to competence—the kind of general learning competence often referred to as self-directedness. We suggest that general competence/self-directedness may be seen as a hierarchy of skills and propose one for consideration. At the bottom is skill in discussion, the basis of learner-centered discourse. Learners with poor literacy skills may be highly proficient (sometimes as a means of compensation) in verbal discourse, although generally this is not the case. Next comes skill in independent study, which is necessary if the learner is to succeed in any nonsupervised method of distance education. The learner must be able to learn from various media, recognize important and unimportant data, and record the meaning of important information in abbreviated form. Next comes the ability to write well, a skill many adults lack. This skill is especially important at a distance because written communications often play a large role in interaction. Without this skill, learners may be unable to accurately and fully express their attitudes and feelings to the tutors and may do poorly on tests requiring written responses.

The ability to research and write on topics related to coursework is the next step up in this hierarchy of competence. Many adults find writing research papers difficult because their reading and writing skills are less developed than their verbal or thinking skills. Research may also prove daunting for adults who do not feel comfortable in a library, and computer access to data bases may circumvent part of this problem for a small group of adult learners. Adults who can take part in discussion, study, read and write well, and create adequate research papers might be said to have all the basic or general competence skills needed for participation in learner-centered distance education and even adult education.

A basic or general level of overall competence may be considered a given upon which postsecondary competencies are built. Knowledge of the competence required in a course is important to learners so that they do not enroll in courses that they later discover are too hard, too easy, or simply inappropriate for them.

Certain fields contain more knowledge of a hierarchical or structured nature than others (Donald, 1983). In some fields, the structured knowledge is tied together into an overall structure, while in others there may be various assumptions, none of which are universally accepted to be valid by those working in the field, that are the basis of a number of unconnected schemata and overlapping schemata. Education is such a field. Yet even in education, there are a number of relatively comprehensive approaches such as history, socioeconomics, and demographics that can be used to provide structure in the discipline. The difference between a high-structure field—such as mathematics—and a low-structure field—such as education—lies in the degree of formality or informality of the overall structure (Beder, 1985).

Generally, a high-structure field will require more specialized knowledge on the part of the learner than will a low-structure field. In a field in which knowledge of one aspect is necessary before a learner can obtain knowledge of another aspect—such as the need to understand algebra before moving on to statistics—the degree of formality is high. But if the previous knowledge needed to participate in a particular course can be gained rapidly—say through readings, as in many education courses—the degree of formality is relatively low. For this reason, the second dimension of the model presented here is called *structure/specialized competence.*

In higher education, the least specialized competence is probably required in courses such as overviews of a subject designed for nonmajors and introductory-level courses in a particular field or discipline. Interdisciplinary courses require similar levels of specialized competence, but they may require considerable amounts of general competence when designed for advanced students. Advanced-level undergraduate courses and professional or graduate-level courses usually require general competence as well as specialized competence to the extent that specialized competence is required in the field.

In the third dimension of the model, termed *general competence/self-directedness,* Moore's view of autonomy (1973) is combined with the self-directivity proposed by Pratt (1988). Authors in the adult education field tend to overgeneralize about the nature of learning sought by adults based on the principles of andragogy and similar philosophies of adult learning, focusing perhaps on how adults would learn in an ideal world rather than on how they actually learn best in reality.

We do not assume that self-directedness is inherently good or bad. For problem-oriented adult and distance education, the idea of general all-around competence in terms of self-motivation and study skills does have some validity. However, it is not logical to expect that every field be equally well suited to the promotion of autonomy through student-shared control of objectives, study methods, and evaluation decisions. Such an approach does not differentiate between general competence, or self-directedness, and the specialized competence that is highly tied to the structure of the subject matter. A better approach to deciding appropriate levels of self-directedness or autonomy might be to determine whether the student is competent in that field at that level, to estimate the student's general competence, and to see if appropriate structure and dialogue have been afforded, given the formality or lack of it in that field.

As Pratt (1988) notes, self-directed learners often enter into formal, highly structured programs in pursuit of professional goals. As self-directed learners, they may actively seek out a high-structure approach that fits the type of knowledge found in the field and that prepares them for various forms of professional certification. Taking highly structured coursework to achieve their objectives does not make these students any less self-directed in terms of their overall educational plan.

The three dimensions together—dialogue/support, structure/specialized competence, and general competence/self-directedness—generate eight possible categories or cases of learning experiences when considered in terms of low or high levels of each attribute. Four more categories can be added to include those cases in which there is no dialogue at all, characteristic of distance learning situations.

The twelve cases follow, along with some of their most common educational applications.

Case 1: Low dialogue/support; low structure/specialized competence; low general competence/self-directedness. Few educational situations fit this category. One example, however, is the experience of a participant in a general interest videoconference at a site with one-way video and little chance for audio interaction via telephone—a typical situation, unfortunately.

Case 2: Low dialogue/support; high structure/specialized competence; low general competence/self-directedness. If structure is high and competence and dialogue are low, the instructional design of the coursework must be good if the learners are to succeed, since they will not always be able to get feedback if they encounter problems. Much correspondence study, particularly the vocational-technical distance study available through proprietary schools that accounts for nine out of every ten American distance education enrollments, falls into this category.

Case 3: Low dialogue/support; low structure/specialized competence; high general competence/self-directedness. Most problem-oriented distance education falls into this category. Learning contracts and independent study courses typify such low-structure, low-dialogue, and high-competence types of distance education. Both in terms of structure and competence, this is the most andragogical of the low-dialogue cases.

Case 4: Low dialogue/support; high structure/specialized competence; high general competence/self-directedness. Distance and conventional education for further vocational or professional credentials often require both high structure and competence, while necessitating only low dialogue. Now we turn to the high-dialogue cases.

Case 5: High dialogue/support; low structure/specialized competence; low general competence/self-directnesss. The University of Wisconsin-Extension's Educational Telephone Network is a good example of this category. Ninety-five percent of ETN's offerings are noncredit wide-ranging discussions on topics of interest to people gathered at its statewide audioconferencing sites. Although much of ETN programming is continuing professional education with specialized competence, many general-interest audioconferences offered by ETN come under Case 5. Conventional educational experiences such as Freirian consciousness-raising groups and many postsecondary-level class discussions also fit into this category.

Case 6: High dialogue/support; high structure/specialized competence; low general competence/self-directedness. Perhaps most elementary and secondary classroom study and most study of formal subjects at any level (except for large lecture classes, which fit better into Case 2) fall under this category. Even informal subjects often have a body of rules in which learners must become competent before autonomous study is possible.

Case 7: High dialogue/support; low structure/specialized competence; high general competence/self-directedness. Many advanced classroom study courses in the humanities belong in this category, including graduate seminars and continuing professional education in fields such as education.

Class 8: High dialogue support; high structure/specialized competence; high general competence/self-directedness. Advanced classroom study in the sciences, including graduate seminars and continuing professional education fits this category. Obviously, some courses of study may be better described as a combination of the cases cited here than as examples of a single case alone.

Finally, we turn from cases that cover distance and conventional education to those that may be used to describe distance learning. In these cases, no dialogue at all exists between learner and education provider.

Case 9: No dialogue/support; low specialized competence/formality; low general competence/self-directedness. Much basically unplanned distance learning from media fits this category. Unsystematic distance learning about a topic of interest achieved by watching television talk shows is a good example of Case 9 learning. It is difficult at times to differentiate between people watching to learn and those watching for entertainment, especially among regular viewers. But if the large majority of programs in a series can be used for education, distance learning may be occurring.

Case 10: No dialogue/support; high specialized competence/formality; low general competence/self-directedness. Distance learning using textbooks intended for students of high-structure subjects belongs in Case 10, although learners low in self-directedness may have poor results in such self-study efforts.

Case 11: No dialogue/support; low specialized competence/formality; high general competence/self-directedness. Much of the continuing learning of professionals in low-structure disciplines consists of reading journals in the field, and this clearly falls into Case 11. An interesting nonformal learning example in this category occurs when professionals eat as they listen to a speaker.

Case 12: No dialogue/support; high specialized competence/formality; high general competence/self-directedness. Continuing professional distance learning in high-structure fields such as medicine through the reading of journals is an example of this category.

It is probably more useful to think of segments of courses rather than entire courses in applying these categories. Almost every subject being taught at a particular level includes at least some high-structure/specialized-competence material that is best taught pedagogically and some low-structure/specialized-competence material that is best taught andragogically. However, in the real world, it appears, based on the work of Gorham (1985), that teachers adopt and maintain a teaching style that is basically either andragogical or pedagogical, regardless of the age of students or the subject matter. Gorham found that most educators of both children and adults subscribed to andragogical principles in teaching their adult students. However, when they were observed teaching in the classroom, they exhibited only minor changes in their teaching styles as they moved from teaching children to teaching adults, engaging in less overtly directive behavior and avoiding criticism. Gorham found little variation in teacher behavior across the subjects as well.

Although the consistently pedagogical educators Gorham surveyed were all men, the few women in Gorham's study did change from pedagogical behavior with children to andragogical behavior with adults, facilitating this change by moving desks into a circle, effectively changing the power relationship in the classroom. However, these female teachers maintained their andragogical styles in high-structure coursework with adults where pedagogy might have been more appropriate.

While this inability to shift from one teaching orientation to another when teaching adults may be problematic for conventional adult educators, it may offer opportunities for distance educators who wish to offer high-quality educational experiences to their students in all situations. To provide socialization, face-to-face contact with the teacher, and opportunities for intuitive evaluation of competencies and changes in behavior, distance educators should, if possible, require students in advanced courses to travel to a central location for intensive seminars. Much of this classroom study might be replaced by high-dialogue group-study distance methods such as audioconferencing and videoconferencing, which offer similar real-time interaction. By arranging course content so that high-structure elements such as theories, principles, history, and examples of practice come first then moving into low-structure aspects such as present-day implications of theories, especially in areas of interest to the student, distance teachers in low-structure subjects might be able to make the transition from a pedagogical distance education course segment to an andragogical classroom study segment. Teachers in high-structure subjects might follow a pedagogical section at a distance with an in-person laboratory segment that was also pedagogical. This technique might prove especially useful in higher education courses usually taught through intensive seminars in which valuable time is spent acquainting learners with concepts fundamental to coursework with a higher cognitive objective that may, because of time restrictions, get short shrift. In other words, by choosing teachers to fit subject matter and requiring intensive classroom work, distance education providers might maximize the achievement and satisfaction of students through proper matching of teaching methods, teaching orientations, and subject matter.

The reader may have noticed that our model did not address the cases in which the degree of structure of the course content and the specialized competence of the learner differed. If structure is high and specialized competence is low, optimal learning is impossible. If structure is low and specialized competence is high, students would have no difficulty with content and might even be bored.

In many problem-oriented adult education situations, specialized competence is fairly irrelevant, but self-directedness is important. In self-directed distance learning by professionals, both are important. Specialized competence and self-directedness are treated as separate factors since the need for specialized competence is directly related to the degree of subject structure, and the need for self-directedness in the sense of general learning competence tends to remain fairly constant overall.

Which of the eight cases of the model seem to work best for adults or children studying conventionally or at a distance? Adults generally have higher specialized and general competence, which gives them an edge in low-dialogue situations in which direction is less available. Of couse, there are exceptions, especially when adult education serves a social function. In general, children have spent less time building specialized competence and self-directedness and therefore need more dialogue.

Clearly, adults are more suited than children for study at a distance since distance study by definition involves constraints on dialogue. Where children do succeed in distance study, such as in Alaska, the distance system usually includes the use of a monitor, usually the mother, who enforces study periods and provides supportive dialogue. It appears that the high-dialogue cases, Cases 5 through 8, typify adult conventional study, although distance teleconferencing and other high-dialogue distance study techniques also belong in these categories.

In conventional education of children, Cases 5 and 6 are perhaps emphasized, stressing high structure and high dialogue. But since children also build progressively on previously developed competencies, children's study also involves Cases 7 and 8.

Adult education at a distance usually falls into Cases 2, 3 and 4. Children's distance study falls in the same categories. However, it should probably be noted that many secondary students successfully complete college correspondence study courses, and that these individuals have probably developed the sort of higher self-directedness usually associated with adult students. Age is a continuum, too, with no absolute categories. Adults who have not attended school in a long time or who dropped out of high school may have levels of competence and self-directedness similar to those of teenagers. Nevertheless, they have much more life experience than pre-adults, which may help them keep their learning deficits in perspective while providing a valuable resource for use in their studies.

If Cases 2, 3, and 4 best fit the distance education process, what are some general implications of their uses? In all cases, dialogue, although low in comparison to other situations, must still be maintained to a good degree in order to ensure the support adult learners need (Garrison, 1989). Even though dialogue in these cases is low by definition, its presence must be ensured to encourage adult learning and continued motivation; reciprocal communication is critical.

Instructional design and media development are critical in

Case 2 because of the high structure and low feedback. The entering knowledge base of the adult also can be important, particularly if the course or learning unit builds on previous ones.

In Case 3, the problem definition and establishment of learning contracts must receive careful attention if learning is to take place. The adult learners must also have general competence in problem solving and researching a topic.

In Case 4 the assurance of both specialized and general competence must be established for successful completion of the learning unit. However, this method of delivery would only be used with students who have considerable knowledge, expertise, and experience in the topic they are studying.

The quality of the learning in all cases, of course, depends on the subject matter under study and the needs and entering behavior of the adult students. Assessment and decision making by the distance educator are critical when working with adults to ensure that a mismatch does not occur and that meaningful learning will take place.

Andragogy and Learning Theories

Further support for our model comes from some of the ideas associated with andragogy and learning styles. In 1970, Malcolm Knowles reintroduced the concept of andragogy in American adult education, defining it as "the art and science of helping adults learn" (1970, p. 38). The term was orginally coined in 1833 by a German scholar, Kapp, to describe the educational theories of Plato (Nottingham Andragogy Group, 1983). It resurfaced in Europe in 1921, and was in extensive use in several nations on the continent by the 1960s. Lindeman (1927) first introduced the term in the United States, and Knowles (1980) revised the work of Lindeman and stated the basis of a theory of andragogy in terms of four assumptions about adult learning: (1) as people mature, their self-concept moves from dependency toward self-direction, (2) the accumulated experiences of adults may be used in learning, (3) the readiness of adults to learn is closely related to developmental tasks or social roles, (4) learning becomes more problem oriented and less subject oriented in adulthood.

Since Knowles reintroduced the term, *andragogy* has been at the center of an argument in adult education over the role of the teacher and the true characteristics of learners. As happens with many schools of thought in education, supporters of andragogy often seem to assume that it is universally applicable. As discussed earlier, Gorham (1985) found that most teachers who believe they are andragogical when teaching adults actually made few changes in the pedagogical style they used in teaching children. Self-directedness, a key concept in andragogy, appears to actually be a situational attribute (Pratt, 1988). In addition, the formality or informality of a discipline may be a stronger influence on appropriate choice of teaching style than the age of the students (Beder, 1985). It is best, perhaps, to see andragogy as a set of ideals that can only be successfully applied in a minority of adult education situations.

Behavioral and cognitive learning theories may best describe pedagogical study, in which the teacher is an expert source and the learners are basically passive recipients of knowledge. Humanistic theories appear to best explain andragogical learning situations, in which students are more capable of self-direction and the teacher is more facilitative than directive. Instead of attempting to take an entirely behavioral, cognitive, or humanistic approach, we have tried to combine applicable parts of each on a situational basis.

Knowle's assumption that readiness to learn is tied to adult developmental tasks is based on Havighurst's work in this area (Knowles, 1980). When Merriam and Mullins (1981) surveyed 540 adult residents of Roanoke, Virginia, they found that Havighurst's life stage tasks were most important to women and middle-income adults and least important to low-income adults. Also, some tasks did not seem to need to be completed in certain stages of life, as Havighurst had contended. This finding is similar to the work of Alderfer (1972) who posited that the needs of Maslow's hierarchy did not necessarily have to be completed in order. Some authors such as Gilligan (1979) believe that the conclusions of the developmental stage theorists are not generalizable to all people because the research samples used, such as the one used by Maslow, were generally white middle-class males. Those adult and distance educators who wish to take the developmental tasks for their learners into account when attempting to decide the learners' readiness for a particular topic need to remember that developmental tasks and the progression through them may vary considerably among chronologically similar students.

Field Dependence and Independence

Perceptual fields may influence the motivation and participation of adult and distance learners. Field dependence and independence can be seen as extremes on a continuum. The Embedded Figures Test (EFT), which is used to test the speed with which students can distinguish a geometric pattern, is one of several instruments used to determine degrees of field independence. Field independents have a preference for solitary situations and self-defined goals, strategies, and reinforcement. Field dependents, on the other hand, prefer group situations, externally defined goals and reinforcements, and explicit instructions or definitions of desired outcomes (Witkins, Moore, Goodenough, and Cox, 1977). Field dependence is usually defined in the literature as a low degree of field independence since there is no instrument available to test for it, but this definition overlooks the possibility of adaptive behavior by students who have high levels of both field-dependent and field-independent behavior (Bonham, 1987).

In a study in which field-dependent and field-independent students were matched with teachers having the same or a different field orientation, slightly higher achievement and satisfaction were found among students matched with a teacher with the same orientation (Garlinger and Frank, 1988). Walters and Sieben (1982) found that field-dependent children were less competent in an unstructured learning environment. While field independents worked better independently, field dependents worked better with extra guidance (Jacobs and Gedeon, 1982). Pietrowski (1982) found that field independents tended to take a hypothesis-testing, participatory role in learning. They seemed to function on intrinsic motivation, were perceptive of the nonsalient cues in the field, and appeared to be motivated by intrinsic rewards. On the other hand, field-dependent individuals tended to ignore nonsalient cues in the field and seemed to be motivated by extrinsic rewards. They were more susceptible to social influence and tended to comply with and conform to experimenter demands.

Clearly, adult education theorists such as Knowles and distance education theorists such as Moore promote field independence when they propose andragogial ideas such as self-directedness. Yet at the same time they call for the kind of caring, supportive teacher behavior that is more effective with field dependents (Even, 1982). Moving everyone from field dependence to field independence, which seems to be one goal of the proponents of andragogy, may not be desirable. Perhaps it is better for people to have both skills, especially if the most effective teaching orientation in a given situation varies between andragogy and pedagogy, based on the formal structure of the subject matter, as Beder (1985) proposes.

Several researchers have found that people enrolling in distance education courses are likely to have higher than average levels of field independence. Chickering (1976) suggests that field-dependent enrollees might be contributing heavily to the high dropout rate in distance education. Moore (1976) reported that field-independent students were more likely to enroll in correspondence study, although his fourteen subjects were too small a population for him to draw any statistically meaningful conclusions.

Thompson and Knox (1987) administered the EFT to 102 of the 106 students enrolled in selected correspondence courses at the University of Manitoba in 1984–85. The subjects, 76 females and 26 males, were classified as field independent or field dependent based on whether their EFT scores fell above or below the median score. Forty-nine females and 9 males were classified as field dependent, while 33 females and 17 males were rated field independent. Compared with same-sex normative groups, females were significantly more field independent and males were marginally more independent than subjects in the female and male populations used as norms. This finding supported the hypothesis that correspondence students were more field independent than conventional learners. However, Thompson and Knox found no differences in retention rates among the more or less field-independent students completing the course or in their satisfaction with the course.

Experienced students may learn to adjust to teaching styles and to field-dependent or field-independent learning environments.

Thompson and Knox (1987) suggest that some field-dependent students may be less sensitive to the lower level of interaction or dialogue found in correspondence study. Perhaps if courses are taught either at a distance or conventionally using a combination of andragogical or pedagogical methods, the resulting methods are likely to be mixed in terms of perceptual fields.

Correspondence courses are usually highly pedagogical, consisting of structured segments building one upon the other. This type of structure may appeal to the field-dependent learner. Yet at the same time, the low dialogue and need for independent study habits may drive field dependents away even as they attract field independents.

In conventional education, an andragogically oriented graduate seminar in which students sit in a circle drives away field independents and attracts field dependents in terms of learning environment, yet it attracts field independents and repels field dependents in terms of individual control over curricula and required work. Both field-dependent and field-independent behavior in conventional and distance education situations should be promoted to produce balanced and adaptive learners who can cope with all kinds of learning experiences.

The picture of teaching and learning becomes quite complex when the idea of mixed perceptual field orientations is combined with the concept of situational andragogy and pedagogy. Obviously, more research is needed in this area.

Summary

This chapter proposes the foundations of a theory that might help explain the phenomenon of distance education both subjectively and objectively and that may provide a framework by which distance education can be related to adult and conventional education. The theory of Moore (1973) provided a theoretical base for this effort.

A new concept, distance learning, which is defined as any use of media for self-study, covers a much broader variety of learning situations than does distance education. This concept does not appear to have been fully developed previously, yet virtually everyone engages in distance learning, perhaps making it a bridge to distance education.

Moore's concept of dialogue, or two-way communication, is sound, but it should include the idea of support since the basic reason for dialogue is to provide support of one kind or another to the distance learner. For this reason, the first dimension of our model is called dialogue/support.

Generally, a high-structure field will require more specialized knowledge on the part of the learner than will a low-structure field. Therefore, the second dimension of the model is called structure/specialized competence.

Self-directedness, or autonomy, refers to general learning competence, not to specialized competence built up in a field. Thus the third dimension of the model is called general competence/self-directedness.

Cases 2, 3 and 4, described earlier, best fit the distance education process because of the low dialogue present. High structure with good instructional design and media development are critical in Case 2, which is used often in correspondence study. Case 3, the most andragogical in orientation, requires careful problem definition with learning contracts and independent study. High competence is critical. Case 4, used extensively in continuing vocational and professional education, requires both a good knowledge base and high competence on the part of the distance education student.

Although the inability to shift between pedagogical and andragogical teaching orientations may be problematic for conventional adult educators teaching individually, it may offer opportunities for distance education providers who can maximize the achievement and satisfaction of students through proper matching of teaching methods, teaching orientations, and subject matter during the various segments of the course. Experienced students may learn to adjust to different teaching styles and to environments conducive to field-dependent or field-independent learning preferences. Much research supports the idea of promoting both field-dependent and field-independent learner behavior in distance education and exposing learners to andragogical and pedagogical teaching styles to produce balanced and adaptive learners.

7

Teaching and Learning

In designing a process for distance education, a careful examination of adult behavior, how it works and how it changes, is important because the basic job of distance educators is changing adult behavior. Further, a review of the major domains of behavior—cognitive, affective, and psychomotor—is critical because, again, distance education operates within these domains to enhance the learning of adults. Also, since distance educators is in the business of delivering instruction to clients who are not normally in a contiguous setting, an instructional delivery system should be explicated. And, since dialogue/support is vital to the entire process, some discussion on a communication system is important, including some mention of a climate in which the learning would take place.

Perceptual Approach

One view of behavior, learning, and behavior change that holds strong meaning for distance education is the perceptual theory of psychology (Bills, 1959; Combs, 1959). This theory suggests that how individuals view (perceive) people and the objects and events in their environment will have much to do with how they behave; behavior is the product of perceptions existing for individuals at the moment at which they exhibit the behavior. For example, if an adult perceives the need to learn a new mechanical operation, the adult will be motivated to learn it. If an adult sees the values derived from gaining a college degree, that adult will be more motivated to gain such a degree. If the adult sees little need to study art, that person will more than likely avoid taking any art courses. The perceptions of various objects and events in adults' environments can have a strong impact on the total behavior of adults and can, therefore, cause adults to move in one direction or another.

The perceptual approach operates under three assumptions. One is that behavior is a function of perceptions; how people perceive something or somebody will have a lot to do with how they behave. The second simply suggests that people are self-actualizing; people are self-starting and will move toward things that have personal meaning. Third, a person's basic need is to maintain or enhance self-organization. People want to maintain their existing personality organization. However, at the same time, they want to develop more adequate self-images or self-concepts. The "need for adequacies is expressed in man's every behavior at every instant of his existence" (Combs, 1959, p. 46). The need for more self-adequacy is a driving force in human life. Given these three assumptions, which seem reasonable within the dimensions of adult learning and distance education, some thought then has to be given toward changing behavior.

If behavior is a function of perceptions, then educators should examine the factors that give rise to adults' perceptions. Students come to a learning situation for new information and skills, and educators so design the environment to foster the acquisition of the new information and skills. If behavior is a function of perception and if the job of educators is to change human behavior, then educators must change perceptions. Moving an adult toward a new behavior can be accomplished by modifying the way an adult perceives a particular part of the world.

Each adult possesses a perceptual field that is the individual's universe "including himself, as it is experienced by the individual at the instant of action" (Combs, 1959, p. 21). The perceptual field can be consciously or unconsciously constructed through several interactions with the environment. Adults construct their world by perception and it is through this construction (always incomplete and precarious) that they tend to display behavior. The perceptual field is indeed the individual's life space from which the individual's behavior constantly emerges.

Perceptual Determinants. Because of the significance of people's perceptions for behavior and learning, it is most important for educators to consider those things that determine or affect human perception. There are several perceptual determinants. The identifiable ones are beliefs, values, needs, attitudes, and self-experience.

What adults believe to be true affects their behavior. *Beliefs* take the form of faith, knowledge, assumption, or superstition, and they are real to individuals. Individuals behave as if their beliefs were true.

Values are adults' beliefs about what is important. Values could include ideas, people, material objects, or a way of life. Each adult values certain things.

Needs are what individuals require to maintain or enhance themselves. Needs can be divided into two types: physiological needs (maintenance)—need for food, water, air, and shelter—and social needs (enhancement)—need for approval and acceptance, status, prestige, and power.

Attitudes are emotionalized beliefs about the worth or lack of worth of someone or something. All adults have attitudes about certain objects and events in their environment.

Self-experience, or *self-concept,* denotes how people see themselves, how they feel about being the kind of person they think they are, how they think others see them, how they see other people, and how they feel about all of this. Self-experience includes individuals' concepts of the roles they play and how they feel about these and their ideal role concepts.

Adults have lived in the world for a given number of years and have had the opportunity to gain many different perceptions of their environment and all the objects and events in it. The sum total of all of these perceptions forms the *past experiences* of the individual. Past experiences and an individual's reactions and interpretations of them have an impact on the individual and actually form a perceptual package that governs what the individual does. Adults bring this perceptual package into a new learning experience when they engage in distance education. The package actually is the starting point for the development of new behaviors. Changing these perceptual packages is the task of the distance educator.

Another concept in the perceptual approach to human behavior that has relevance to distance education is the notion of *threat*. Threat is the perception of an individual of an imposed force requiring a change in behavior, values, or beliefs. Requiring a change in behavior when there is no change in beliefs, values, or needs can cause a person great difficulty. Adults can be most threatened when they are forced to change the ways in which they seek to maintain or enhance self-organization.

Threat in turn elicits defensive behavior and a narrowing of the perceptual field. When threatened, adults seek to maintain themselves, not to grow or be enhanced. Imagination, initiative, and creativity can be destroyed as people tend to concentrate on the safe and secure. In the absence of threat, however, adults can gain new perceptions; begin to review their personal attitudes, values, needs, and beliefs; and thus begin to form new and different behaviors. Minimizing external threats definitely makes it easier for adult learners to explore and change (Knox, 1986).

Implications for Distance Education. Perceptions are, therefore, dependent upon several factors and are most readily changed through the reexamination of beliefs, values, needs, attitudes, and the personal meanings of previous experiences. These factors can be modified through an openness to new experiences. By questioning the past from the perspective of the present, adults can understand their perceptual package and the influence of it upon their search for the more adequate self. Intelligent and improved behavior is, therefore, the function of the richness of, extent of, and availability of perceptions. The exposure to new and different experiences must take place in the absence of threat because threatening situations hinder perceptions. This idea goes hand-in-hand with the major construct of dialogue/support in distance education; freedom to experience new perceptions is imperative and appropriate dialogue and support should enhance this freedom.

Past experiences cannot change, but interpretations of them can change. Learning or changing behavior, then, is a very personal, individual process—actually the discovery of a personal meaning of things.

Since beliefs, attitudes, needs, and values are such important determiners of perceptions, perhaps educators should seek to help adult students know what beliefs, attitudes, values, and needs are important to these students and have the students consider them fully and in relation to one another. This assessment could then lead to change since perceptions are most readily changed through a reexamination of these factors and the possible meaning of previous experience. It appears then that to teach people, educators must understand them, which is most easily accomplished by trying to see the world and the students from the students' viewpoint. Educators' perceptions of the individual and the world may be quite different from the adult student's view.

Adults learn in response to their needs and perceptions, not necessarily to those of their instructors. If incongruity exists, adults may drop out of a learning situation. If the course material is critical over the long range, distance educators must indicate the importance of it to the students so as to eliminate, as much as possible, any incongruity or misperceptions of value. Having adults know why they are studying a given area should encourage them to participate more in the learning experience.

Meaning is difficult to communicate at a distance. When interaction is made less complete through loss of visual stimuli or, in the case of correspondence study, both visual and aural stimuli, expression and tone that might have communicated meaning are lost. Give-and-take between educators and students is not possible in distance education settings without two-way immediate interaction, so misunderstandings and misperceptions may arise that threaten the students' continuation in the course.

Knowledge is but one determiner of human behavior. Adults' knowledge about something may or may not have an impact on their behavior (for example, an adult may know smoking is detrimental to health but may continue to smoke). Therefore, personal perceptions are not readily changed through the introduction of objective evidence. Education should begin with the beliefs of adults and relate knowledge to their peculiar perceptions. This, again, is difficult in some distance education programs such as those found in institution-centered models, in which course design and media development are highly prescribed ahead of time.

It appears that distance education, to be truly effective, must assess the issues that are important to learners and relevant to their needs. Determining these issues can ensure better learning experiences for adults. Also, distance education should start at the level of the adult learners and permit them to determine their own direction and pace.

Individualizing instructional programs is not an easy task because, again, some programs are highly prescribed prior to use and the heterogeneous nature of distance education programs and adult learners complicates individualization. However, changing the behavior of each individual is a unique process and should be treated as such. Individual progress is especially critical for adult learners; they must know that they are achieving and moving toward individual goals and not wasting time in a learning situation. Keeping the individual moving toward the professed goals will do much to retain the adult in the learning situation. As has been noted, retention is a problem in many distance and adult education programs, so progress toward goals should be evident.

Some adult learners do not progress in achieving goals because of their low self-concept and lack of self-confidence. Many adults, particularly those who are undereducated or have not participated in schooling for some time, may have acquired rather poor self-concepts in regard to education. However, if adult learners recognize their progress toward meaningful goals their self-concept and behaviors may change, particularly in the areas of motivation for more learning.

Praise and positive acknowledgment of the students' achievement by the instructors are important. Through achievement and success, adults develop a positive pattern of experiences that can help them move to more extensive and complex course content. Success breeds success, and the more positive and healthy the perception of self, the more adults will be willing to explore the new experiences. A positive self-concept provides a readiness that is a prerequisite for all learning. Unfortunately, the kind of support services needed for this approach are, with notable exceptions (see

Chapter Three), not sufficiently available in American distance higher education today.

Finally, adults must be given appropriate time and guidance to gain new behaviors. Individual differences include different rates of learning; some adults learn things more slowly than others, especially those who possess low scholastic skills. However, with the exception of people who are severely learning disabled, most adults can learn or accomplish most tasks. The aptitude to learn something, therefore, is really a function of time. It takes more time (more guidance) for some adults to learn certain tasks and perhaps less to learn others. Again, distance education should be individually based whenever possible.

Certain general instructional strategies and techniques appear to be effective when working within the dimensions of the perceptual theory of human behavior and learning. Group work has been found effective for changing perceptions and behaviors. Within a democratically led group, individuals can retain beliefs and attitudes until they have had the opportunity to reexamine them carefully and can then change when they feel it is necessary. The open and nonthreatening group allows individuals to interact with others who possess different beliefs and attitudes and permits an interchange of ideas. This interchange may cause individuals to rethink their position and undergo affective growth. With this in mind, some distance education programs incorporate the use of small groups. In Wisconsin, discussion groups are joined with lecturers through teleconferencing (Reid and Champness, 1983). In some places, campus telecourse groups meet with a discussion leader after viewing a television lecture (Hult, 1980).

Individual problem solving and personal investigation are also effective means for achieving significant behavior change in individuals. Through these procedures, individuals can pursue areas of personal meaning, seek out alternative solutions, and make the decision that seems appropriate.

Learning through hands-on activities is an appropriate method of changing behavior, particularly for those adults who possess low scholastic skills. Words in a book may bother such an adult, but learning through an activity would ease the process and bring about appropriate learning and change. Vocational postsecondary study at a distance, much of which is accredited by the National Home Study Council (Young, 1984), often involves the use of kits. For example, television or computer repair skills may be learned through kits. Experimental learning is often a component of distance higher education programs in "hands-on" areas such as health care (Sullivan, 1984). Materials and experiences, linked to real life, can offer ways to arouse interest and provide for affective as well as cognitive and psychomotor growth.

It appears, then, that to reach many adults, instructional activities should be task oriented and include active participation by the learner. These adults need to experience success in completing activities and demonstrating skills in new situations.

Most adults will be reached if the instruction is adult centered and presented in an open, nonthreatening atmosphere with a high priority on personal needs, interests, and goals (Loewenthal, Blackwelder, and Broomall, 1980). Distance education instructors working closely and cooperatively with adults can be the key to significant behavior change. Personal tutoring by telephone and computer, as well as face-to-face meetings at study centers, have been very successful at the Open University of the United Kingdom (Keegan, 1986; Rumble, 1986).

Three Forms of Behavior

When thinking of a new behavior state (or end product of learning), an educator and a student are really thinking of a goal for a particular instructional experience; the new behavior is actually a goal or objective deemed important to acquire by the instructor or the student or both. Objectives or goals for instruction can be divided into three major areas: cognitive, affective, and psychomotor. As was discussed earlier, Knox (1980) in his theories on adult education, suggests that proficiency is a key construct and is actually the capability to perform effectively in a given situation. This capability usually depends on some combination of knowledge (the cognitive domain), physical skills (the psychomotor domain), and attitudes (the affective domain) that the adult possesses. Therefore, to enhance an adult's proficiencies and capabilities to perform and to facilitate significant learning, educators must place the three major domains at the center of instructional thinking and planning for adults (Cranton, 1989).

Major taxonomies, or category systems, of the three domains can assist instructors as they think through and specify goals for adults. In the taxonomies, a hierarchical order exists whereby each category is included within the next higher categories. These systems focus on process and internalization factors and not subject matter or the content variable. In other words, these three systems are actually free of subject matter in that they can be applied to any subject matter. Their strength lies in the fact that they combine the factors present in each domain—logical, psychological, and educational factors for the cognitive domain, attitudinal and internal factors for the affective domain, and perceptual and motor skills for the psychomotor domain—into a total system for analyzing and stating goals.

Cognitive Domain. Bloom's taxonomy offers a systematic way of viewing cognitive growth (Bloom and others, 1956) suggesting that there is one category, knowledge, and five additional categories of the skills and abilities to use knowledge. The six categories are as follows:

    1.00   Knowledge
           1.10   Knowledge of Specifics
                  1.11   Knowledge of Terminology
                  1.12   Knowledge of Specific Facts
           1.20   Knowledge of Ways and Means of Dealing with Specifics
                  1.21   Knowledge of Conventions
                  1.22   Knowledge of Trends and Sequences
                  1.23   Knowledge of Classifications and Categories
                  1.24   Knowledge of Criteria
                  1.25   Knowledge of Methodology
           1.30   Knowledge of the Universals and Abstractions in a Field

1.31 Knowledge of Principles and Generalizations

1.32 Knowledge of Theories and Structures

2.00 Comprehension

    2.10 Translation

    2.20 Interpretation

    2.30 Extrapolation

3.00 Application

4.00 Analysis

    4.10 Analysis of Elements

    4.20 Analysis of Relationships

    4.30 Analysis of Organizational Principles

5.00 Synthesis

5.10 Production of a Unique Communication

5.20 Production of a Plan, or Proposed Set of Operations

5.30 Derivation of a Set of Abstract Relations

6.00 Evaluation

6.10 Judgments in Terms of Internal Evidence

6.20 Judgments in Terms of External Criteria

This taxonomic system suggests that the first level of cognition is pure knowledge and deals with the simple knowing of a bit of information from low-level facts to complex theories. The next level, comprehension, indicates that the knowledge defined at the first level is understood by the adult and that this understanding can be shown in a number of cognitive tasks; after something is known and understood, it can be put to use. Application involves taking the understood information and applying it to new situations. The next level, analysis, occurs when applied information is broken down into component parts through such tasks as comparing, contrasting, or distinguishing and reviewing the information itself. Synthesis is the mental transformation of information into a new or different structure, design, pattern, or solution. Evaluation involves the making of judgments or assessments of information based on some criteria specified beforehand. Thus the hierarchy presents a continuum from simply knowing something to making precise personal judgments about information confronting the learner.

This system allows for more precise goal statements and instructional development in cognitive processing for adults. Since it is hierarchical in nature, the lower levels must be achieved before later levels are achieved. Decisions on what level of cognition are required for the adult are left to the instructor, content utilization, subject matter, and the student.

Affective Domain. The affective taxonomy (Krathwohl, Bloom, and Masia, 1964) works primarily with the change or inner growth of learners as they receive, become aware of, and begin to adopt certain attitudes and principles that in turn form selected value judgments. These value judgments begin to have an impact on the learners' behavior because adults will behave according to the value system that they possess. The learners will be characterized by a consistent behavior pattern or way of life upon complete internalization of the value system. An outline of the major levels of the affective domain follows.

1.00   Receiving (Attending)
      1.10   Awareness
      1.20   Willingness to Receive
      1.30   Controlled or Selected Attention
2.00   Responding
      2.10   Acquiescence in Responding
      2.20   Willingness to Respond
      2.30   Satisfaction in Response
3.00   Valuing
      3.10   Acceptance of a Value
      3.20   Preference for a Value
      3.30   Commitment (Conviction)
4.00   Organization
      4.10   Conceptualization
      4.20   Organization of a Value System
5.00   Characterization by a Value or Value Complex
      5.10   Generalized Set
      5.20   Characterization

In this system the formation of attitudes and, ultimately, total behavioral characterization begins when an individual receives some external stimuli regarding some phenomenon. These stimuli are introduced in an instructional setting. The first level reflects an awareness of the stimuli. If the stimuli have some personal meaning, the learner will exhibit a willingness to receive them. If the stimuli continue to have meaning for the learner, the individual will give them selected attention. The next level after receiving is responding, in which the adult continues to find meaning to the stimuli. The adult will possibly give in or acquiesce in the form of a response, but if continuous meaning is present, the individual will express a willingness to respond and then a satisfaction in response to the phenomenon will occur.

If the phenomenon under study takes on more personal meaning and gains in internal importance for the adult, the adult may begin to value it to some degree. The process of valuing has three steps: accepting the value, preferring the value, and actually having a commitment to the object or event under study.

Since many values confront adults in learning and other life situations, some ranking or prioritizing may occur. Some values simply are more important to people than others, and thus some conceptualizing and organizing of values into a value system occurs. A value system develops as an adult reviews what is important to the maintenance and enhancement of the self, and, therefore, the adult's overt behavior will begin to reflect some of the more important values held by the individual. This overt behavior is then seen as the characterization of the adult, or the way the adult appears to operate consistently in many different situations. The total characterization of the individual really is the consistent overt behavioral state that is affective in nature and governs the individual's responses to a variety of situations in a generally consistent and coherent manner.

The affective domain is an interesting and important, but complicated, one to work with. It will be no easy task to move individuals to new attitudes and values in selected areas of study during the instructional process. Each adult must see the personal meaning of something before a movement up the hierarchy is possible. Adults have had a long time to formulate their own values and value systems, so it will not be easy for educators to introduce new information into the affective realm and produce some change in the total behavior of students.

Adults can gain new cognitive and psychomotor behaviors relatively quickly, but it takes time for adults to experience change and inner growth in affective behaviors. Attitude change and the development of new values do not happen overnight or during a short instructional learning session. Adult learners must have time to review their existing beliefs and values and then look carefully at any new ideas before they will assimilate them into their current value system. However, this domain is important because of its impact on values, attitudes, beliefs, and an adult's total way of behaving.

The affective domain is omnipresent; stimuli are always present in a learning experience, and adults will react to them in some fashion. In a new learning situation, adults may be excited or discouraged by the subject matter or methodology. They are in fact making judgments regarding the value or lack of value of what they are perceiving mentally in an instructional setting. When adults are engaging in a cognitive or psychomotor learning experience, they are also going through mental processes that help to establish the value of the experiences. Since the affective stimuli are always present in all learning experiences, a close interrelationship of the behavioral domains exists, and it is very important to consider in learning situations.

Psychomotor Domain. A third major behavioral domain, the psychomotor, involves work in vocational-technical, esthetic, and recreational and leisure areas as well as others of interest to distance education students. A significant taxonomic system developed by Simpson (1972) can guide the thinking and activity of distance educators. An outline of the major components of this domain follows.

    1.00   Perception
          1.10   Sensory stimulation
                 1.11   Auditory
                 1.12   Visual

1.13   Tactile
1.14   Taste
1.15   Smell
1.16   Kinesthetic
1.20   Cue selection
2.00   Set
2.10   Mental
2.20   Physical
2.30   Emotional
3.00   Guided response
3.10   Imitation
3.20   Trial and error
4.00   Mechanism
5.00   Complex overt
5.10   Resolution of uncertainty
5.20   Automatic performance
6.00   Adaption
7.00   Origination

This taxonomic system suggests that the first step in the hierarchical process is that of the simple perception of, or becoming aware of, objects, qualities, and relations through the sense organs, and then, the adult decides what cues to respond to in order to satisfy the requirements of the task at hand. When perception is complete, the adult moves to step two—set, or readiness for a particular kind of action or experience. Set includes mental readiness, physical readiness, or making anatomical adjustments; and emotional readiness, a favorable attitude toward the motor acts taking place.

At the next level, guided response, the adult begins to make an overt behavioral move to learn the particular psychomotor activity, either under the guidance of an instructor or on the basis of a model or some criteria. A guided response could be carried out through imitation or by trial and error. Trial and error usually involves some rationale for each response in the act until an appropriate response is achieved.

At the mechanism level the learned response has become habitual. The adult has achieved a degree of confidence and proficiency in the performance of the act. The learned act is part of the behavior of the adult client and can be used when various situations demand it.

With the development of more sophisticated psychomotor behavior, the complex overt response enters into the picture. At this stage, the adult can perform a motor act that is considered complex because of the movement pattern involved. The adult has attained a high degree of skill. When the adult can perform without hesitating and form a mental picture of the task sequence, the learner has achieved resolution of uncertainty. Automatic performance is achieved when the adult performs a finely coordinated motor skill with a great deal of muscle control and ease.

The next level, adaptation, comes when the adult alters personal motor activities to meet the demands of new problem situations requiring a physical or motor skill. And, the ultimate psychomotor behavior, origination, comes into play when the adult can create new motor acts or ways of manipulating materials out of the abilities, understanding, and skills developed in the psychomotor domain.

As with the other domains described, a hierarchy is present in this taxonomic system. Lower levels must be treated before moving to the higher levels. This, too, takes time, as the adult learners move from beginning levels to a point where they may adapt or originate in a given psychomotor area.

Use of Domains. The use of the three behavioral domains in distance education is manifold and lends a good level of sophistication to the entire process. Since everything in the educational process is contingent upon goals, a hierarchical system stating the new behaviors to be gained can lend precision to the instructional process and make the distance educator's job easier. Measuring or evaluating the growth of adults in learning situations is also easier and more precise if the taxonomic systems are used for setting goals. Clear, precise goal statements in behavioral terms at whatever level will give a good indication as to what the terminal behaviors (outcomes) of the instruction will be. All the instructor needs to do is see (measure) if the new behaviors are present after the learning experience has been completed. The educator's basic mission is, of course, to define the appropriate behaviors to be gained from instruction, either cooperatively with the student or from some other source, design the learning experience so that the learner can gain these behaviors and know when to use them, and then check to see if these behaviors resulted from the entire activity. The taxonomies give organizational strength, direction, precision, and ease to the instructional process from the opening activity of goal stating to the end activity of evaluating.

Verduin (1980) argues that educators can use the taxonomies effectively at the course-design level. After broad, general goals for entire programs are established, more precise goals are needed for courses, modules, and units of instruction that reflect the general goals but give sound direction to the teaching-learning process. Effective use and instrumentation of these taxonomies are discussed further by Verduin (1980).

Instructional Delivery System

An instructional delivery system must be designed to help adult learners gain new behaviors. The term *instruction* in this case means the planning for and delivering of learning experiences for adults. It involves planning, teaching, interacting, learning, and assessment.

A modification of an existing model from Verduin, Miller, and Greer (1977) can assist the distance educator in instructional delivery. It is a model, not a theory, although it does satisfy some of the conditions for an instructional theory set forth by Bruner (1966) in that it does specify experiences to predispose the individual toward learning, it does define a structure for information and knowledge, it does specify some sequencing for presentation of material, and it does allow for feedback. Further, it gives consideration to the theory of teaching offered by Holmberg (1986) in such items as student motivation, individual needs, promoting learning pleasure, rapport/climate, accessibility to course content, and the importance of communication between learner and distance educator. Finally, it takes into consideration some of the key constructs of distance education such as dialogue/support, structure/specialized competence and general competence/self-directedness. It is

general in nature, identifying major variables for consideration and
decision making by distance educators. As Holmberg (1986) suggests, a specific model or theory applicable to all individual students, with great differences in their life backgrounds and learning
styles and working in all imaginable study areas, is an impossibil-
ity. It is difficult to prescribe specifically, but guidelines can be
useful.

Our model (Figure 1) appears at the outset to be a popular
industrial model of delivery and highly behaviorally oriented, but
it does not have to be. It can be used for highly prescribed curricula,
with external or societal controls, or individualized, small-scale
open learning experiences. It is, in fact, an individualized approach
to fostering adult learning. Because of the individual nature of adult
clients with their differing beliefs, values, needs, attitudes, past experiences, and goals, the model must be individualized in order to
be effective.

An effective model identifies the major variables that mediate
in a given situation and places them in a coherent and logical order.
Such a model does not provide for any direct answers to specific
concerns, it just identifies the important factors for use in decision
making by the professional in given situations. This model identifies six major factors for use in decision making: assessing entering behavior, specifying behavioral objectives, specifying learning
units and procedures, presenting learning units and tasks, performing of tasks by students, and assessing the performance of the students. The first three factors deal with the planning process, the
second two with the learning and interacting process, and the final
one with evaluation by instructor or learner or both.

Entering Behavior. Assessing entering behavior is the process of determining the background of adult learners and what they
desire from the formal learning situation. Such an assessment looks
beyond the students' present knowledge and skills. It should also
assess motivation goals, learning styles, tendencies and preferences,
competence/self-directedness, beliefs, discrepancies in proficiencies,
needs, and background and past experiences of the students. The
entering behavior signifies the point at which educators must begin
work with the students. Understanding the students' needs, goals,

Figure 1. An Instructional Model.

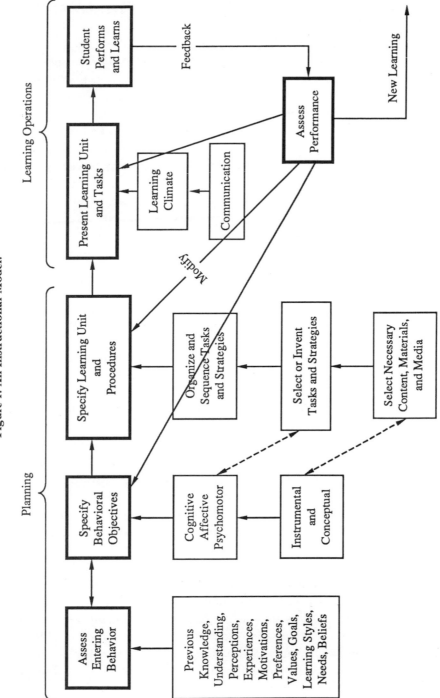

and discrepancies enables the educators as well as the learners to deal with the diversity of backgrounds, assess readiness, and clarify aspirations in order to help adult learners move to higher levels of learning and development (Knox, 1986). Further, assessment is the beginning of the climate/rapport building because it focuses in on the individual, the importance of the individual, and on the educator's desire to help the individual move to new learning and behaviors in as effective and meaningful a manner as possible. As Loewenthal, Blackwelder, and Broomall (1980) emphasize, there is no substitute for getting to know something about the students, about their reasons for taking the course, and the circumstances under which they will be working.

If the course is highly prescribed and defined ahead of time, educators can identify the knowledge and skills required before instruction begins and can discuss these with the adult students. If there is less structure and more openness to the course, educators can plan more directly and cooperatively with the students.

Instructional Objectives. Next, in conjunction with the entering assessment, the goals or objectives for the instructional experience are defined. Assessing behavior and specifying objectives are necessarily coordinated with one another (note reversible arrow in the figure) to ensure compatibility and logical progression in the development of new behaviors. If, for example, the terminal objectives are considerably beyond the entering behavior, little or no learning may take place. If the entering behavior exceeds the objectives, the program will be a waste of time for the learner. Objectives must be useful, meaningful, and feasible for adult learners (Knox, 1986) and, therefore, should be closely coordinated with the entering behavior to assure progress in learning. Again, in a highly prescribed instructional unit, the objectives could be specified ahead of time and in the absence of any input from the adult learners. If this is the case, distance educators should indicate the rationale for such goals to the learners so that the learners can see the value of the goals and know where the instruction is going (Cranton, 1989). If the instructional unit is less defined or is open to learner input, educators and learners can define the goals cooperatively, thus giving more personal meaning to the instructional endeavor.

The objectives are actually expressions of what the adult will be able to do after the instructional session is completed; they are expressions of the new behaviors resulting from learning. Behaviors include knowledge, skills, and attitudes as well as the actual use of these three factors or the actual performance of the behavior by the individual. Thinking of objectives in terms of behavioral change is helpful to educators. The three major behavioral domains come into play and should be utilized here. Being able to handle a new mechanical process (psychomotor), developing a new attitude about something (affective), and understanding a new theory (cognitive) can all result from an instructional experience and are actually new behaviors for the learner.

Behavior changes as adults interact with the objects and events in their environment. Thus, the structure of content or subject matter is important. Adults will not learn about new mechanical processes without interacting with them. They will not gain new knowledge and understanding (for example, about European history) without interacting with the subject matter. Every teaching activity has some content that influences adult learners through interaction with it. Educators provide various environmental conditions, both real and simulated, to which the adult students react. And the environmental conditions will vary with the kind of behavior desired, be it simple or complex.

To teach some rather simple behaviors, termed *instrumental*, little logical conceptual content is required, and a form of operant conditioning will effect the desired behaviors. For example, adding or subtracting numbers, translating foreign words into English, using proper grammatical expressions, spelling correctly, and many other behaviors do not require adults to have direct exposure or contact with the environment to learn them; adults simply perform these tasks without any high conceptual input. These behaviors are important, but simple presentation and practice and rewards are all that are necessary to accomplish them in a conditioning setting. Therefore, they require a different and straightforward teaching design, without any real conceptual content.

Other behaviors, termed *conceptual*, require learners to interact with the object and events (content) in the environment. Through instruction, adults perceive the objects and events in the environment, form concepts about them, use the concepts for decision making, and act on these decisions. Forming concepts about objects and events gives adults the raw material with which to think about, judge, and act upon their world. As adults, for example, learn about welding, nursing, colonial history, accounting, or macramé, they will gain conceptual information (form concepts) about these areas through designed instructional activities. Once they have the conceptual information, they can use that knowledge in personal situations or they can be required by the instructor to put it to use in higher cognitive processing.

Forming concepts or learning about some substantive subject matter moves adults to the knowledge and possibly the comprehension level in terms of cognitive learning. If this is all that is required for the learning, then the instructor would specify behavioral objectives at those levels. However, if the instructor desires the adult to apply the knowledge in further learning, then higher cognitive objectives would be specified. The same would hold true for the affective and psychomotor domains. Conceptual input—absorbing of content—must take place before it can be used and displayed in some behavioral form as advocated in Verduin, Miller, and Greer (1977).

Designing the Learning Unit. Once the appropriate conceptual goals are specified, a learning unit that will help adults acquire the needed experiences to form new behaviors must be designed. This phase of planning is a critical step for distance educators because of the noncontiguous nature of the entire process (Loewenthal, Blackwelder, and Broomall, 1980). The first step is to select the necessary content, materials, and interactive media needed for the design. These, of course, are dependent on the nature of the conceptual or instrumental goals that were specified earlier (connected by a dotted line in the model). Books and other materials on a subject, for example, colonial history, can be easily defined. However, the selection of materials should be a little more precise in the sense that they should be geared to the learning styles and preferences of the adult students as much as possible. This entails the provision of varied materials to allow students to select those best suited to their learning styles (Knox, 1986).

The selection of the various learning tasks and strategies, the next step, is contingent upon the nature of the objectives stated in the behavioral domains. (These two areas are also connected by a dotted line in the model.) If the instructor wishes the student to achieve, for example, a goal in the cognitive domain after the student acquires knowledge and understanding, then varied tasks leading to that level are specified. If a goal in the psychomotor domain is required after the basic learning, then tasks for that level are suggested. If a goal is required in the affective domain, then experiences, tasks, and strategies for that level will be required. Organizing and sequencing of the various tasks and strategies are also important (Cranton, 1989). Adult learners can then move logically from task to task for the acquisition of new behaviors.

At this important stage in the planning, educators should consider preferred learning styles, adequate materials, organization of the experiences, possible use of group work, use of tutors, modes of delivery or interactive media, and feedback opportunities or interpersonal communication. During this stage, development of study guides to assist the students in the course or unit of study is an important consideration (Loewenthal, Blackwelder, and Broomall, 1980). These guides can give students instruction on the mechanics of the course such as assignments, submission of work, and deadlines; additional explanatory materials and evaluation self-checks; and, more important, guidance on the mastery of the subject matter. Discussion sections within each lesson are critical to help adult students acquire the needed knowledge and also to keep students involved and interested in the subject at hand. Finally, a guide can provide continuity to the course by relating assignments to one another and to separate activities. As Loewenthal, Blackwelder, and Broomall (1980) state, "The study guide will be most helpful if it serves not only as a substitute for the experiences available to students attending class but also as a source of encouragement" (p. 37).

Presenting and Performing. Even though the next two major components, presenting and student performance, actually occur simultaneously, they are separated in the model for purposes of examination and development. Presenting learning units and tasks involves more than just handing adult students a package of instruction with which they will interact. At this point, interaction, facilitation, and teaching begin.

Gage (1963) defines teaching as a form of interpersonal influence aimed at changing behavior. Obviously, teaching and influencing adult clients toward new behaviors occur in distance education. Influence is a key when looking at the teaching process; the teacher's influence on the student and the student's on the teacher are reciprocal (Rowntree, 1975).

Instructors should look at their verbal and nonverbal behavior as a part of influencing students since it is through these behaviors that influence is achieved. Verbal and nonverbal behavior is, of course, communication, often two-way because of the interpersonal nature of the process. Verbal factors such as the written and spoken word and nonverbal factors such as pictures, overlays, numbers, and even gestures on television and intonations on audiotapes (and those used by the tutor in learning situations) convey messages to adult learners who in turn "read" these messages.

Further, these factors are a major part of the climate within which the learning can take place; they help create a climate of dialogue and support between instructor and institution and adult student that is critical to many adult learners (Garrison, 1989). Dialogue, as explained earlier, is the two-way communication between the teacher and the learner. The greater the dialogue in distance education, the smaller the transactional distance between the two parties. Effective dialogue leads to support of one kind or another of the distance learner. While field-independent learners perhaps need only dialogue, field-dependent learners can gain, through effective dialogue, emotional support for their efforts. Therefore, through effective communication, even at great distances, educators can create an open, supportive, and encouraging climate that lets adult learners know that they are important and that learning is a cooperative, collaborative effort of learner and educator working together (Garrison, 1989). This responsive, supportive climate is important to adults (Knox, 1986) and is critical in distance education, since little face-to-face interaction takes place.

Assessing Performance. As the adult learners perform the tasks and engage in the learning, opportunities for feedback must be present (Garrison, 1989; Rowntree, 1975). Adult learners want to know how they are doing and do not want to waste time. Feedback comes from the instructor directly or from some materials provided for the students. If learning is progressing, then a new direction must be defined. Feedback is, therefore, important to instructors and to the instructional process but holds considerable meaning to the adult learners as well (Cranton, 1989). As Knox (1986) suggests, "Feedback is important to learners because knowledge about the progress they are achieving and what affects it aid in their decisions about persisting and adjusting their efforts" (p. 159).

The final variable in the model, assessing performance, simply involves looking at the degree to which the objectives specified earlier have been achieved by the students; the instructor looks for the desired behavior resulting from the learning experience. Two processes, formative and summative, are used depending on the nature of the results desired.

Formative evaluation is used to collect information during the learning experience or during the "formative" state of learning. The instruction is still fluid and flexible and quick remediation can take place if undesirable outcomes are apparent. Formative evaluation can be used during most instructional activities and gives the instructor and adult student some idea of the student's growth. If the desired outcomes do not seem forthcoming, then a modification of the goals, learning unit and procedures, or presentation methods should be made. Quick redirection or remediation can turn the process around so that learning will continue. Formative evaluation is very effective in small learning units.

Summative evaluation comes at the end or "summation" of the learning unit and is usually a major task. It gives information on the general behaviors that have resulted and is more global in nature. This evaluation helps in grading or certifying major learning units.

In these evaluation processes, distance educators may use either internal means or external means or both. Internal means include criterion based measures that generally have been designed to measure behavioral objectives set by the instructor. External means refer to norm-referenced or standardized measures that compare a student's outcomes from learning with the outcomes of other students of the same type. In any case, the criterion of acceptable performance for passing or satisfactorily completing a learning unit should be established by the instructor ahead of time so that this is clear to the adult learner.

If the performance resulting from the learning is satisfactory in all domains specified—cognitive, affective, or psychomotor— then learners move on to new learning, if that is desired. If the performance is not satisfactory, then, again, some redirecting of the learning experience should occur.

Overriding and influencing the instructional process is the variable of time. Adults learn at different rates and spend different amounts of time on a given learning unit because of outside influences. These differences, therefore, cause adults to complete learning units at varying speeds. It may simply take some adults a little longer to learn something than others. If completion time is critical to a given unit because of outside demands, then these time demands must be specified for the learner. If time lines are not specified, then the task is much easier. In any case, educators should keep in mind that most adults can learn most things if given enough time and guidance.

Summary

Each adult learner is different from other adult learners. Each adult possesses different beliefs, values, needs, attitudes, self-concept, and past experiences that must be considered as planning for the learning experience progresses. The movement of the individual adult learner from one behavioral state to a desired new behavioral state that has personal meaning to the learner is no easy task for distance educators. But to achieve the desired outcomes, individual considerations must be made.

The understanding of each adult student's behavior can give distance educators a background from which to build the needed learning experiences. This understanding is the first step in the instructional process. Some definition of where the individual is upon entering the situation to where the adult wishes to go should help clarify the entire process. With that understanding, the definition of new behaviors can be made.

Clear, informed statements of the new behaviors (objectives) in the three major behavioral domains, or hierarchies, add strength and precision to the instructional process. Everything else in the process is contingent upon them. Also, objectives offer the standard to which the evaluation measures will be applied. From this point, the content, materials, modes of delivery, strategies, and tasks are outlined to guide the adult's learning.

During the learning experience, the communication lines must be open for interpersonal interaction. Open communication can lead to instructor-learner rapport, which reassures the client of support, encouragement, and progress in learning. Critical feedback of progress to the adult learner is necessary to further ensure the success of the learning experience. If progress is not being attained, then some redirecting or remediation can take place. If progress is being achieved, the adult client can then move on to new learning experiences and gain a further measure of success.

8

Organization
and Administration

Successful distance education programs meeting the needs of adult
learners demand effective organization and administration. Organizational plans must be defined first, and then an administrative
structure to carry out those plans is designed. Communication
throughout the design process is the major variable. Effective communication will help all organizations and administrative designs
become more successful. Also, the important dimension of evaluation must be incorporated into the total distance education program. Structures must be designed and utilized to assure the
performance of any program. Educators need to consider a number
of factors as they define the ideal organization and administration
to fulfill the needs of the adult learners. Discussions on these important topics, along with a discussion of communication and program evaluation, should assist distance educators in designing
appropriate structures for programs.

Organization

The organizational pattern and operating practices of a distance education establishment are, of course, based on the educational philosophy of that institution as well as some economic and
political restrictions. If the prevailing philosophy of the institution
suggests that the school's mission is to dispense instruction to adults
outside of the system, the institution will be organized one way. If

the philosophy seems to emphasize a more society-based set of activities, then the organization and practices will be quite different. Although hybrids and variations exist, Rumble (1986) suggests that there are three potential models for organizing distance education: institution centered, student centered, and society centered.

Institution Centered. In the institution-centered model, sometimes called the industrial model, large numbers of adults can be handled with highly controlled and technical experiences emanating from the institution. Little student input occurs on goals, directions, and content other than the students' decision to enroll in a given course or set of courses. The materials and learning packages are developed by "experts" whose major concern is to develop the protocols and have them delivered to students. Interpersonal communication is almost nonexistent, and limited guidance is available to the students. Many proprietary schools offering distance education would fall in this category.

Escotet (1980) terms this model more *instruction* than *education* because little permanent contact between student and instructor or student and student is available. Also, little sociocultural interaction and feeling, mutual respect and dialogue, and interpersonal communication, which would make this model education, are present. This model basically transfers information from the institution to the client in a rather straightforward manner. The advantages of this model are that large numbers of students can be served and that it is an economically advantageous way to conduct programs in this day of limited economic resources. These features make the model politically expedient and can result in good support for this mode of operation.

Student Centered. The second model, the student-centered model, allows for more individualization of learning experiences. As Rumble (1986, p. 30) suggests, "The learner is an 'independent' consumer of the products of the system, be they educational materials or services." The programs within the model, like the Empire State College model discussed earlier, are personalized and afford students more individualized instruction and greater contact with individual tutors and other educational personnel if the student so desires.

Under this model, students can choose a contractual arrangement whereby they can use the materials, teaching, and other services of the school to reach a degree or certification of some sort but still pace their studies and, in some cases, modify course content in reaching their goal. Or, they can simply become independent users of the materials in their personal studies, receiving no help from the institution. This, as mentioned earlier, is a form of distance learning, not distance education.

A third option within the student-centered model is a contractual relationship with the institution, allowing students to utilize the learning materials the school provides to learn only what they want to learn and not what is prescribed for them. This type of contract learning is generally designed by the learner, sometimes with institutional assistance, for the purpose of attaining a personal educational goal.

The advantages of this second model are obvious. It allows for an individualized and personal approach to learning that appeals to adults who want and need different kinds of learning experiences. Further, this model provides for direct teaching and guidance if desired, and it can provide numerous materials and other services for use by adult learners. It can lead to a degree or certificate at the pace and convenience of the adult learner.

The highly personalized nature of this model, which involves utilizing tutors and other personnel, does not allow it to handle a large number of students, as can the institution-centered model. This and accompanying costs and administrative procedures are disadvantages of this model.

Society Centered. The third model identified by Rumble, society centered, is actually a form of community education whereby the distance educator goes into the field to help people with adult needs and community problems. In addressing these problems, adults meet in groups and are assisted by an educator or guide who helps to identify what is to be learned, what the needed resources are, and how the process can be evaluated. The problem addressed could be process centered, such as cleaning up a neighborhood,

social planning oriented, such as achieving certain social or economic goals by solving specific problems, or social action oriented,
by helping selected populations (such as economically deprived
people or minority people) in the community. If large numbers of
people in the community are involved, additional facilitators may
be needed.

Unlike the institution-centered model, in which emphasis is
placed on pure instruction, this model draws heavily on group process and problem identification. This changes the role of the distance educator and the use of learning materials. In the first case,
the educator is more a facilitator and process person than direct
instructor, and the learning materials obviously cannot be developed until the learning direction is established. Feedback to materials developers is critical so that the materials help in the solution
of the problem. And, since most community problems are never
totally alike, the materials have to be focused precisely for each
learning effort.

The advantage of this approach is that it allows groups of
people to attack social problems of common interest in a community and learn about and solve the identified problems. It can, as in
the case of the Highlander School in Tennessee, be a way to address
major social concerns by having adults learn about solutions and
then put them into action. However, the development of appropriate learning materials needed for such activities is labor intensive
and costly, and a number of different educators and facilitators must
work with each community problem identified—also labor intensive and costly. The unstructured and unprescribed nature of this
approach makes it quite different from the other two approaches.

In terms of the definitions offered in this book, the society-
centered model is questionably a form of distance education since
it is built around a face-to-face teaching function that is the basis
of an experiential learning contract carried out by the participants.
It is debatable as to just where the teaching function lies in this
model. In a way, it might be considered another variation on the
student-centered model.

Transaction Centered. The problem with learner-centered or
institution-centered approaches to developing models for distance

education is that both can lead to an overemphasis on one participant in the process underway. A more recent model focuses attention on this concern. Writing about strategic marketing, Kotler (1982) emphasizes the need to recognize the symbiotic exchange of values between parties to a marketing transaction. By following institution-centered marketing models, organizations may try to change consumer attitudes toward their product or service, rather than trying to fit their offerings to consumer wants and needs. On the other hand, organizations following consumer-oriented marketing models may go so far in attempting to please consumers that their organizational identity is lost, organizational constituencies are alienated, and standards are not upheld (Simerly, 1989).

The exchange model of marketing instead places the emphasis on a constant assessment of the degree of balance between consumer perceptions of value and their perceptions of the benefits of the products or services being offered. A similar approach can be discerned in distance education. Moore (1973) first characterized the distance education process as a transaction between teacher and learner based on dialogue and structure. He advocates an approach that falls between low-dialogue, or high-structure, models, which place too much emphasis on the message of the teacher, and low-structure models, in which students may not have the level of support or independence they need. The transaction-centered model calls for a balance between dialogue and instruction and for the optimization of both factors. Like Kotler's theory, transaction-centered distance education requires the adoption of a systems approach in which entities involved in the process cannot be considered in isolation from each other (Saba, 1989).

Transaction-based distance education makes extensive use of formative and summative evaluation techniques in an attempt to continually readjust the match between values and benefits in the exchange or transaction taking place during instruction or other institutional activities. The Open University of the United Kingdom has both institution-centered and learner-centered aspects (Rumble, 1986) and also takes a transaction-centered approach in some of its programs and projects. Indeed, as with most models, a hybrid approach may most acccurately characterize organizational realities. Detailed formative evaluation by the OUUK, for example, in the development of CYCLOPS, and the planning efforts of Nova University give an idea of how postsecondary distance education providers, like many organizations in the corporate world, may invest in the kind of continual assessment, adjustment, and proactive strategic planning characteristic of the transaction-centered organization.

Philosophical Considerations. As stated earlier, the philosophical position of the institution will dictate the nature and quality of the institution's distance education program. This philosophical position, of course, is tempered by political and economic considerations. Most educators would perhaps aspire toward a more student-centered, multifaceted organizational model, while politicians and economics would possibly dictate a more institution-centered approach, in which greater control and larger numbers of students are possible.

In the development of an ideal organizational structure based on a philosophical statement, it is important for educators to analyze some of the variables associated with philosophical statements (Verduin, 1980). Briefly, in answering the following questions, educators can make decisions on institutional direction and purpose and, in turn, can decide organizational pattern. The pattern can be tempered and modified later, based on the prevailing economic and political considerations.

What is society like, and what meaning does the nature of society have for distance education? The dynamic, ever-changing nature of society, with its social, technical, and scientific changes and advancements has a great impact on the process of education. Adults must keep abreast of changes, advancements, and modifications in existing social systems to function satisfactorily in society; it appears quite clear that society demands continued education for adults. And if postsecondary institutions and organizations are to accomplish their mission of assisting adults in learning, they will have to respond to social changes and the myriad of accompanying adult needs.

Why do adults want continued education? Perhaps the main purpose of adult and distance education is to help to improve the quality of life for individual adults. As discussed earlier, adult education can be designed and used to help the undereducated, those who have inadequate learning to function successfully in society. Further, it can serve adults in the occupational and vocational domain and can serve the individual leisure, self-enrichment, and self-enhancement needs of adults.

What is the adult learner really like? The qualities of adult learners have been discussed extensively in previous chapters. One word might sum up these qualities—*individuality*. Individual needs, interests, values, beliefs, self-concepts, experiences, goals, attitudes, roles in life, and motivations describe adults, and they complicate the lives of distance educators planning adult learning experiences.

How does adult learning take place and for what purpose? Again, some discussion on this topic has occurred previously. Adult learners are continuous, informal learners as they function in daily life, and much of this learning is of a pragmatic nature. They learn as they interact with the objects and events in their environment that have personal meaning to them; *personal interest* and *personal meaning* are key terms for adult learning. Adults learn at different rates, want guidance and feedback, prefer self-paced and hands-on experiences, and like to feel they are making progress in their studies. Some adults like structure and direction, while others prefer a more open and self-directed learning method. In most cases, the goal of adult learners is to use and apply the new knowledge and skills immediately. As mentioned earlier, most adults can learn most things if given enough time and attention.

How shall the learning material be organized? Adult students are generally full-time workers who must study at other than working hours. This dictates the use of evenings, weekends, and other free-time periods for study. Self-paced, short, manageable packages of instruction seem desirable. Appropriate guidance and feedback also appear important to adult learners. When group meetings are necessary, it appears that a "school" setting of some sort is preferred. Open and adequate communication, minimum cost and red tape, and easy access to learning experiences are most helpful.

What is the role of the distance educator in the institution, in curriculum work, and in the profession? Most adult educators in general work in the field part time. In distance education, most professional educators also share responsibilities with other areas of interest, even though they are in the general field of education. This complicates matters in terms of their commitment and allegiance, staff development, instruction and curriculum building, student advising, and total interaction with students. A "second-class" orientation could result from such a situation. In any case, it appears that distance educators must be, among other things, communicators, teachers, tutors, guidance personnel, evaluators, sometimes friends and placement personnel, and administrators as they facilitate the growth and learning of the adult students. In addition, they probably need to develop the learning modules and units for adult students. Finally, personal professional growth should be of importance to the educators. Putting all of this together in one package makes for quite a role. However, since distance education in this country is still embryonic in nature, a strong professional commitment and effort are required for it to advance and for educators to do the necessary job.

Answering the preceding questions should alert educators to the necessity for an organizational structure with a very comprehensive set of learning experiences for the diverse needs of adults. It should further alert them to the considerable professional effort demanded of distance educators. Although educators cannot be all things to all people, it would behoove distance educators to strive for a maximum educational effort.

Administration

Organizational philosophy will have an impact upon, and to some extent influence, the administrative structure controlling a distance education program. A major concern for effective distance education is who manages, controls, or administers the program and in what kind of institution the program is located. How a program fits into an existing sponsoring institution or organization will determine much of its direction and effectiveness.

Sole Responsibility. Rumble (1986) identified three different modes of operation that reflect the possible administrative designs under which distance education could operate. In the first model, the institution and its administration have as their sole responsibility distance education; the only purpose of the institution is distance teaching, much like the OUUK originally. Unencumbered by conventional teaching and other activities, institutions in this mode can focus on developing and managing distance education. At these institutions, the faculty is involved in all the production and teaching processes and thus can respond to the needs of distance students with new course and program designs when necessary. Autonomy and control of the program rest with the institution, and they do not need to be shared by or subservient to other faculties and administrations as in multipurpose institutions. This mode can be effective because it allows a focus on the distance students, who are often quite different from the on-campus students and their characteristics. Adults learning at a distance are especially different from younger students on campus. Finally, in a single purpose institution, greater focus can be placed on research, including the development of teaching techniques and innovative practices designed for use in distance education.

Mixed Mode. The second arrangement, which is much more common, is the mixed mode, one in which both distance education and conventional education occur. A variety of designs exist under this mode. In some cases, a single department within a conventional institution offers distance education. In other cases, several departments offer distance education. Or, a distinct, separate unit may offer distance education in a variety of areas. In the first instance, the central administration of the entire institution would administer the program. In the second, a separate administration is usually set up to manage all departments' functions. In the third, the administrative process is carried out by a unit solely devoted to distance education.

A major advantage of this mixed mode of operation is that it can draw upon the considerable resources of resident faculty and others to conduct the distance teaching. This might ensure that the distance student's learning experiences are comparable to those of the campus-based students. For example, on-campus faculty could teach both at a distance and conventionally, using similar materials, content, and processes, as at the University of New England in Australia or at the University of Wisconsin. A dual arrangement like this could ensure that certain standards are maintained within distance education.

Having a dual administrative and delivery system is not without problems. Some faculty and administrators may consider distance education to be less important or effective than campus-based instruction, which could easily result in a second-class status for the distance education program. Senior instructors may not wish to participate in the program because of their attitudes, so junior instructors may be relegated to this task. In this case, the quality of instruction could be questionable. The amount of work needed to prepare special materials, lectures, and assignments could also deter full participation by selected faculty. Also, faculty members may use the same teaching techniques in distance teaching as in campus-based activities, and this may cause problems for the special external population to be served. Finally, some distance education programs, because of their special needs for technology or instructional design, can become expensive, sometimes even more so than conventional education, and this can jeopardize the whole effort. The administration must be apprised of these concerns and must be prepared to cope with them for effective and continued programming.

Consortium. The third mode of operation is through a consortium of institutions, or a federation of structures, devoted to distance education. The number of distance consortia in the United States is growing rapidly, involving mostly conventional educational institutions engaged in cooperative distance education activities such as audioconferencing and videoconferencing. Attempts to develop complete distance education programs through consortia have not met with considerable success, as witnessed by the demise of the University of Mid-America. One common use of consortia is to set up a central agency for the production of learning materials and strategies, such as the International Consortium at the University of Maryland, to be used by participating institutions in the instruction of their students. The students simply register with their own institution and work with the centrally developed learning materials. Upon successful completion, of course, students obtain credit from their home institution. If only one institution offers a distance course that others do not, the credit can be transferred to or credited to another institution in the consortium.

Although consortia appear to be viable for the administration of distance education, collaboration between institutions is not without problems. Philosophical and ideological differences, the potential dominance of one institution over others, problems with sharing costs, problems with developing learning materials and sharing their use, and poorly matched institutions cause collaborative efforts to become fragile at best and ineffective in carrying out their missions. Distrust in using other institutions' teaching packages, unequal contributions by the institutions, different administrative structures for processing distance education, and different media and teaching techniques can cause further problems. Anyone with experience in collaboration between educational institutions, particularly ones in higher education, can attest to the inherent problems of a consortium. However, the consortium, if well designed, could link institutions with diverse strengths, could bring more political pressure to bear when needed, and could meet some common goals for distance education that might not be possible for the institutions individually.

Perhaps the ideal administrative mode would involve a unit that has the autonomy and authority and at the same time the faculty and resources to produce and carry out the learning experiences for external adult students. Whether a program is linked with, separated from, or integrated into other programs is immaterial as long as development, production, and the execution of distance education programs and courses can be done by able faculty and staff to meet the needs of adults.

Administrative Concerns. The administration unit has several key personnel concerns for effective operation. As in any conventional education unit, the distance education unit must contain a clearly defined faculty or faculties, counselors and tutors if different from faculty, media and learning materials development experts, and marketing and distribution personnel. A team approach to distance education on a permanent basis would be the most effective approach. The interactive team would assess adult needs, design the appropriate learning packages, provide guidance, and assess performance. A more holistic treatment could occur under this functional team approach.

The development of learning materials and media is particularly critical in distance education and could be approached by a team with a good degree of sophistication. The development team should include content specialists (academics); instructional designers; writers and editors; media specialists, if different from designers; and specialists in adult learner behavior and curriculum development. An interactive team approach can minimize the production-line concept, in which people add bits and pieces to courses as they come down the line. Course development is a highly skilled area of expertise and should be treated as such to ensure quality control of the program. Effective administration of distance teaching programs also involves record keeping, finances, equipment acquisition and maintenance, support personnel, and printing, storing, and mailing of materials.

If regional or local centers or both are part of the distance education concept, their coordination with central activities is critical. Counseling services, discussion groups, additional learning resources, information services, recruiting and support services, and direct tutorial assistance, when required, must be available to the participating adult students. All of these services and activities must be consonant with and supportive of the central institution's philosophy and goals and must be closely coordinated with the total mission of the distance education program.

In most cases, adults desire some direct contact and interaction, assistance, and feedback from not only faculty but also other students. Local or regional centers can provide these important human interactions (Tomlinson, 1984). Also, the centers, in concert with the home base, should handle registration, transcript interpretation, program requirements, course payments, timing of learning experiences, provision of materials, and other barriers to successful learning that can bother and hinder the busy adult learner. Also, centers can provide a modern and well-equipped media resource station, where students can use the latest technological resources that they may not have available elsewhere (Tomlinson, 1984).

Counseling adult learners at a distance is another important administrative concern, especially if local or regional centers are not available. Adults have educational, personal, and career problems that must be resolved in order for them to learn effectively. The professional staff can provide counseling. Research on counseling adult learners at a distance is fairly sparse, but this is not a new subject (see Arbeiter, Aslanian, Schmerbeck, and Brickell, 1978; Thornton and Mitchell, 1978). Wertheim (1981) notes that the use of media to advise adults is quite extensive, but that the counseling rarely goes beyond advising.

Written correspondence, both one-way and two-way, is a highly traditional form of counseling that is, nevertheless, nontraditional (Woolfe, Murgatroyd, and Rhys, 1987). Such counseling can be highly structured, as in the Indiana University courses in career planning and decision making in which individual lessons requiring answers to both general and personal questions are completed over an extended period. The telephone is similarly a traditional medium for counseling, but not in comparison with face-to-face methods (Wertheim, 1981; Woolfe, Murgatroyd, and Rhys, 1987). The telephone has been used for academic counseling at the OUUK (Thornton and Mitchell, 1978) and is used a great deal at other distance education institutions as well, because it makes possible fast and effective communication. But effective tutoring and counseling by telephone necessitates highly developed communication skills that many counselors lack (Paulet, 1987).

Audiocassettes, again one-way and two-way, can provide a kind of cross between telephone and written communication (Woolfe, Murgatroyd, and Rhys, 1987). They may be mailed back and forth, serving the same purpose as writing but providing more cues to the counselor, or they may be reached by telephone by the learner wishing to obtain information without personal contact. Call-in radio and television counseling is another innovative method of reaching learners (Wertheim, 1981). Finally, computer-based contact is suggested as another source for some counseling services (Woolfe, Murgatroyd, and Rhys, 1987). This technique would assume, of course, computer linkages.

In any case, counseling assistance, at least of an academic nature, either through a center or at a distance must be provided to help adults reach their educational goals. Counseling by the administrator, teacher, tutor, or a counselor is necessary and should encourage a one-to-one relationship with the students (Loewenthal, Blackwelder, and Broomall, 1980).

Administering and coordinating an effective distance education program is not an easy task and requires considerable planning, support, and interaction. The distance education program should not be relegated to a second-class position in the participating institution. It must have authority, autonomy, and cooperation with other units. It must have adequate personnel, faculty, and other staff, and it must have a sound funding base to carry on its mission.

Communication

Another important consideration in the organization and administration of distance education programs is communication. Communication is critical because in distance education the instructor and the student are physically separated during the majority of instruction. And, as Garrison (1989) states, education is a collaborative experience that depends on communication. Communication is also important in conveying other information in addition to instructional information to external students and between the administration, faculty, and staff of the distance education program.

Communication is a process of sharing ideas, needs, and perceptions and can be used to build considerable unity and rapport between educational staff members, adult clients, and the institution. It is, by definition, the giving and receiving of meaning, and at the concrete level it is actually the mutual exchange of ideas, needs, perceptions, options, facts, and other items of interest. To be effective, communication should flow multidirectionally (to all people concerned) and should be two-way in nature. This will ensure that people are informed and also that they may react to the information accordingly.

To tell someone something has many implications. First, the information must reach the individual, which means more than just placing information in a person's mailbox or on a person's desk or printing pertinent information in a newspaper, newsletter, or bulletin. Second, the individual who receives the information must be able to understand and interpret it; this includes thought process as well as content. Finally, provisions must be made for the individual to react and respond to the information if this is perceived as necessary by both the sender and receiver.

Communication Variables. Boles and Davenport (1975) have identified six variables that are at work during the communication process: the sender, the message, the medium, the receiver, the environment, and feedback. Figure 2 presents a model incorporating these variables based on their work. A brief discussion of each variable follows.

The *sender,* who in distance education can be an administrator, instructor, tutor, counselor, and others at the home institution, should have a knowledge of the receivers and their behavioral "package" so as to make the communication as effective as possible. This empathic ability requires the sender to know the individuals, their ability to decode the given message, and the impact of the message. Senders should also be aware of their position in the social institution (credibility) and should present a trustworthy attitude and authenticity in their behavior. Senders should check the intent of the message, such as to reinforce behavior, change behavior, increase knowledge, or form or change attitudes, before sending the message. If the sender and receiver are face-to-face, the sender must be aware of nonverbal signals, such as intonations, gestures, and other body movements. The message itself can be affected by the sender's tone of the voice, facial expression, or choice of words. All of these factors have meaning for the receiver of the communication. Improper choices could inhibit instead of encourage communication.

The *message* can occur in two forms, verbal and nonverbal. In distance education, most messages are transmitted verbally in written or spoken form, but nonverbal messages, as suggested above, can come into play also. Careful selection of symbols and words in verbal communication can help the sender to avoid ambiguity. The message should be explicit and to the point in distance education. If a response to the message is required, this should be made clear to the receiver. Interpretation of messages is critical to the distance learner so messages should be carefully planned and their intent critically assessed.

Figure 2. Communication Model.

Distance Education
Environments: Physical and Social

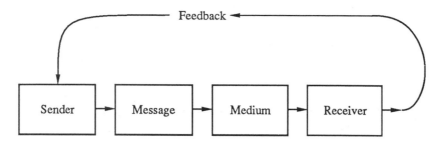

Source: Adapted from Boles and Davenport, 1983.

The *medium* or method of sending a message from one person to others can be either formal or informal. Transmission relies mostly on the senses of sight and sound in distance education and includes the use of conferences, meetings, group discussions, radio, television, the press, notes, memoranda, telephone calls, reports, letters, visits, and other combinations of media. Interpersonal methods of sending a message, or one-to-one interactions, appear to be effective in changing attitudes and beliefs, and mass media channels are effective in the dissemination of information and awareness of ideas (Boles and Davenport, 1983). Communication channels with provisions for feedback appear to be more effective than those that do not include such provisions.

The sender must decide the type of medium used to convey information on the basis of the nature of the receiver and the kind of message sent, important considerations in distance education. Effectiveness is determined by the impact the medium has on the receiver. As Boles and Davenport (1983) suggest, the amount of reliance on and trust in a medium of communication experienced by the receivers is probably related to "(1) the degree to which the medium and channels reduce uncertainty, (2) the extent to which feedback is invited or welcomed, and (3) the freedom from message-garbling 'noise'" (p. 185). This last point suggests that extraneous and confusing verbiage or nonverbal moves must be eliminated from the medium presentation. The message/medium variables are important ones, particularly in the development of course materials and media for distance learners because of the absence of face-to-face interaction.

As previously mentioned, the sender should have a knowledge of the *receiver*, the fourth major component in the communication process. Each receiver, who in most cases is the adult learner in the field, is different and thus may interpret messages differently. In fact, receivers are more receptive to and more likely to retain messages that are consistent with their knowledge level, attitudes, and beliefs. Therefore, the receivers' entire perceptual background will determine how they react to the message. For example, if the receiver is a subordinate (student, secretary), he or she is likely to pay greater attention than if the receiver is a superior (full professor, president). People bring to bear what they currently know and not what they are expected to know regarding the message. Further, the receivers' position or status in the social environment has an impact on how they receive messages. Also, positive communication, as might be expected, has a favorable impact on receivers, and communication oriented toward the receiver and not the message or sender is more effective.

The *feedback* loop provides the opportunity for the receiver to respond to the sender if this is perceived as important or is required. The sender can know if the message is being received, understood, and acted upon only through feedback. In the distance education process, feedback is required by educators to determine if students are progressing toward educational goals. Feedback enhances and encourages the dialogue/support concept so vital in distance education (Garrison, 1989). In other cases, feedback may only be desirable or implied. Although opportunities for feedback by the receiver are important in assuring effectiveness in the communication process, often feedback does not occur unless it is specifically requested.

The *environment*, both social and physical, is the general arena within which communication takes place. In distance education, the environment is generally large, dispersed, and diverse in nature; it is both formal and informal in terms of educational activity. The social environment includes faculty, technical staff, support staff, and others from an institution generally devoted to both campus-based and distance education. It includes adult students living at varying distances from the institution who possess different needs, goals, and motivations. The physical environment is equally diverse at the institution and in the field. This great diversity means that if communication is to succeed, openness and trust must characterize the environment—again, the dialogue/support construct of distance education. Distrust, defensiveness, and extraneous factors (noise) must be eliminated from the system. Whether the environment is informal or formal, an open, multichannel, two-way communication system must be utilized so that the sender and the receiver can share the information needed to make the distance education program as effective as possible.

Evaluation

The term *evaluation* means many things to many people. In one form or another, evaluation is used in every kind of formal education. This diversity of use is reflected in expressions such as *teacher evaluation, curriculum evaluation, materials evaluation, student evaluation,* and *organizational evaluation.* Almost any object or event can be evaluated.

Evaluation is a process of making judgments or applying values in a given situation. It is the means used by educators in judging the worth or value of something or the lack of it. The root word of evaluation is *value,* which comes from the Latin *valere,* meaning "to be strong, to have worth." Values are always a significant part of the evaluation process.

Program evaluation takes on additional meaning in distance education. Distance educators tend to assume that distance education reduces certain barriers to learning, provides for more learner-centered instruction, is more convenient, and meets the needs of adults more effectively than conventional education. However, how do educators know if these assumptions are valid or if certain goals are being met without assessment?

Thorpe (1988) suggests several important reasons for evaluation in distance education. With little face-to-face interaction, it is difficult for educators to gather information about learners, their needs, and their wishes and desires as in a conventional educational program. Educators should be responsive to learners' needs and they cannot know these needs without some formal assessment.

Thorpe also suggests that evaluation is needed because distance education is still in an embryonic, innovative stage, with considerable developmental activities taking place. Different models, strategies, and systems are being tried and tested, and educators need to determine effectiveness on a comparative basis. Consistent evidence through regular evaluation can provide for a more structured process and prevent random activity.

Good evaluation will also assist distance educators in thinking about what they are trying to do and achieve as they implement programs and activities. Continued development in distance education is essential, and evaluation can reveal what is effective and what is not. Just as business and industry evaluate their products, distance education must do the same to see if their "customers" are satisfied and what more can be done. Evaluation leads not only to development of courses, programs, and materials but also to the development of the professional staff.

Thorpe also says that evaluation can provide information needed by external bodies. Legislative bodies, funding agencies, businesses, colleges, and other clients want to know if distance education accomplishes what it sets out to do. Evidence of the effectiveness of distance education can further enhance a distance education program that is being implemented.

Program evaluation, therefore, is a critical aspect of the administration of distance education. If this alternative form of education is to continue to grow and meet the needs of adult learners, educators must have evidence as to its effectiveness. Program evaluation can move distance education from a trial-and-error effort to one with more sophistication.

Types of Evaluation. Grotelueschen (1980) suggests three major purposes of the evaluation of educational programs involving adults. The first deals with evaluating the past outcomes or activities that generally lead to justification or accountability of program operations. This form of evaluation, which Scriven (1980) terms *summative,* gives quantitative and qualitative data at the summation of distance program activities and can present a global review of just what has happened.

The second form of evaluation focuses on current progam efforts and is used to determine if a program needs improvement. This evaluation process seeks information about and monitors the program during its implementation stage and is conducted to ascertain any problems or shortcomings that need remediation. This evaluation, termed *formative* by Scriven (1980), takes place when distance education activities are still fluid and when new directions can still be defined.

The third form identified by Grotelueschen is *future-oriented* evaluation and helps decision makers in planning a future distance education program. Although similar to a needs assessment, it can go beyond such an assessment to look at potential alternatives and ascertain their merits. It can identify new goals, procedures, and potential clients as well as other data vital to the continued development of distance education.

Combinations of these three forms of evaluation are possible and highly likely. For example, a formative study may lead to a future-oriented study as new data are revealed. And summative data could lead to a future-oriented study as an analysis occurs.

Scriven proposes two other evaluation processes that have direct meaning for the distance educator. In program evaluation, the educator can employ a comparative construct or a noncomparative one. The comparative approach involves the comparison of similar characteristics across programs. If distance educators wish to compare their program in certain areas (such as cost, achievement, and accessibility) with more traditional programs, then the comparative approach can be utilized. Examples of the use of this approach are found in the Resource. Of course, there must be a valid basis for comparison. On the other hand, if distance educators wish to gather data on factors not generalizable across institutions or programs, the noncomparative model would be used. Generally, noncomparative evaluation involves numerical studies and generates data that give an idea as to how much and what kind of educational activity is taking place. Here the institution is usually compared over time with itself. This noncomparative mode has a definite place in distance education. Data from both evaluative modes should be collected and analyzed in terms of their relative value.

Evaluation generally involves the establishment of criteria that are relevant and important to the program as well as the collection of information. The collected information is then analyzed to determine if the criteria are being met and just how effective the program is or can be.

Key Program Goals. Overall goals or important criteria must be determined and specified early on so that the evaluation process can proceed. Gooler's (1979) seven criteria, discussed in Chapter Five, appear significant and useful in the evaluation process. These criteria, or general program goals, set the stage for determining the effectiveness of a distance education effort. Use of these seven criteria—access, relevancy to needs and expectations, quality of program offered, learner outcomes, effectiveness and efficiency, impact, and generation of knowledge—encourages the development of a broad outlook concerning the goals of distance education. They can be applied in summative evaluation to present a holistic picture of the program.

The first criterion is *access,* or who is being served, both in terms of absolute numbers and numbers in special target groups. Access may be easy to measure if registration for courses is required but difficult to measure in open learning situations such as mass-audience telecourses. Evaluation of access may involve assessing the participation of target populations for which programs have been developed, gauging the extent of geographic coverage, and determining the availability of media needed for participation among the student population. The effectiveness of efforts to promote the awareness of programs among potential students is another factor because programs will do little good if students are not aware of them.

The second and perhaps most critical factor is *relevancy to needs and expectations,* whose importance stems from the fact that if needs are ignored, then quite obviously little of educational value can result. Broadly based and varied programs will generally meet the needs of more students than programs that are not as widely based. Identifying societal, individual, and employment-related needs is no easy task. High application rates may indicate that needs are being met, but they do not necessarily indicate the level of potential demand among adults not yet enrolled. Some form of needs assessment or market research is necessary to identify the diverse needs and desires of adults and to assess levels of demand. The ideal method for the prioritization of those educational needs that are identified is to determine their relationship to the basic mission and goals of the situation and the specific program or unit in question.

To judge the *quality of the program offered*, educators must look at a number of factors. The quality of the learning materials used is one important factor since distance education relies so heavily on teaching materials. Also, the ease with which these materials can be successfully used by students must be assessed. Multimedia approaches can cause problems when learning media are ineptly combined by educators who do not understand their properties, either alone or in combination. Finally, to assess overall quality, a look at the total educational experience of students, and at the short- and long-term impact of the learning on them and their lives, is important. Educators must ask, Has the experience been an education or just training, and have students moved toward appropriate diplomas and certificates and found satisfaction and recognition in their social environments, when compared with their conventionally educated peers?

To assess *learner outcomes* is to answer the general question, who learns what? Again, are students moving at a satisfactory pace toward degrees, diplomas, or certificates as a result of participation in the distance education program? Rumble (1986) emphasizes the importance of outcomes by stating, "It is clearly important to evaluate success or failure in this endeavor, particularly as the evaluation of learner outcomes has been the historical focus of much evaluation effort and remains a major indicator of success or failure in the eyes of funding bodies" (p. 210). Evaluating learner outcomes involves looking at the output/input ratio used to measure the numbers of graduates in relation to the number of students entering a course or program of study and the amount of time taken to complete the studies. These measures allow evaluators to take into account course failures, repetition rates, and dropout rates. This is a complicated and somewhat misleading process since some students just want to learn more about a subject and do not really care about getting course credit or a diploma. Poor completion rates are well documented in distance education. Further, entry qualifications may vary between programs. Some institutions have strict admissions requirements, and others have open entry policies. In addition, institutions vary in terms of their time and progress requirements for the completion of coursework. Finally, time taken to complete a program could vary because of the differences in students' needs and goals.

The *impact* or overall success of the program is gauged in terms of outcomes relating to students, graduates, employers, other educational institutions, and society. Both monetary and nonmonetary impact can be assessed such as if students do well after completing their degree, diploma, or program, whether other institutions use one of the programs as a model, and whether greater overall enrollment occurs following the success of one program. Conclusions about the impact or success of a program should be based on long-term as well as short-term measures.

Effectiveness is a measure of the extent to which outputs are meeting the needs and demands of students and society, while *efficiency* refers to the cost of achieving these outputs. Effectiveness, of course, is an overriding issue because the mission of distance education is to meet those needs and demands of potential students and society in general that are within its role and scope. Cost, too, is an issue since administrators need to know the cost per average student per unit of study, particularly if distance and conventional systems of education are in competition or are being considered for use to reach a given student population. Cost calculations are tricky since variations exist in the amount the student pays, dropout rates, the quality of the program, the kinds of media used, and the population reached.

Finally, the rather embryonic state of distance education today makes the *generation of knowledge* an important consideration. Greater understanding of the problems and issues in this field and new practices should result from careful research on current distance education programs. It behooves the professional administrator and evaluator to seek out new directions and ideas for use in this evolving field.

Within these broad, general program goals, the educator should state subgoals or objectives that are more precise and measurable and that will give direction to program development activities (Verduin, 1980). For example, under the major goal area of access, an objective may specify that all appropriate media for a given course be available to all students for their use at all times. Or under the goal of relevancy to needs and expectations, a subgoal may state the employment-related needs of clients within a given agency, jointly cooperating with the distance education institution, will be met. These and other goal statements are the value expressions that give direction to distance program operations and are the goals to which the evaluation process is applied.

Although the goals for any phase of a distance education program are expressed prior to the evaluation process, it is important that the institution, administration, and staff review these goals early on to determine if they are of value and importance. A basic question here is, Are these worthy goals for a distance education program? If the goals and objectives are not applicable, or are out-of-date, little value results regardless of how well they are achieved. Careful attention should be paid to this area since in some distance education courses and programs objectives are locked in for some time because of the difficulty of revising materials due to the cost of courseware production and other factors.

The emphasis on goals of value is consistent with some of the constructs offered by Scriven (1980). He maintains that the criteria for judging evaluation must be based on the goals, and that the criteria must indicate the worth of the goals. He also says that the purpose of evaluation is to establish and justify merit or worth and that the emphasis in assessment should be on holistic program evaluation. In other words, all parts of the program should be assessed in terms of worth.

Further, Scriven views the evaluation process as the gathering and combining of performance data that are then prioritized through the use of a weighted set of goals. This means that as one evaluates a distance education program, certain goals or sections of the program may be held more important than others. If, for example, access is more important than cost to the evaluators, it will be weighted more heavily. If generation of knowledge through evaluation holds little meaning for program administrators or evaluators, it will be given little weight. The weighting of the factors depends largely on program philosophy and direction, says Scriven, coupled with outside political and economic forces. So while Scriven's approach to evaluation is a holistic one, it does allow for distinctions based upon the relative importance of goals and objectives in a distance education program.

Evaluation Matrix. Combining the seven important goals of distance education as defined by Gooler (1979) with the three types of evaluation advanced by Grotelueschen (1980) can offer an evaluation matrix for use by evaluators of distance education programs (see Table 2). The major goals of the program, with some ideas or areas for subgoals or objectives, are listed. Then evaluators can identify major evaluation designs and can determine if formative, summative, or future-oriented modes of evaluation are needed using comparative and noncomparative measures and even weightings as deemed appropriate. Using the matrix can provide a holistic design for evaluation and for viewing the worth of selected aspects of the program as might occur in the formative and future-oriented modes. Further, time schedules and the assignment of personnel to conduct the work could be defined. If utilized correctly, the matrix could provide for effective feedback on the entire distance education program.

Evaluation Planning. Before engaging in evaluation studies of any magnitude, educators must give considerable thought to the planning of these studies, so that effective results are ensured. Planning an effective distance education evaluation program is not a simple task. Grotelueschen (1980) has identified eight major considerations that must receive attention for effective program evaluation.

The first major consideration is that of *purpose*. The reasons for a study could vary from an external mandate to the educators' desire to know how well a given program is doing. Of course, the major goal of evaluation is to ascertain the worth of something and to give the appropriate data to decision makers. But, this goal is

Table 2. Evaluation Matrix for Distance Education.

Goal Evaluation Factors	*Formative*	*Summative*	*Future*

1. Access
    Numbers
    Target Group
    Geographic Coverage
    Media Availability
    Awareness			

2. Relevance to Needs and
Expectations
    Societal
    Individual
    Employment-Related
    Needs Assessment–Related
    Market Research–Related			

3. Quality of Program Offered
    Instruction
    Learning Materials
    Education/Training
    Total Learning Experience
    Diplomas/Certificates
    Satisfaction/Recognition			

4. Learner Outcomes
    Output/Input
    Time
    Failures/Repetition/Dropouts
    Entry/Exit Qualifications			

5. Impact
    Overall Success
    Students
    Graduates
    Employers
    Enrollment			

6. Effectiveness and Efficiency
    Needs
    Demands
    Cost			

7. Generation of Knowledge
    New Practices
    New Ideas
    New Directions			

multifaceted, and as Grotelueschen states, "Evaluation may thus serve the purpose of program planning, policymaking, program improvement, or program justification or accountability" (p. 96).

The second consideration is that of the *audience* for the evaluation results. Audiences in distance education can range from the teachers and administrators in the program to program participants to community groups to funding agencies to legislators. Each prospective audience must receive attention, and different audiences may require different kinds of information. Since the various audiences are generally decision makers, this concern is a major one also.

In discussing the evaluation with potential audiences, the program evaluators will determine the critical *issues* of the evaluation. The right questions must be asked in evaluations to get appropriate responses. The right questions come from an analysis of the issues. The issues must be closely related to the needs and interests of the audiences and could entail such things as program outcomes, cost, attainment of goals, and the extent to which needs were addressed.

The next consideration is that of the *resources* available to conduct the evaluation. The total scope of the evaluation may not be set until the cost, time, and expertise needed to carry out the work are addressed. A formative self-study by staff members takes their time away from other duties. A summative study done by external personnel with good expertise can be costly. Education at a distance can cost varying amounts of money, and so can the evaluation of it. These costs must be weighed in terms of the urgency and relevancy of the evaluation outcomes, and a determination must be made as to what costs can be borne to get significant results.

The questions asked in an evaluation give *evidence* as to outcomes. Evidence leads to critical judgments utilized by decision makers. Therefore, program evaluators must determine what kinds of evidence should be collected. Evidence can come in many forms, from descriptions of participants, programs, and costs to statements about the value of the programs. As might be expected, the relevance of the evidence is contingent on the demands of the issues and audiences. Since the definition of appropriate evidence can be a highly technical process, specialists in this area may need to be employed.

Once the evidence has been determined, evaluators must turn their attention to *data collection*. They must determine not only how much data to collect but also data sources. Data sources are people and things within the domain of the distance education program and can include staff members, participants, other people, and also documents. Data collection can include informal inquiries into the participants' feelings about the program, the construction of highly formal instruments, observations, rating scales, interviews, and so forth. The methodology depends on the nature of the evidence needed and can be restricted by time and costs. Again, data collection can be a highly technical process, so outside specialists may be needed to design instruments and procedures to collect the information.

After the data are collected, an *analysis* must determine the worth or lack of worth of the program and its elements. An analysis is important because "good data analysis will provide descriptions of the program being evaluated, highlighting those aspects relevant to particular issues or audiences" (Grotelueschen, 1980, p. 101). Analyses may include comparisons between current and past performances, thus documenting change over time, or they may simply describe the current status of a program. Specific as well as general outcomes can be documented by the analysis. If highly quantitative statistical data are analyzed, a specialist may again be employed. But in the main, the type of data analysis that will occur is contingent on the nature of the evidence, the audience, and the audience's ability to comprehend the information.

The final consideration in evaluation of programs is that of *reporting* the evaluation in a meaningful and comprehensive manner. In most instances the nature of the audience will dictate how the findings are reported; the individual differences of people and groups must be considered. Some people may be able to understand highly statistical and technical findings while others may not. Nonstatistical and nontechnical descriptions can be useful and in many instances quite appropriate to most people. As Grotelueschen suggests, "The criterion for selection of the appropriate procedure is simple: use the procedure that best communicates findings in the particular issue to the specific audience" (Grotelueschen, 1980, p. 103). Further, if the evaluators are asked for conclusions, implications, and recommendations resulting from the findings, they should be cautious. It would be better to have the audience itself draw conclusions and implications if possible.

Although they may appear to be tedious, these considerations can be quite helpful to administrators, evaluators, and others who are preparing for any kind of an evaluation study. Using such procedures encourages them to think through and prepare for every event in the assessment process. A more comprehensive approach to the evaluation of a distance program is possible through this careful planning.

Summary

The organizational pattern of a distance education program should be based on the philosophical position of the institution or agency delivering it. This position determines who will be receiving the education, how it will be presented, how much will be presented, and the purposes of such an educational effort.

A distance education program may be institution centered, or organized to deliver basic instruction in a straightforward manner to large numbers of adults with little if any input by learners. It may be student centered, allowing adult learners greater input, control, and feedback opportunities in the process. It may also be society centered, focusing on learning about and bringing solutions to problems confronting adults in their everyday living. It may be transaction centered, offering a balance between the institution/ instructor's and the adult student's definition and control of the learning experiences. Or it may be a combination of the above.

Any social institution delivering distance education faces political and economic constraints. Once the constraints and philosophical positions of the institution are meshed, the form and direction of the organization can be defined. The qualities, characteristics, and needs of adult learners should be given careful consideration during this process.

Three major methods of administering the distance education program can be used. In the first design, the distance education program comes under direction of a single administrative unit with accompanying staff in a single-purpose institution. Here the only mission of the institution is to provide distance education. The second administrative design is a mixed mode, characteristic of institutions in which both distance and conventional education are used. Administration of distance education in this design involves working with faculty who may be part of both programs and attempting to ensure that distance education does not receive second-class treatment. The third design involves a consortium of institutions that cooperatively attempt distance education. The complications of consortia may make this form of administration difficult.

Whatever mode is used to administer and carry out the distance education program, adequate funding, staffing, control, and freedom must be present to ensure a successful effort. Autonomy and authority are critical to the success of distance education programs.

Any organizational and administrative structure must have effective communication for it to succeed. Distance education, with its diversity of activities and staffing, the nature of its students, and externally based instructional programming, requires truly effective communication. Information must flow in such a manner that all parties are apprised of common goals, activities, and procedures and that appropriate feedback is possible whenever necessary.

Any effective distance education organization, because of its unique place in educating adults, must have a plan for evaluating the program to determine its value and accomplishments. A sound evaluation plan would be holistic in nature to ensure that all parts of the program are functioning successfully. Formative measures can be employed to determine worth during the execution of program activities. Summative measures can be utilized to evaluate the total effectiveness of a program or program segments at their completion. And future-oriented evaluation can be used to determine future directions for program development. An important initial step, if this has not been done previously, is to ascertain the key program goals and their validity. Then each segment of the program can be assessed, even if some aspects are deemed more important than others.

Before effective program evaluation can be instituted, careful planning for all events must take place to ensure that the procedures and results will be meaningful and appropriate to all parties. Evaluation, as a critical process in distance education, generates information that the distance educator and others can use in effective decision making for the good of the program and its clients.

9

Conclusion:
Opportunities
and Challenges
for the Future

Before attempting to extrapolate future trends in distance education in the United States, it is important for educators to consider
the societal context and demographic patterns projected for the next
decade. Related trends and predictions about adult education, educational technology, and distance learning should shed some light
on the potential of this educational delivery method.

The Setting for Education in the Future

Forecasting by the government provides a great deal of information useful to people interested in future educational trends. The
Bureau for Labor Statistics (BLS) has made projections on the basis
of low, medium, and high growth in education jobs for the years
1986–2000.

On the basis of projections of moderate growth, the BLS
predicts an 18 percent growth rate in American jobs between 1986
and the year 2000 (Silvestri and Lukasiewicz, 1987). This rate does
not compare favorably with the growth achieved between 1972 and
1986, when the U.S. labor force expanded by 35 percent, nearly twice
the projected 1986–2000 increase. Women, Hispanics, and blacks are
expected to account for almost 80 percent of the net increase in the

197

labor force by the year 2000, and women alone are predicted to account for nearly 60 percent of new workers.

High birthrates prior to the Great Depression, the baby boom following World War II, and low birthrates over the last twenty years have resulted in a U.S. population with more middle-aged and older adults, and fewer children and youths. With continued low birthrates in the overall population, this trend should go on well into the next century (Kutscher, 1987).

However, even this lower population growth will increase demands for goods and services and, therefore, will increase demand for workers in many fields. The West and South are expected to be the fastest growing regions, with projected population increases of 45 and 31 percent, respectively. Little population change is likely in the Midwest, and in the East, the population may even decrease slightly (Kutscher, 1987).

The aging of the population will be reflected in the work force. Seventy-five percent of workers in the year 2000 will be between twenty-five and fifty-four years of age. However, contrary to popular belief, the proportion of workers over the age of fifty-five is expected to be only slightly higher in 2000 than in 1986 because of increased early retirement. Early retirement, of course, dictates a future focus on programs for retirees in adult education (Spear and Mocker, 1981). Forecasters tend to see a bright future for the mostly middle-aged job force described in government projections, which is expected to "result in improved labor productivity, especially since in recent years the educational attainment of the labor force has risen dramatically. . . . [This] emphasis on education will continue. The fastest growing jobs will be in executive, managerial, professional and technical fields requiring the highest levels of education and skill. . . . Opportunities for high school dropouts will be increasingly limited" (Kutscher, 1987, p. 9).

But such forecasts may be overly optimistic. According to statistical derivations by the Hudson Institute, a Washington-based think tank, more than 75 percent of the 21 million new workers entering the work force between 1986 and 2000 will have limited verbal and writing skills that will qualify them for only 40 percent of the jobs created during the same period. The institute's staff estimates that to attain the gains in productivity predicted by the government forecasters as many as fifty million workers will have to be trained or retrained in the next twelve years—twenty-one million new entrants and thirty million current workers (Bernstein, 1988).

While this estimate may be overly gloomy, it suggests a tremendous need for more and better education in the United States in the near future. Distance education and other forms of adult education should play a significant role in this expansion of educational opportunity. Distance education may become of far greater importance in America in the years ahead because it is so cost efficient in most applications and because it allows for in-place learning by working adults. If society is to cope with this growing need for continuing education, the role of the adult educator must take on new meaning and importance.

Table 3 shows the predicted trends in employment for adult educators and other teachers to the end of this century. The projected moderate-level growth in employment of adult educators is expected to fall between that of elementary and secondary teachers. The number of faculty members employed in higher education, on the other hand, is expected to decline.

These projections show that there will be an increase in the employment of adult educators even as higher education employment decreases. Yet this increase does not seem sufficient to meet the growing needs of adult education that the Hudson Institute and others have predicted. What role, then, might distance education play?

Distance Education. Bates (1984a) postulates some major trends in distance education since the establishment of the Open University of the United Kingdom that are related to recent technological developments. Media are becoming more diverse, he says, as is access to these media, even as expensive media are becoming less costly. These new interactive media allow more student control of learning. Feasley (1983) also notes the trend toward interactive media, but he asserts that the new media increase the cost of programs, making access dependent on the wealth of learners, even as they lessen the control of faculty over courseware.

These new media present something of a dilemma for dis-

Table 3. Employment in Education: Actual 1986 and Projected to 2000.

Occupation	Total Employment (numbers in thousands)				% Change Moderate Projection
	Actual 1986	Projected/2000			
		Low	Mod.	High	
Education administrators	288	316	325	336	+13
Teachers, preschool	172	233	240	248	+36
Teachers, kindergarten and elementary	1,527	1,771	1,826	1,833	+23
Teachers, secondary school	1,128	1,246	1,280	1,320	+13
College and university faculty	754	703	722	745	-4
Other teachers and instructors	1,097	1,296	1,340	1,386	+22
Teachers, adult and vocational education	427	489	509	529	+19
Instructors, adult nonvocational education	202	229	241	251	+19
Teachers and instructors, vocational education and training	225	260	268	278	+19

Source: Adapted from Silvestri and Lukasiewicz, 1987.

tance educators. Computer, videodisc players, and teleconferencing equipment are expensive but bring a badly needed interactive component to distance education. However, less affluent adults may be unable to afford this high-technology kind of distance study, even though serving such adults is an important rationale for distance education. A possible solution is to set up learning centers that give the less affluent access to the new technology. Attempts to increase educational activities during the period of projected slower economic and, therefore, tax base growth between now and the year 2000 appear to face formidable problems, but some authors see such dispersed learning centers as an important aspect of expanding educational opportunity (Hankin, 1988; Brockett, 1987).

As Bates (1984a) notes, the pervasiveness of media usage is one way to judge access: "There are still major obstacles and limitations to the introduction of new technology for distance education. . . . [Distance education] requires technology which is so cheap, reliable, and easy to use that it can be found in nearly every home. Apart from books, broadcast television, radio, audiocassettes, and the telephone, technology at the moment cannot actually meet homebased needs" (pp. 224, 226).

Both Feasley and Bates mention increases in the number of specialized staff members who may become an unwanted buffer between faculty and educational media. Bates (1984b) suggests that distance teaching units should have internal training for distance teachers on the best use of media so that the faculty can take part intelligently in course preparation. Bates also sees changes in professional roles, such as academics doing their own typing on a computer, leading to conflicts with educational organizations. He predicts that the educational innovations possible with existing technology such as the development of courses via computer conferencing and word processing may not become common until fifteen or twenty years hence because of the refusal of academics to adapt to new methods. Consortia will probably continue to increase in importance in the future as institutions offering distance education attempt to mitigate costs of the new media (Hankin, 1988).

In 1982, the National Home Study Council asked twenty-one panelists representing a cross section of the distance education community to take part in a three-stage delphi survey (National Home Study Council, 1982). The predictions finally agreed upon by the panelists, for example, "The adult population (18–70 years) will be the prime source for D/E [distance education] enrollments," illustrate the difficulty in achieving any new insight through such a process. Perhaps surveying subfields of distance education would have led to more specific and useful answers.

Moore (1987a) suggests some trends in distance education for the near future that generally reflect its continued growth. He believes that there will be growing use of distance education by adults whose educational needs are not fully met by more traditional methods of educational delivery. This demand will be filled through increased integration of distance and traditional institutions and by an increase in the specialization of professionals who teach adults at a distance. Small distance teaching institutions may evolve into research and resource centers designed to meet the initial and continuing education needs of these professionals. Moore also foresees the weakening of state university boundaries and the development of appropriate courseware at the local, regional, and national levels as a natural outgrowth of this new emphasis on distance education.

Morrison (1989) offers six challenges that he believes reflect changes in society that distance educators must overcome. These may be summarized as follows:

1. Some barriers to students' success in distance education cannot be surmounted by overcoming barriers to access. A broader definition of distance education as a kind of open-learning system with these features is needed: (1) the absence of discriminatory entrance requirements, (2) a results-driven concept of equality, (3) a success-based concept of program and service design, (4) a multiple-strategy model approach to program delivery, (5) a developmental concept of quality.

2. Rather than serving only institutional concerns, distance education should provide equality and success in learning. This can be achieved by adopting a systems perspective, linking distance education with other education agencies through activities such as collaborative program development.

3. Distance education is a method of managing learning that is by nature innovative, and, therefore, it must innovate continually. Distance educators must apply strategic management principles to distance education that will allow them to react successfully to change and uncertainty.

4. Distance educators should develop models or frameworks for judging the appropriateness of new technology applications in their field, rather than assuming that use of new distance technology will revolutionize learning.

5. Distance educators must adopt a global vision and assist in the development of a global learning network based on common technology.

6. Distance educators must strive for an equitable distribution of education benefits, not just for a large quantity of learners. They must use strategies designed to stimulate economies, accelerate rural development, and meet the basic needs of disadvantaged people.

Distance Learning. Distance learning, or the deliberate use of educational media by learners in the absence of formal evaluation and two-way communication with an educational agency, is likely to play an important role in the future learning efforts of adults. The slow growth of the economy will probably fuel the do-it-yourself, or self-help, phenomenon already underway in the United States. As Harris (1986) notes, "The average citizen may perceive that self-help is the most promising way to maintain the level of goods and services to which the American householder has become accustomed" (p. 47). Self-help methods may also be used, says Harris, "to acquire the knowledge and skill that will qualify one to advance in a job or career position or to remain competitive in one's existing position" or to "enhance the quality of leisure time" (p. 47).

Distance learning techniques may also be used to reach those most unlikely to participate in formal adult education. Creation of highly appealing educational media products targeted for one-way reception by urban economically disadvantaged adults might be one way of taking advantage of the pervasive ownership and use of radios, television, and cassette players in our society. As more affluent consumers move on to cable television, videocassette recorders, and satellite dish reception, the commercial broadcast TV sources most watched by the urban poor may decline in revenue and educational value. Public television broadcasting still mainly appeals to a narrow audience.

Targeted media projects could be developed through the use of consortia and grants that are specifically intended to reach not only the small percentage of adults likely to enroll in a telecourse but also incidental and distance learners. Incidental learners are those educational media users who are just watching the program without enrolling, without a deliberate educational purpose. Typically many more incidental learners than adults enrolled in the course are watching a program. Distance learners are those viewers who deliberately make the program part of their own learning project without enrolling. Adult learners who do not enroll can be characterized as distance learners in much the same way as adults learning on their own are engaging in adult learning, not adult education. For any distance education program offered via mass media, participants probably include a large group of incidental learners, a smaller group of distance learners, and a very small group of learners actually enroll and therefore are taking part in distance education.

Incidental learning and distance learning might furnish new target markets for educational media producers trying to justify the funding of their projects, just as the serving of incidental learners has been used as a justification of public television expenditures since its inception, based upon its educational and cultural mission. Distance and incidental learning may also lead to formal enrollment in distance and conventional education programs. Distance educators should be aware of the broad-based potential for adult learning through educational media and should work toward its realization.

Educational Technology. Robins and Hepworth (1988) note that the use of media in instruction not only creates new educational opportunities but also creates or exacerbates societal problems as well. While electronic media make it possible to transcend the historical boundaries of time and space, there are signs, say Robins and Hepworth, that they may also create new social divisions and conflicts in the future. By making it possible to work, shop, and perform other common functions electronically from one's home, the emerging media make possible the "electronic cottage" which "threatens to ensnare [women] again in a domestic identity. [Along] with the loss of workplace sociability, there goes also the protection of . . . trade unions. . . . Expensive safe places and cheap unsafe places [will proliferate in] cities. . . . Surveillance will grow. . . . [There will be] a new segmentation of the work force into a core of permanent workers, a periphery of temporary and part-time workers and an outer ring of external contract labor" (Robins and Hepworth, 1988, pp. 164, 168, 173).

This pessimistic future scenario seems unlikely to occur in the near future. Problems associated with technology, such as mandatory overuse of visual data terminals by workers or the imposition of piecework rates on salaried employees through the use of computer monitoring, illustrate the need for dialogue among educators about the future use of technology.

On a more positive note, educational applications of emerging media in the home or learning center already can provide great interconnectivity and versatility to learners. Computer users have access to a wide variety of conferences, courses, information data bases, learning groups, and bulletin boards related to their subject of interest.

The workstation is a recent result of the trend toward more interconnectivity and versatility in media. The workstation was described by Watson, Calvert, and Collins (1987) as "an integrated technological learning environment which supplements teacher to student interactions (p. 14)." The prototypical workstation they describe includes a computer, videodisc, cassette player, and other media. They were most interested in using the workstation to facilitate in-school learning from sources external to the K–12 school, although they worry that such systems may be misused as an alternative to achievement of educational equity between schools in rich and poor districts. If workstations become commonplace in schools, however, they may also be used widely in learning centers accessible to distance higher education students and distance learners.

Another example of this trend toward interconnectivity and versatility is *hypermedia,* or computer delivery of information in a simultaneous rather than a linear manner. It allows the student to have access to more than one data base at a time through the use of high-power desktop computers not available before the 1980s. Apple Computer's president, John Sculley, believes that hypermedia, computer simulation, and artificial intelligence (computer duplication of some advanced functions) will be the core technologies in a new learning environment in the future (Sculley, 1988).

Of course, it is important to keep in mind that only a relatively small proportion of the U.S. population are likely to become active computer users because of constraining factors such as learning preferences, computer phobia, and cost. However, there may be a broadening of the segment of adults participating in computer-based learning and education, in part because of the availability of computers in the workplace (U.S. Bureau of the Census, 1989).

Dailey (1984) posits that the forecasting of an invention means that there is a good chance it will be invented. However, he said, some inventions are absolutely unpredictable, and it is impossible to predict which educational medium will be dominant any time in the future. As new communications technologies emerge, said Dailey, they do not make old ones obsolete.

On the surface Dailey's observations seem reasonable, but it seems likely that most future educational technologies can be safely predicted to be permutations on, or combinations of, print, audio, video, and computer media. Physiological or psychological methods for the delivery of the outputs of the various media directly into the brain may be invented, perhaps in combination with sensory signals convincingly simulating the subjective experiences of educational events. Unfortunately, the potential for misuse of such devices is great. It is difficult to see how some existing media can fail to be the dominant media for quite a while, although direct-to-brain hookups may add new personal dimensions to learning at some time in the next century.

In the near future, print will probably continue to be the dominant medium, although computers, offering as they do a new format for the printed word, will probably one day supplant many uses of print and graphics on paper. Computer notepads capable of reading individual handwriting may become widespread and cheap, just as reprogrammable, portable minicomputers may to some extent replace books. However, paper will certainly continue to be used to copy documents, conduct correspondence, and perform many other tasks. Its relatively low expense, portability, rapid analog search capability (thumbing through the pages), and utility in the absence of any external power source or electronic machine mean that print, whether on paper or on a similar material, may never become obsolete.

It is important to remember that the dominant instructional medium in one nation or region is likely to be different from that in another, especially when comparing developing and developed nations. Almost all media predictions, including the preceding one, focus on the future of the developed nations. Different nations and cultures will be at different stages in their own unique evolutions of media usage, at least for the foreseeable future. For instance, some instructional functions of radio may give way to print study in developing nations with rising literacy rates, leading to markedly increased, not stable or declining, use of correspondence study at times when high-technology media are growing most rapidly in developed nations.

Dailey's assertion to the contrary, advances in media do sometimes render older media obsolete. For example, the audio-cassette has just about made the phonograph record and open-reel tape educationally obsolete. Even in developing nations, the audio-cassette is cheaper, easier to use, and easier to mail than these media. Audiocassette itself may fall victim to a recordable, highly portable version of audiodisc. Similarly, the use of film in American class-rooms has been eclipsed by the use of videocassette. Videocassette may itself lose part of its market to videodisc, although its home recording function is not likely to be usurped. Obsolescence occurs when a new medium can perform all the important functions of a competing medium that serves the same purpose.

It is easy to wax rhapsodic about the future of educational media, predicting that there will be a workstation or hypermedia system in every den and that a plethora of telecommunications car-rier systems will make possible virtually instantaneous audio, video, and computer communication around the world. The problem with such a rosy scenario is that only a small proportion of the world's population will be able to afford such services.

Applications of Technology to Higher Education. Lewis (1989) cites a number of ways in which university-based adult educators have brought educational technology into their profession. For example, in 1986, the editors of the journal *Lifelong Learning,* based at Texas A&M, began to permit the submission of manu-scripts via computer bulletin board. In the same year, the Computer Task Force of the Commission of Professors of Adult Education created a directory of adult education professors who used BITT-NETT, a network often employed for bulletin board communica-tion between student and teacher and for the purpose of facilitating networking among professors. At Syracuse University, the Kellogg Project has, since 1985, been entering documents from the univer-sity's large collection of adult education materials into a computer data base. Eventually, these materials will be made available via computer to adult educators worldwide through the Adult Educa-tion Network, already in existence.

Lewis also cites a description by Middletown (1986) of the Educational Utility, another large data base currently in development. The utility will be composed of a computer center, a distribution system or network, a storage computer that can hold information until the least expensive time of day for transmission, and finally, computers and peripherals at the user end that will be used to gain access to information. Proponents of the Educational Utility say that it will significantly lower the cost of on-line computer use. After describing trends in artificial intelligence, Lewis cautions her readers that "in order to ensure the successful integration of these new technologies to promote adult learning, adult education must take an active role" (p. 624). Like Gooler (1987), she emphasizes the need to adapt technology to learners, rather than to adapt learners to technology.

How will future higher education faculty members carry out their duties? Slatta (1987) describes a prototypical use of electronic communications at North Carolina State University, Raleigh, which provides data and text sharing, electronic mail, and other on-line services to its faculty through a contract with a local videotex company. Called ScholarNet, this amalgam of services is customized to serve the needs of individual educators. Using ScholarNet, North Carolina State professors have engaged in academic projects with colleagues scattered across the state, including preparation of classes and editing of books. Professors at other institutions can "visit" classes on the Raleigh campus via computer conferencing and teleconferencing. In the future, ScholarNet may be used to transmit publications internationally, reducing the time lag between publication and reception of books and periodicals (Slatta, 1987).

Dunn (1983) predicts that in a few decades faculty members will perform the same tasks that they undertake today, but in different ways. "The reputation and future of the University will still rest on them," says Dunn (p. 58). Professors will supervise mini-educational systems that will allow individualized, criterion-referenced testing of students, he predicts, and courses will likewise be individualized. Dunn thinks that the teacher's duties in the twenty-first century will be similar to the one-on-one teaching methods common in medieval universities. He sees faculty attitudes toward the adoption of such innovations as crucial for their success and thinks that adequate rewards and positive experiences for the first faculty members who get involved will make acceptance more rapid.

Some Final Thoughts

What do all of these predictions, trends, and potential developments mean to those of us in distance education? For one thing, the large number of adult clients to be served means that greater opportunities for educational experiences will be required. Informal learning and traditional adult education will continue to help, but distance education needs to and will move ahead and serve many other adults and their learning needs. Distance education can fit into adults' busy schedules and provide knowledge, skill, and attitudes so vital to adults and their well-being.

As distance education continues to develop, specialized staff with media and instructional design backgrounds will need to be trained and utilized. Many other postsecondary educators of all persuasions will need to be trained, retrained, and brought into the process. Educators must first recognize the potential and efficacy of distance education. They must understand the philosophy and methodology of distance education. They must recognize existing and emerging technologies that could help distance education and must not consider these technologies a threat but as an adjunct to the traditional instructional process (Garrison, 1989). And they must be motivated and encouraged to try this alternative mode of educational delivery. The development of staff or the training of distance educators, not touched on significantly in this text, must be emphasized so that educators can gain the new required behaviors of teaching at a distance.

New and existing interactive media must be incorporated into the learning experience. However, these media must be capable of supporting feedback to adult clients (Garrison, 1989) in order to provide for the dialogue/support concept so vital to learning. With the increase in media utilization, media must somehow be made available to adults through learning centers, organizational designs, and administrative philosophies of both distance and traditional institutions.

Innovation and testing in educational designs, structures, and procedures need to be emphasized. The embryonic nature of distance education in the United States requires that development, testing, and evaluation be continued to afford adults more and better learning opportunities. Innovation will be critical to developing the new alternatives needed for delivering distance education (Garrison, 1989).

It appears evident that greater interaction between traditional adult education, discussed throughout this text, and distance education needs to take place. Although adult education is further advanced than distance education here in the United States, the cooperative interaction could benefit distance education. In fact, Garrison (1989) sees a strong interrelationship between the two fields because of similarities in missions and believes professionals from both domains should work together to provide more learning opportunities for adult clients.

Finally, adults must have greater access to education within the structure of distance education. Adults currently participate in many self-help experiences and informal and incidental learning. This will continue in the future. However, distance education can help these and many other adults, from rural to urban, from young to old, and from rich to poor, where perhaps other delivery systems cannot. And with greater access to formal distance education, regardless of existing boundaries and domains, perhaps adults can better meet their learning needs in a more appropriate manner. This is no easy task either, but certainly one worthy of our attention and best efforts.

Summary

There is an urgent need in the United States for more and better adult education in the near future, as the gap between the education of workers and the skills required for jobs continues to grow. Distance education may play an important role in this effort, which will occur during a period of slower growth when such cost-effective methods may gain in importance.

The future of distance education and related fields has been the subject of considerable speculation in recent years. Media will continue to become more diverse, but new media will be more costly than those they replace, which may result in a narrowing of access. Distance educators should strive for equal access and quality despite the dilemma created when access, a major rationale for distance education, meets cost, which may render interactive media out of the reach of many individuals. Those teaching at a distance should recognize incidental and distance learners as target audiences, just as enrolled students already are, since such nonformal use of media may lead to participation in distance or conventional education.

Although the use of exotic techniques may become common, many low-technology media, especially print, will continue to be used to serve educational functions. Learning centers, consortia, and other cost-sharing innovations will be needed to maximize access to distance education. And innovation and research in distance education must receive new support if the field is to reach its full potential. These are not small tasks, but the potential of distance education for adults in the United States makes trying to accomplish them a worthwhile effort.

Resource:
Academic Achievement
in Distance and
Higher Education

The overview of academic achievement studies in Chapter Five included only meta-analyses and reviews, not individual studies. In the Resource, available studies located through ERIC and through the periodical holdings of the Morris Library, Southern Illinois University, Carbondale, are presented. Most of these items were located by the second author during preparation of his master's thesis.

The Resource has four sections, devoted to comparing academic achievement of conventional education with television, computer-based, videodisc, and correspondence study. The methodological rigor of the studies varies greatly, and most cannot be called truly experimental since they do not involve choosing subjects for the experimental and control groups. However, the more recent studies, which are in general more rigorous, reach much the same conclusions as do the bulk of the studies—that distance education methods achieve similar, if not superior, results when compared with conventional methods of teaching.

Television Study

Stromberg, E. L. "College Credit for Television Home Study." *American Psychologist*, 1942, 7, 507–509.

Sixty-six Western Reserve University students watched an introductory psychology telecourse in their homes during the fall semester of 1951. The course consisted of thirty-nine televised lectures, written assignments, and an on-campus final examination. Of those students who did not drop the course in the first few weeks (thirty-five of fifty-three students), 66 percent completed the course and took the exam. The final was a 110-question multiple-choice examination that had been administered to students in the on-campus conventional course for the past few years. On-campus students had a median score of 54 and a range of from 31 to 95. The telecourse students scored from 35 to 95, with a median score of 68, significantly higher than the median score of conventional students over the period the examination had been given.

Husband, R.W. "Television Versus Classroom for Learning General Psychology." *American Psychologist*, 1954, *9*, 181–183.

Fifty-four Iowa State College students (fifty women and four men) watched a course in general psychology on television in their homes during the winter quarter of 1953. They were one of four groups taking the same class from the same teacher (Husband). The other groups included a class that was present in the studio during the live TV lectures; a class that watched films of the TV lectures and participated in twenty minutes of discussion afterwards; and the conventional class, actually two groups taught face-to-face by the same instructor. No demographic information was provided except for the at-home viewers. Retention of at-home students was extremely high—fifty-six students originally registered, and fifty-four completed the course. The retention rate was 98 percent. The typical at-home student was a thirty-seven-year-old housewife with two children, currently unemployed and with no prior college credit. The at-home group achieved better grades for the course than all the on-campus classes except the class viewing films.

Meierhenry, W. C. *A Study of Teaching by Television Under Two Conditions*. Lincoln, Nebr.: University of Nebraska Press, 1955.

At the University of Nebraska in 1954, twelve students viewed a kinescope lecture on TV at home and twelve viewed the same kinescope lecture in a campus classroom. Each group saw twenty-eight filmed lecture-demonstrations that were thirty minutes in length, read the same assignments in the textbook, and took the same final examination. The on-campus group held discussions for twenty minutes after each film, and the off-campus group turned in written assignments.

There was no significant difference between the scores of the two groups on the final exam. Retention rates for both groups appear to have been 100 percent.

Lepore, A. R., and Wilson, J. D. *Project Number Two: An Experimental Method of College Instruction Using Broadcast Television*. San Francisco: San Francisco State College Press, 1958.

This study compared the performance of three groups of students—those watching TV at home, those watching TV in the classroom, and those receiving conventional instruction—who were taught by the same instructor in six college credit courses at San Francisco State College. A total of 1,261 students taking classes in science, English, and creative arts took part in the study. Students learning by TV at home or in the classroom were matched with students receiving conventional face-to-face instruction. The students in both groups watching TV compared favorably with the conventional students in five of the six subjects. Students of high, low, and average ability learned equally well when taught by TV or conventional methods. No study date, demographic breakdown, or completion rates were given.

Grant, T. S., and Merrill, I. R. *Television in Health Sciences Education*. San Francisco: University of California Medical Center Press, 1963.

In this study, nurses, 40 in each of three cities, were equally divided into groups of 20 home and 20 hospital classroom viewers. Each group watched two programs on each of three medical topics—emotional illness, emphysema, and cerebral-vascular accidents. Each broadcast was twenty-eight minutes in length and included ten questions. Hospital and home groups, all female, were equated in terms of age, number of children, and hospital work shift. The programs were broadcast for six weeks beginning on April 16, 1963. Dropout rates were 9.2 percent for hospital groups and 9.0 percent for home groups. An evaluation session held during the seventh week in each city revealed that learning was greater for those in the home viewing group that for those who watched as a group in the hospital.

Janes, R. W., and McIntyre, C. J. *Televised Instruction in University Residence Halls with Trained Undergraduates as Discussion Leaders.* Urbana: University of Illinois Press, 1964.

In this study, 3,511 students—2,540 in campus classrooms and 971 in residence halls—watched a televised four-credit introductory social science course twice a week or attended a live class. Most of the students (83–89 percent each semester) were women, and almost all were freshmen or sophomores. When the twelve midterm and final examinations offered in the course during the three years of the study were compared, students in live or TV lecture classes performed significantly better on only one of the tests. No significant difference in performance between the residence hall and classroom groups was found on the other eleven tests. Residence hall viewers watched as individuals with no monitoring of attendance. Completion rates were not given.

Grimmet, G. "Improving the Skills of Remote Teachers." In O. MacKenzie, R. Postgate, and J. Scupham (eds.), *Open Learning.* Paris: United Nations Educational, Scientific, and Cultural Organization (UNESCO), 1975.

Grimmet reported the results of a study of the academic achievement of 177 students who watched an introductory course in psychology on television at off-campus group viewing sites at the University of Newfoundland in Canada. These students were compared with 124 day and 78 evening students who took the same course in conventional on-campus classes during the same 1969–70 school year. Grimmet noted, "In all cases the dropout rate was extremely low (5 percent or less) and in the final marks there appeared to be no significant difference between the performance of the various groups" (pp. 133–134).

Agler, L. S. *Evaluation of the English 101 Telecourse "Writing for a Reason."* Dallas, Tex.: Dallas County Community College District, 1976. (ED 136 868)

Agler compared the academic achievement of all telecourse learners and twelve representative on-campus classes taking English 101 in the Dallas County Community College District during spring semester of 1976. No significant difference was found between the grades of the two groups. The telecourse students averaged 2.8 on a four-point scale (*B* minus), and the classroom students averaged 2.7. Eighty-seven percent of the conventional students completed the course, and about 55 percent of the telecourse students had completed their work by the cutoff date.

Agler, L. S. and Linn, T. B. *Telecourses in Dallas: The First Three Years.* Dallas, Tex.: Dallas County Community College District, 1976. (ED 126 969)

This study of eight telecourses offered in the Dallas County Community College District from 1972 through 1975 suggested that the new telecourse program had problems to overcome. Students in equivalent on-campus classes performed better in all eight subjects. Overall, classroom student pass rates were significantly higher than telecourse student pass rates. In one course, only 40 percent of telecourse students passed. This is the only study comparing distance and conventional education we have found that portrays distance achievement as highly inferior. It is important to consider that distance students dropping out after a deadline or failing to complete a course by a deadline may have been given failing grades. Most programs seem to use more open requirements. The student populations being studied may also have been extremely different demographically or academically.

Brown, L. A. *Employment of an Open Learning Course with Traditional and Nontraditional Learners.* Working Paper, No.

13. Lincoln, Nebr.: University of Mid-America Press, 1976. (ED
159 966)

The final grades of 151 telecourse students enrolled in an
introductory accounting course at the State University of Nebraska/
University of Mid-America during the fall semester of 1974 were
compared with the grades of 61 University of Nebraska, Lincoln,
students taking the same course and using the same course materials
in conventional classes during the spring semester of 1975. Ninety-
six percent of the students in both groups passed, and telecourse
students averaged *B* grades while classroom students averaged *C+*
grades. Completion rates were not given.

Dallas Community College District. *Evaluation of the Business
Telecourse, "It's Everybody's Business."* Dallas, Tex.: Dallas
County Community College District, 1977. (ED 143 382)

During the fall semester of 1976, 216 telecourse students and
98 classroom students taking an introductory business course with
the same teacher were given the same final achievement test as part
of the course evaluation. While both groups mastered the course
objectives, the telecourse students' mean score, 89.9 out of 100, was
significantly higher than the 80.0 mean score of the classroom students (p. 1). Females and older students attained higher scores in
both groups. Telecourse students were on average six years older
than classroom students. Classroom and telecourse students twenty-
eight years old or older outscored their younger classmates by an
average of 91 to 80. Age was apparently a factor in the higher mean
score of telecourse students. Completion rates were not given.

Hult, R. E. "The Effectiveness of University Television Instruction
and Factors Influencing Student Attitudes." *College Student
Journal*, 1980, *14*, 5–7.

Ninety-six students enrolled in a graduate-level course in human development at the University of Southern California were
divided into three groups. One group watched a telecourse version
of the class with no instructor contact. The second group also

watched the telecourse but had instructor contact. The third group attended a regular class in the subject. Hult maintained tight control over variables such as instructor, course materials, course content, and final examinations. Examination results did not significantly differ among the three groups. The date of the survey and completion rates are not available.

Mount, G., and Walters, S. "Traditional Versus Televised Instructional Methods for Introductory Psychology." *Journal of Educational Technology Systems,* 1980, *9,* 45–53.

In this study, the academic performance of students watching a telecourse and students in the classroom taking an introductory psychology course at Mountain View College (Texas) was compared. Telecourse students achieved significantly higher test scores. Information on variables affecting achievement was not available.

Smith, J. "Evaluation of the Telecourse Program at Saddleback College: Student Retention and Academic Retention." Unpublished doctoral dissertation, Nova University, 1983. (ED 239 684)

About 120 telecourse students and students taking the same four courses on campus were compared in terms of scores on the final examination. The same instructor taught both telecourse and classroom students in this study conducted during the spring semester of 1983 at Saddleback Community College (California). There was no significant difference in the final examination scores of the two groups of students in any of the courses studied. Completion rates of telecourse students were lower. Older and female students performed better in both groups.

Keston, C., and Burgess, J. *A System Evaluation of the University of Regina Project to 1984.* Saskatchewan, Canada: University of Regina, 1984. (ED 273 245)

Four courses were offered during the fall semester of 1984 at the University of Regina via live television transmission and telephone communication (one-way video, two-way audio). On-campus classes acted as the studio audience for the TV broadcasts concerning administration, computer science, and film. Off-campus students watched in groups at five locations. Fifty-seven students enrolled on campus and 114 off campus, for a total of 171 participants. On-campus students performed a little better academically—84.2 out of 100 as an average final exam score as opposed to 79.1 for off-campus students—but if only the grades of those who passed are counted, the grades are not significantly different. There was little difference in completion rates—about 11 percent of off-campus and 12 percent of on-campus students dropped the course. Both groups were referred to as adult students, but no demographic breakdowns were given.

Computer-Based Study

Because there are so many studies of computer instruction versus classroom instruction, only large-scale reviews and meta-analyses of conventional versus computer higher education were included in Chapter Five. Three individual studies that did not fall within the scope of previous reviews and analyses are presented here. All three are concerned with adult education at a distance. Most computer instruction studies (as opposed to face-to-face, classroom studies) are difficult to classify as distance or conventional since the teacher may be present in the learning environment, but these three are clearly examples of distance versus conventional study.

Schwartz, H. A., and Haskell, R. J., Jr. "A Study of Computer-Assisted Training in Industrial Training." *Journal of Applied Psychology,* 1966, *50* (5), 360–363.

The authors compared the academic performance of twenty-five electronic technicians who learned from a remotely located computer with the achievement of seventy-nine control students who studied programmed texts. No significant differences in exam scores were observed, although the distance group (computer group) had slightly higher scores.

Schwartz, H. A., and Long, H. S. "A Study of Remote Industrial Training via Computer-Assisted Instruction." *Journal of Applied Psychology,* 1967, *51* (1), 14–17.

In this subsequent experiment, the control group did significantly better, but as in the 1966 study, the distance group working on the computer took 30 percent less time to complete the course.

Broussard, R. L. "Homebased Computer Assisted Adult Education Project—Phase III." Unpublished manuscript, University of Southwestern Louisiana, 1983. (ED 234 181)

This is the only example of computer distance study compared with conventional education that was located in the adult education literature. ABE educators in Lafayette Parish, Louisiana, conducted three one-year phases of home-based CAI. Traditional students outperformed those using computer-assisted instruction at home in 1980–81, but the group using computers significantly outperformed the control group in the second phase, 1981–82, and also exceeded the control group by a borderline significant amount the last year of the project. Overall, the CAI group performed somewhat better than the control group.

Videodisc-Based Study

Holmgren, J. E., Dyer, P. N., Hilligos, R. E., and Heller, F. H. "The Effectiveness of Army Training Extension Course Lessons on Videodisc." *Educational Technology Systems,* 1979, *8* (3), 263–274.

The authors compared the test scores of 298 soldiers who were given short periods of instruction—two or three lessons—in their military specialty. Soldiers from each specialty were randomly placed in four treatment groups. The first group watched a film, the second watched a standard videodisc, the third watched a modified videodisc that allowed them to replay sections, and the fourth group received no instruction but took the final exam. The groups watching the videodisc scored significantly higher than the group watching the film, which in turn scored significantly higher than the group receiving no training. However, students watching the modified videodisc did not show the expected superiority over those watching the standard videodisc.

Bunderson, V.C.A., Olsen, J. B., and Baillio, B. *"Proof of a Concept Demonstration and Comparative Evaluation of a Prototype Interactive Videodisc System."* Orem, Utah: WICAT Systems, 1981. (Mimeographed.) (ED 228 989)

The authors of the study recounted a study funded by the National Science Foundation in which students taking an introductory-level university biology course by interactive videodisc scored significantly higher on a reliable post-test than a control group taught using the traditional text-and-lecture method. The average total study time required by the group watching the videodisc was 37 percent less than that needed by the conventionally taught control group.

Gibbons, A. S., Olsen, J. B., and Cavagnol, R. "HAWK Training Systems Evaluation Report." In M. Debloois, K. C. Maki, and A. F. Hall (eds.), *Effectiveness of Interactive Videodisc Training.* Falls Church, Va.: Future Systems, 1983. (ED 278 370)

In this study, three groups of students were trained in the use of the HAWK ground-to-air missile system. The first group, sixteen students, received conventional instruction. The second group, ten students, received lessons from the videodisc training system. The third group, twenty students, received both lessons and simulation problems on videodisc. All of the students from the groups using videodisc solved a test problem after training, but only 25 percent of the students in the first group could solve the problem. Students in the third group, who had simulation experience, completed the problem in half the time taken by group two, which received lessons alone.

Bush, M. "Personal Conversations with M. Debloois About USAF Academy Videodisc Training Study." In M. Debloois, K.C. Maki, and A.F. Hall, (eds.), *Effectiveness of Interactive Videodisc Training*. Falls Church, Va.: Future Systems, 1983. (ED 278 370)

The author found that when twenty air force cadets were split into groups watching interactive and noninteractive videodiscs and were taught German, the group watching the interactive video-disc achieved significantly higher scores than the group watching the noninteractive program.

DeBloois, M. "The Final Report and Documentation of the Simu-lation and Training in Agriculture Project (SIMTAB)." In M. Debloois, K. C. Maki, and A. F. Hall, (eds.), *Effectiveness of Interactive Videodisc Training*. Falls Church, Va.: Future Sys-tems, 1983. (ED 278 370)

DeBloois offered an interactive version of "simulation train-ing in agribusiness" to twenty randomly assigned dairy farmers. Another twenty were given a noninteractive version of the same course, prepared by the same designer, and accompanied by an il-lustrated workbook. Instruction took place in a mobile van at the farm site. Post-test but not pretest scores of the two groups were significantly different. The group using the interactive videodisc made a large learning gain. This research is interesting, but it might have been more convincing if the author had included completion rates, numbers of subjects in each treatment, same or different in-structor, and other variables considered important in determining validity.

Gale, L. "Evaluation of the Effectiveness of Student Controlled In-teractive Videodisc Lesson." In M. Debloois, K.C. Maki, and A.F. Hall, (eds.), *Effectiveness of Interactive Videodisc Training*. Falls Church, Va.: Future Systems, 1983. (ED 278 370)

The author reported on a study in which a control group watched a Spanish-language videotape, and the experimental group viewed the same material on an interactive videodisc system that asked questions at critical points in the presentation. The experimental group scored significantly higher than the control group on a 200-item multiple-choice test.

Crotty, Jill M. "Instruction via an Intelligent Videodisc System Versus Classroom Instruction for Beginning College French Students: A Comparative Experiment (Computer)." Unpublished doctoral dissertation, University of Kansas, 1984.

Seventy air force academy cadets enrolled in a beginning French course were assigned randomly to videodisc, classroom, or no instruction groups. Groups one and two received ninety minutes of instruction. All groups were then given a twenty-item test. Subjects receiving videodisc instruction scored slightly better than their classroom counterparts, but the difference was not significant.

Pieper, W. J. *Interactive Graphics Simulator: Design, Development, and Effectiveness/Cost Evaluation.* Lowry Air Force Base, Colo.: U.S. Air Force, 1984. (ED 253 211)

The author compared twenty-two students using videodisc-based simulation training with twenty-one students using a conventional equipment trainer to learn procedural equipment operation troubleshooting activities. No significant differences were found between the two groups in performance on exams, ability to perform procedural equipment operation, or field assignment readiness, but the group using the videodisc did significantly better on the troubleshooting test.

Stevens, S. M. "Surrogate Laboratory Experiments: Interactive Computer/Videodisc Lessons and Their Effect on Students' Understanding of Science." Unpublished doctoral dissertation, University of Nebraska, 1984.

The author studied the performance of forty-nine subjects enrolled in an introductory college physics course at George Mason University. Twenty-seven were assigned to the control group and received traditional laboratory instruction while the twenty-two experimental subjects used an interactive videodisc program. On both task performance and a test of course content, no significant difference in performance was found between the two groups.

Wankel, M. J. "Student Performance on Cognitive and Content Tests: A Comparison of Optical Videodiscs to Laboratory Learning in College Physics." Unpublished doctoral dissertation, University of Nebraska, 1984.

Wankel used randomly assigned matched subjects, thirty as controls and thirty in an experimental group, in an experiment that gauged the learning of specific physics concepts through actual and simulated laboratory work. Students were quizzed on their understanding of the standing wave phenomenon before and after using their simulated or real laboratory resources. Groups using videodisc and traditional lab equipment had similar post-test scores.

Gale, B. G. *Nebraska Videodisc Science Laboratory Simulations.* Lincoln, Nebr.: University of Nebraska, 1985 (ED 264 821)

The author described a field test at seven American colleges and universities of six videodiscs containing laboratory experiments in undergraduate biology, chemistry, and physics. A total of 506 students performed experiments via videodisc while 183 did their experimentation in a traditional "wet" laboratory. Since graduate assistants are usually employed in the several labs for one professor, it seems likely (although it is not stated) that different instructors were used in control and experimental groups. Only two of the seven schools involved randomly assigned students to one of the two treatments. Despite the variable conditions, it appeared that "videodisc students performed as well as or better than their 'wet' counterparts" (p. 7).

Balson, P. M., and others. "Videodisc Instructional Strategies: Simple May Be Superior to Complex." *Journal of Educational Technology Systems,* 1986, *14* (4), 273–282.

The author randomly selected 246 subjects from an entering group of 500 army paramedic trainees. Three groups were subdivided into sections and then taught in one of three ways: the first group was taught conventionally, with a videodisc played through once as an audiovisual aid; the second group had limited access, through the instructor, to preplanned segments in the videodisc program; the last group was taught by an instructor, with full access to the videodisc programs. The second and third groups received significantly higher scores on performance tests than the conventional group using the videodisc only as an audiovisual aid, but the group with full access to the videodisc did not do better than the group with limited access.

Dalton, D. W. "The Efficacy of Computer-Assisted Video Instruction on Rule Learning and Attitudes." *Journal of Computer-Based Information*, 1986, *13* (4), 122–125.

    Dalton compared videodisc with CAI and stand-alone video instruction. The 134 subjects in the study (64 females and 70 males) were chosen from six junior high shop classes. Forty-eight subjects were given interactive videodisc instruction. Forty-two were taught by CAI, and forty-four were instructed by a linear video (video played straight through) alone. The content and methods of instruction used in the three versions were extremely similar. The groups using CAI and interactive videodisc outperformed subjects receiving the video alone, but the students using CAI outperformed those using interactive videodisc by a statistically insignificant amount. This, however, is a K-12 study.

Smith, S. G., Jones, L. L., and Waugh, M. L. "Production and Evaluation of Interactive Videodisc Lessons in Laboratory Instruction." *Journal of Computer-Based Information*, 1986, *13* (4), 117–121.

    This study used a videodisc to provide prelaboratory instruction and to simulate a laboratory experiment. Videodisc instruction was given to forty-seven students, and fifty-six students received a prelaboratory written assignment and then undertook the same experiment in the laboratory that was simulated for the group using videodisc. Students who used the videodisc lessons scored significantly better on a lab report and quiz than did students who prepared a traditional lab report and performed an actual laboratory experiment.

Correspondence Study: U.S. Studies

Because international achievement studies often compare conventional education with a mixed "external" method of educational delivery, including both correspondence study and off-campus education, this section has been broken down into two parts: U.S. studies and international studies.

Ziegel, W. H. "The Relation of Extra-Mural Study to Residential Enrollment and Scholastic Standing." Unpublished doctoral dissertation, George Peabody College for Teachers, 1924.

Writing about Ziegel's work, Mathieson (1971) says, "This monumental study is of more than historical importance because (1) it applied statistical analysis for the first time on a comprehensive basis in correspondence study research; (2) the population sample used was a fairly large one; and (3) it examined many variables not examined since" (p. 14).

Ziegel used a population sample from five state teachers colleges in Missouri and Illinois to study the relation of extension and correspondence study to resident enrollment and scholastic standing. He found that "when the three types of study are compared, grades are lowest in residence study, medium in extension study, and highest in correspondence study" (Mathieson, 1971, p. 14). Ziegel found that age and grade level were chiefly responsible for the fact that students with residence *and* extension or correspondence study had higher grades than students with residence study only. The time of the study and completion rates were not available.

Schwin, M. L. "Analysis of Correspondence Course Grades in the University of Colorado." Unpublished master's thesis, University of Colorado, 1929.

Schwin surveyed records at the University of Colorado for her master's thesis and concluded that the average grades made in correspondence courses were higher than the average grades made in all university courses. This finding was tempered by a 50 percent dropout rate by correspondence students and the fact that correspondence students usually took first-year or second-year courses. Dropout rates for conventional students were not available. The date of the study was not given.

Feig, C. A. "The Effectiveness of Correspondence Study." Unpublished doctoral dissertation, Pennsylvania State University, 1932.

Feig's doctoral dissertation included a comparison at several universities of the academic achievement of correspondence students and on-campus students taking the same course with the same instructor. He concluded that correspondence students performed better in terms of academic achievement than did their on-campus counterparts. Age was a possible factor. Feig also found that correspondence students on the whole had better grades than resident students. Completion rates and the time period of the study were not available (study cited in Mathieson, 1971).

Ames, B. W. "A Study of Correspondence Instruction Based on Eleven Years of University Extension Work at the University of Florida." Unpublished master's thesis, University of Florida, 1932.

Ames compared the work of correspondence and resident students at the University of Florida from 1919 through 1931. He used enrollment data and the grades of 868 correspondence students in reaching the conclusion that grades earned by correspondence and resident students were fairly uniform, with no appreciable difference in standards (study cited in Mathieson, 1971).

Crump, R. E. "Correspondence and Class Extension in Oklahoma." Unpublished doctoral dissertation, Columbia University, 1928.

Crump's doctoral dissertation was a comparative evaluation of correspondence, extension, and residence work at Oklahoma colleges and universities from 1909 through 1928. As part of this study, groups of students were taught a course in psychology by the same teacher using one of the three instructional methods. It is not clear from existing records where this study occurred. On the basis of achievement testing, no significant differences were observed in student retention of knowledge among the three methods. (Study cited in Mathieson, 1971.)

Larson, E. L. "The Comparative Quality of Work Done by Students in Residence and in Correspondence Work." *Journal of Educational Research*, 1936, *25*, 105–109.

Larson examined the grades of fifty-six University of Arizona students who had taken both residence work and correspondence courses. The grades earned in correspondence study tended to be slightly higher than those earned by the same students in residence study. The time period of the study and completion rates were not available. (Study cited in Mathieson, 1971.)

McDowell, J. "An Experimental Study of the Effect of Supervised Correspondence Lessons on Achievement in Academic Subjects." Unpublished doctoral dissertation, University of Oklahoma, 1940.

McDowell studied paired samples of students taking supervised correspondence courses and students who had taken correspondence courses but who now were taking only residence courses. He did not find that correspondence work had any significant effect on later residence work, but he did find that students achieved grades approximately one letter grade higher in their correspondence work than in their residence work. Time period of the study and completion rates were not available. (Study cited in Mathieson, 1971.)

Dysinger, D., and Bridgeman, C. S. "Performance of Correspondence Students." *Journal of Higher Education*, 1957, *27*, 387–388.

In this study an instructor in 1955 at the University of Wisconsin taught introductory psychology to 167 conventional and 41 correspondence students using the same text and giving certain multiple-choice questions to both groups of students on the final examination. No significant difference was found between the achievement of the two groups on those final examination questions even when students were compared on the basis of age or ability.

Allen, C., and Wedemeyer, C. A. *Extending to the People*. Madison, Wis.: University of Wisconsin-Extension, 1957. (ED 016 185)

Writing in a book commemorating the first fifty years of the University of Wisconsin-Extension, Allen and Wedemeyer chronicled UWEX's tremendous success in extending the "boundaries of the university to the boundaries of the state" (p. 13) through many modes of educational delivery, including vocational courses and academic courses at both the high school and college levels. Comparing the success of correspondence and resident students in the University of Wisconsin system from 1907 through 1957, they state: "Because of the way in which Extension teaching is related to residence teaching, a comparison of teaching results can be made. Such comparisons consistently indicate that instruction by correspondence is at least as effective as resident classroom instruction" (p. 13).

The overall completion rate for correspondence courses was only about 55 percent during this period, although for-credit students had "much higher" completion rates (p. 14). The completion rate of conventional courses was not given.

Parsons, T. S. "A Comparison of Instruction by Kinescope, Correspondence Study, and Customary Class Procedures." *Journal of Educational Psychology*, 1957, *48* (1), 27–40.

Parsons had forty university upperclassmen divide into two groups. Twenty enrolled in developmental psychology and twenty enrolled in an unrelated course in the psychology department to serve as controls. The twenty subjects in the experimental group were then randomly assigned to one of three groups: correspondence study, kinescope (TV) study, and regular instruction. All groups were taught by Parsons. Borderline significant differences favoring correspondence study over the other two methods in terms of academic achievement were reported both at the end of the course and as a result of follow-up testing four months later. Completion rates were not given.

Spencer, O. "Factors Associated with Persons Who Complete Correspondence Courses." *The Home Study Review*, 1965, 5 (4), 10–24.

Spencer evaluated the grades received in all credit and noncredit courses by all correspondence students (a total of 3,303 grades) at the Pennsylvania State University between July 1, 1962, and June 30, 1963. The grades earned by correspondence students in credit courses were better than those earned by full-time students during the spring term of 1963. Completion rates were not given. (Study cited in Childs, 1966, as quoted in Wakatama, 1983.)

Thordarson, T. W. "Classroom Versus Correspondence Instruction." In R. S. Sims (ed.), *Research in the Correspondence Instruction Field*. Madison, Wis.: U.S. Armed Forces Institute Press, 1967.

Four hundred students taking freshman high school subjects by supervised correspondence study in rural schools were compared with students taking the same subjects conventionally in city schools during a five and one half month experimental period. Both groups compared favorably on standarized tests with the average achievement of freshmen throughout the nation in all subjects measured.

Crissy, W.S.E. "Evaluation of Effectiveness of Naval Officers Correspondence Courses." *The Home Study Review*, 1966, 7, 22–35.

In order to evaluate the effectiveness of a correspondence course entitled "Security of Classified Matter," an experimental group of 115 naval officers taking the course by correspondence was tested for knowledge of the course's content immediately after and four months after completing the three-assignment course. Similar tests were administered to 475 officers who had completed the course through regular classroom study and 472 officers who had recent security experience related to the course's content. Two control groups of 115 and 128 officers with no knowledge of the contents of the course were also tested. Those subjects learning in the classroom or by experiential means had scores no higher, on average, than those who studied by correspondence. (Study cited in Macken, Vanden Heuval, Suppes, and Suppes, 1976.)

Green, G. F., Jr. "The Effectiveness of a Correspondence-Study Method for Teaching Mathematics to In-Service Elementary School Teachers Using Programmed Instruction and Television." Unpublished doctoral dissertation, Florida State University, 1967.

Green studied an independent-study-style system at Florida State University used to teach in-service teachers both in conventional classes and by correspondence. A pretest was administered to 142 subjects enrolled in her mathematics classes after four conventional classroom lessons. On the basis of this test, students were labeled low, middle, or high achievers. Each of the five classes was divided into two sections that closely approximated each other in terms of the previous achievement of its members. Seventy-seven subjects completed the next six lessons by correspondence while 65 control subjects took the same lessons in class. A common test was then administered and a retention test was given six weeks later. Differences between the two groups on each test were not statistically significant. (Study cited in Childs, 1971.)

Willingham, J. "A 'Correspondence-Tutorial' Method of Teaching Freshman-College Composition." Washington, D.C.: Office of Education, U.S. Department of Health, Education, and Welfare, 1967.

Willingham compared the academic achievement of two control groups and an experimental group of students in a freshman English class at the University of Kansas each semester during 1963 through 1967. The experimental group met with an instructor once a week for tutoring but otherwise studied mainly by correspondence. One control group followed the traditional classroom method, meeting three times a week with an instructor using lectures and discussion groups, while the other control group was exempted from freshman composition that semester and studied literature instead. Forty students were involved the first year, 80 the second, and 160 in each of the last two years. Numbers in the control groups were comparable. Based on final examinations, papers, and other measures of achievement, the author concluded that "there was no significant difference among the groups involved and that students in Freshman Composition learned equally well in all three groups." Completion rates were not given. (Study cited in Childs, 1971.)

Correspondence Study: International Studies

In Australia, distance education is part of an external study scheme that combines off-campus classes and distance study utilizing seminars and proctored examinations. In addition, internal study, which is very similar to conventional study at American universities is usually available on campus.

While the addition of off-campus classes to the equation makes the external/internal comparison less pure, a comparison is nonetheless useful in that the effectiveness of distance and off-campus classroom study combined may be compared with the effectiveness of on-campus classroom study.

Goodman, R. D. "A Case Study of an Innovation in University Teaching." In R. D. Goodman and others (eds.), *Trends in External Higher Education.* Honolulu: East-West Center/ UNESCO, 1972.

Goodman surveyed the pass rates of internal (day and evening) and external students in seven subjects at the University of Queensland (Australia) in 1965. On average, the day students had a pass rate of 82 percent; the evening students, 76.6 percent; and the external students, 80.0 percent. When the rates of the day and evening students (without knowing the exact number of students) were averaged to get one internal pass rate, this rate, 79.3 percent, was a shade lower than the pass rate of the external students, 80.0 percent.

Freyberg, P. S. "Higher Education Through Correspondence Training in New Zealand." In *Trends in External Higher Education.* Honolulu: East-West Center/UNESCO, 1972.

At Massey University in New Zealand, external or extramural students take part in a fairly rigid distance education scheme that involves submitting written assignments on a regular basis and participating in intensive summer seminars. This system has produced good results, according to Freyberg: "One indication of the success of any correspondence teaching program is the proportion of students who are sufficiently encouraged by teaching and their own performance to complete their courses, whether or not they actually pass the final examination. . . . In the first six years of the Massey University program the proportion of students attempting the final examination increased from 51 percent to 71 percent.

"In those courses offered to both internal and external students, the examination pass rate if all the subjects are considered together, has differed very little. The median difference over a six year period, for example, has been found to be only four percent (in favor of internal students) and in some subjects extra-mural students have consistently achieved at least as high standards as their internal colleagues" (1972, pp. 8-9).

Glatter, R., and Wedell, E. G. *Study by Correspondence.* London: Longmans, 1971.

These investigators conducted a retrospective survey comparing 960 correspondence and 840 part-time conventional students who sat for postsecondary qualification examinations in England in 1963. Of the correspondence students, 23.96 percent, and of the part-time students, 28.21 percent passed both parts of their examinations (p. 321). Glatter and Wedell concluded that there was "little difference in examination performance and the incidence of dropout between students whose main study method was correspondence and those who were following mainly a part-time oral course" (p. 114).

Fawdry, K. "University Distance Teaching Centers in Eastern France." In N. MacKenzie, R. Postgate, and J. Scupham (eds.), *Open Learning*. Paris: UNESCO, 1975.

Fawdry. looked at achievement statistics at France's Centres de Télé-enseignement Universitaire (CTU), l'Entente Universitaire de l'Est (Distance Learning Centers, Association of Eastern Universities). Among the approximately 2,000 students of the CTUs in eastern France, pass rates during the years 1971–1973 averaged 57 percent for first-year students, 58 percent for second-year students, and 69 percent for third-year students. CTU candidates achieve "if anything slightly better results on their examinations than do conventional students. . . . The proportion of dropouts, on the other hand, is a little higher in the case of CTU students" (p. 1).

Kinyanjui, P. E. "Kenya: The Use of Radio and Correspondence Education for the Improvement of Teaching." In O. MacKenzie, R. Postgate, and J. Scupham (eds.), *Open Learning*. Paris: UNESCO, 1975.

The Correspondence Course Unit (CCU) of the University of Nairobi in Kenya was established in 1966 with the help of the foremost U.S. postsecondary distance education provider, the University of Wisconsin-Extension, which was contracted to do the work by the U.S. Agency for International Development. Kinyanjui states:

> Since 1968 the CCU has carried out various analyses of students' performance in the KJSE (Kenyan Junior Secondary Examination—a national exam to certify previously uncertified primary school teachers). The results reveal that candidates who have studied with the CCU have performed better than other candidates sitting for the same examination [1975, p. 260].

The average pass rates for CCU candidates were 42 percent in 1968 and 46 percent in 1969, significantly higher than those of school candidates who achieved 16 to 30 percent in the various provinces, while private candidates averaged 8 to 15 percent pass rates. In 1970 when the government-aided schools averaged 47 percent, the unaided schools 20 percent, and the private candidates 13 percent, the CCU candidates achieved 51 percent pass rates.

> In looking at these figures it is perhaps unfair to compare the performance of private candidates with that of teachers, because, while the the former must pass in at least five subjects at one sitting, the latter are allowed to take examinations in individual subjects until they accumulate passes in five subjects [1975, p. 260].

While the performance of teachers studying by correspondence was superior to that of students studying conventionally, dropout rates were also high. How high was difficult to gauge, since many students did not study in order to take the KJSE, and no time limit was imposed on study. But a dropout rate of 15 to 25 percent was estimated (pp. 259-260).

Cook, W. L. "Practical Project Assessment Problems in Distance Teaching." In J. D. Armstrong and R. E. Store (eds.), *Evaluation in Distance Teaching*. Queensland, Australia: Townsville College of Advanced Education Press, 1980. (ED 223 125)

Cook studied the pass rates of 41 external and 15 internal students taking "Material Science III" at the Newcastle College of Advanced Education (Australia) from 1978 through 1980. He found no significant difference in pass rates—internal students averaged 67.8 percent and external students averaged 65.9—a marginal 1.9 percent difference.

Jevons, F. R. "How Different is the Distance Learner?" In J. S. Daniels (eds.), *Learning at a Distance: A World Perspective.* Edmonton, Canada: International Council for Correspondence Education, 1982. (ED 222 635)

At Deakin University (Australia) comparisons of students in the same courses revealed that off-campus students did marginally better than on-campus students. Jevons compared students in nine humanities and social science courses with off-campus enrollments of 100 or more students. He found no significant differences between student groups in terms of pass rates. Retention rates of off-campus students were slightly lower, 88 percent as compared to 92 percent for internal students, but off-campus students often achieved superior grades.

Misanchuk, E. R. "Correspondence Versus On-Campus Courses: Some Evaluative Comparisons." In I.J.S. Daniels (ed.), *Learning at a Distance: A World Perspective.* Edmonton, Canada: International Council for Correspondence Education, 1982. (ED 222 635)

At the University of Saskatchewan (Canada), Misanchuk conducted three studies in which he compared the performance of correspondence and on-campus students taking the same class. In the first study, the instructor made subjective comparisons of the coursework of nine students studying introductory computer science as part of a pilot project. In the second study, "probably the most rigorous and comprehensive of the three," thirty-eight students took a quantitative business analysis class (p. 122). In the on-campus class, the teacher met with students twice a week, but only to conduct brief quizzes and provide feedback. Both on- and off-campus students used the same independent study materials. Students' academic achievement in this summer session class was also compared with students' achievement in the regular class the previous spring term. Study three involved nine students taking an introductory sociology class either by correspondence or on campus. Misanchuk concluded that "the three studies indicate that independent study students achieve at least as well as on-campus students" (p. 124).

University of New England. *"All Students/Internal Students Units Overall 'Pass' Results."* Unpublished manuscripts. University of New England, Armidale, Australia, 1982, 1983.

This Australian university is perhaps the premiere external teaching university in the entire world. At the University of New England, external and internal students are taught and graded by the same teachers as a matter of policy. From 1955 through 1983, careful records were kept of the pass rates, retention rates, and superior grade rates of both external and internal students. Between 1955 and 1966, pass rates were exactly the same (Wakatama, 1983)— 77 percent for both external and internal students enrolled in the same courses. From about 1955 through 1976, pass rates of students in the same courses who actually sat for an examination were 82 percent for external students and 81 percent for internal students (Dahloff, 1977). Data were not available for the years 1977 through 1981. In 1982 and again in 1983, external pass rates were a little lower than internal pass rates. In 1982, the internal pass rate was 84.7 percent and the external, 82.5 percent—a 2.2 percent difference. The difference narrowed by 1983 to 1.7 percent—85.0 percent external and 83.3 percent internal. Most of the difference between internal and external pass rates in 1982 appears to have resulted from extreme variability between the pass rates within different overall groups of academic subjects studied.

Many of the problems seem to have been substantially remedied during the 1983 school year. It must be remembered that the differences in internal and external pass rates never were great enough to be significant, no matter which group was marginally behind or ahead.

Howard Sheath, the first director of external studies at the university, summarized the results of the ten-year experiment in distance education that he had been largely responsible for as follows: "There is strong evidence to suggest that the standards reached by external students are simply related to the quantity and quality of teaching provided and the extent to which follow-up action is taken throughout the year on students who fall behind in their work. When no teaching whatever is provided as is the case in some institutions, failure rates and withdrawals will be high. When tuition is provided through a highly developed external studies scheme, the performance of external students will not suffer in comparison with that of internal students" (Smith, 1975, quoted in Wakatama, 1983, p. 201).

References

Abrams, H. "Effectiveness of Interactive Video in Teaching Basic Photography Skills." Paper presented at the annual convention of the Association for Educational Communications and Technology, Las Vegas, Jan. 16–21, 1986. (ED 267 754)

Abrioux, D. "Nontraditional Education and Organizational Change: The Case of Athabasca University." Paper presented at the American Educational Research Association/American Society for Higher Education Conference, San Francisco, March 1984. (ED 252 114)

Acker, S. R., and Albarran, A. B. "Implementing ISDN: A Sociotechnical Analysis." Paper presented at the annual conference of the International Communication Association, New Orleans, May 1988. (ED 303 138)

Aggasiz, E. C. "Society to Encourage Studies at Home." In O. MacKenzie (ed.), *The Changing World of Correspondence Study*. University Park: Pennsylvania State University Press, 1971.

Alderfer, C. P. *Existence, Relatedness, and Growth*. New York: Free Press, 1972.

Andrews, K. G. "A Study of the Effectiveness of Instructional Feedback by Interactive Videodisc Instruction." Unpublished doctoral dissertation, University of Texas, Austin, 1985.

Apt, P. H., and Ebert, G. M. "Adult Student Adopters in Open Learning Courses." *Alternative Higher Education*, 1983, 7 (2), 91–94.

Arbeiter, S., Aslanian, C. B., Schmerbeck, F. A., and Brickell, H. M. *Telephone Counseling for Home-Based Adults*. New York: College Board, 1978.

241

Arthur, W. B. "Positive Feedbacks in the Economy." *Scientific American*, 1990, *262* (2), 92–99.

Aslanian, C. B., and Brickell, H. M. *How Americans in Transition Study for College Credit*. New York: College Entrance Examination Board, 1988.

Astin, A. W. "Assessment, Value-Added, and Educational Excellence." In D. F. Halpern (ed.), *Student Outcomes Assessment: What Institutions Stand to Gain*. New Directions for Higher Education, no. 59. San Francisco: Jossey-Bass, 1987.

Bääth, J. A. *Correspondence Education in the Light of a Number of Contemporary Teaching Models*. Malmö, Sweden: Liber Hermods, 1979.

Bääth, J. A., and Manson, N. *CADE—A System for Computer-Assisted Distance Education*. Malmö, Sweden: Liber Hermods, 1977.

Baldwin, T. F., and McVoy, D. S. *Cable Communication*. Englewood Cliffs, N.J.: Prentice-Hall, 1983.

Bartels, J. "Drop-out at the Distance University in the Federal Republic of Germany." Paper presented at the 22nd annual forum of the Association for Institutional Research, Denver, Colo., May 16–19, 1982. (ED 220 037)

Bates, A. W. "Trends in the Use of Audiovisual Media." In J. S. Daniel, M. A. Stroud, and J. R. Thompson (eds.), *Learning at a Distance: A World Perspective*. Edmonton, Canada: International Council for Distance Education/Athabasca University, 1982.

Bates, A. W. "Learning from Audiovisual Media." In *Student Learning from Different Media in the Open University*. Institutional Research Review, no. 1. Milton Keynes, England: Open University of the United Kingdom Press, 1984.

Bates, A. W. *Computer Assisted Learning or Communications: Which Way for Information Technology in Distance Education?* Information Technology Paper, no. 250. Walton, England: Institute of Educational Technology, Open University of the United Kingdom, 1986. (ED 234 131)

Bates, T. "The Growth of Technology in Distance Education." In A. W. Bates (ed.), *The Role of Technology in Distance Education*. London: Croom Helm, 1984a.

Bates, T. "Putting It Together: Now and the Future." In A. W. Bates (ed.), *The Role of Technology in Distance Education.* London: Croom Helm, 1984b.

Battenberg, R. W. *"The Boston Gazette,* March 20, 1728." *Epistolodidaktika,* 1971, *1,* 44–45.

Bear, J. *Bear's Guide to Earning Non-Traditional College Degrees.* (10th ed) Berkeley, Calif.: Ten Speed Press, 1988.

Beaudry, J. S. "A Meta-Analysis of Research on the Effectiveness of Continuing Medical Education." Unpublished doctoral dissertation, University of Illinois, Chicago, 1987.

Beder, H. "The Relation of Knowledge Sought to Appropriate Teaching Behavior in Adult Education." *Lifelong Learning,* 1985, *9* (1), 14–15, 27–28.

Bernstein, A. "Where the Jobs Are is Where the Skills Aren't." *Business Week,* Sept. 19, 1988, pp. 104–108.

Beshiri, P. A. "Answering the Critics: A Cooperative Study on External Degree and Traditional Graduates." *Alternative Higher Education,* 1978, *2* (3), 195–209.

Billings, D. H. "A Conceptual Model of Correspondence Course Completion." *American Journal of Distance Education,* 1988, *2* (2), 23–35.

Bills, R. E. "Perception and Learning." In A. Frazier (ed.), *Learning More About Learning.* Washington, D.C.: National Education Association/Association for Supervision and Curriculum Development, 1959.

Bloom, B. S. *Stability and Chance in Human Characteristics.* New York: Wiley, 1964.

Bloom, B. S., and others. *Taxonomy of Educational Objectives. The Classification of Educational Goals, Handbook 1: Cognitive Domain.* New York: McKay, 1956.

Board of Governors of State Colleges and Universities. *The Board of Governors Bachelor of Arts Degree Program.* Springfield, Ill.: Board of Governors of State Colleges and Universities, 1978.

Boles, H. W., and Davenport, J. A. *Introduction to Educational Leadership.* New York: Harper & Row, 1975.

Boles, H. W., and Davenport, J. A. *Introduction to Educational Leadership.* (Rev. ed.) Lanham, Md.: University Press of America, 1983.

Bonham, A. "Learning Style Instruments: Let the Buyer Beware." *Lifelong Learning,* 1987, *11* (9), 12–16.

Bostock, S. J., and Siefert, R. V. *Microcomputers in Adult Education.* London: Croom Helm, 1985.

Branch, C. E., Ledford, B. R., Robertson, B. T., and Robison, L. "The Validation of an Interactive Videodisc as an Alternative to Traditional Teaching Techniques." *Educational Technology,* 1987, *27* (3), 16–22.

Bratt, J. *Engelskundervisningens Framväxt Sverige, Tiden fore 1850.* Stockholm, Sweden: Föreningen för svensk undervisninghistoria, 1977.

Brey, R. *Telecourse Utilization Survey.* Washington, D.C.: American Association of Community and Junior Colleges, 1988. (ED 301 295)

Brey, R., and Grigsby, C. "Annenberg/CPB Project: A Study of Telecourse Students (Executive Summary) and Telecourse Student Survey." Washington, D.C.: Corporation for Public Broadcasting, 1984. (ED 264 825)

Brigham Young University. *Brigham Young University Bulletin 1989/1990.* Provo, Utah: Brigham Young University, 1989.

Brock, D. "PBS Tunes in to Adult Learning." In E. E. Miller and M. L. Mosley (eds.), *Educational Media and Technology Yearbook.* Vol. 2. Littleton, Colo.: Libraries Unlimited, 1985.

Brockett, R. G. "Postscript: Toward the New Century." In R. G. Brockett (ed.), *Continuing Education in the Year 2000.* New Directions for Continuing Education, no. 36. San Francisco: Jossey-Bass, 1987.

Brookfield, S. D. *Understanding and Facilitating Adult Learning.* San Francisco: Jossey-Bass, 1986.

Brown, J. W., and Brown, S. N. (eds.). *Educational Media Yearbook.* Littleton, Colo.: Libraries Unlimited, 1984.

Bruner, J. S. *Toward a Theory of Instruction.* Cambridge, Mass.: Belknap Press of Harvard University, 1966.

Brush, J., and Brush, D. "Private Television Communications (The Fourth Brush Report)." Cold Spring, N.Y.: HI Press, 1986.

Bunderson, V., and others. "Instructional Effectiveness of an Intelligent Videodisc in Biology." *Machine-Mediated Learning,* 1984, *1* (2), 175–215.

"CAEL Institutional Service Award, Empire State College." *CAEL News,* Jan./Feb. 1988, pp. 6-7.

Cafferata, P., and Tybout, A. M. (eds.). *Cognitive and Affective Responses to Advertising.* Lexington, Mass.: Lexington Books, 1989.

Canfield, A. A. *Canfield Learning Style Inventory Form S—A Manual.* Birmingham, Mich.: Canfield, 1983.

Carey, J., and Dozier, D. "Assessing Electronic Text for Higher Education: Evaluation Results from Laboratory and Field Tests." San Diego, Calif.: San Diego State University Press, 1985. (ED 258 721)

Carnegie Commission. *A Public Trust.* New York: Bantam, 1979.

Carnoy, M., and Levin, H. M. "Evaluation of Educational Mission: Some Issues." *Instructional Science,* 1975, *4,* 385-406.

Cervero, R., and Cunningham, P. "An Evaluation of the Effectiveness of Instructional Televison for GED Preparation." Paper presented at the Adult Education Research Conference, Minneapolis, Minn., Apr. 20-22, 1977.

Chacon-Duque, F. J. *A Multivariate Model for Evaluating Distance Higher Education.* College Park: Pennsylvania State University Press, 1987.

Chickering, A. W. *Education and Identity.* San Francisco: Jossey-Bass, 1969.

Chickering, A. W. *Commuting Versus Resident Students: Overcoming Educational Inequities of Living Off Campus.* San Francisco: Jossey-Bass, 1974.

Chickering, A. W. "The Double Bind of Field Dependence/Independence in Programming Alternatives for Educational Development." In S. Messick and Associates (eds.), *Individuality in Learning.* San Francisco: Jossey-Bass, 1976.

Childs, G. B. "Review of Research in Correspondence Study." In C. A. Wedemeyer (ed.), *The Brandenburg Memorial Essays.* Madison, Wis.: University of Wisconsin Press, 1966.

Childs, G. B. "Recent Research in Correspondence Instruction." In O. MacKenzie and E. L. Christenson (eds.), *The Changing World of Correspondence Study.* University Park: Pennsylvania State University Press, 1971.

Chu, G., and Schramm, W. "Learning from Television: What Does the Research Say?" Stanford, Calif.: Stanford University Press, 1975. (ED 014 900)

Clark, R. E. "Confounding in Educational Computing Research." *Journal of Educational Computing Research*, 1985a, *1* (2), 137–147.

Clark, R. E. "The Importance of Treatment Explication: A Reply to J. Kulik, C.-L. Kulik, and R. Bangert-Drowns." *Journal of Educational Computing Research*, 1985b, *1* (2), 137–148.

Clark, T. A., and Verduin, J. R., Jr., "Distance Education: Its Effectiveness and Potential Use in Lifelong Learning." *Lifelong Learning: An Omnibus of Practice and Research*, 1989, *12* (4), 24–26.

Coggins, C. C. "Preferred Learning Styles and Their Impact on Completion of External Degree Programs." *American Journal of Distance Education*, 1988, *2* (1), 25–37.

Cohen, J. *Statistical Power Analysis for the Behavioral Sciences.* (Rev. ed.) New York: Academic Press, 1977.

Coldeway, D. O. "Learner Characteristics and Success." In I. Mugridge and D. Kaufman (eds.), *Distance Education in Canada.* London: Croom Helm, 1986.

Combs, A. W. *Individual Behavior: A Perceptual Approach to Behavior.* (Rev. ed.) New York: Harper & Row, 1959.

"Computer Chronicles." Carbondale, Ill.: WSIU-TV, Southern Illinois University, 1990. Public Broadcasting Service informational program.

Conti, G. S., and Welborn, R. B. "The Interaction of Teaching Style and Learning Style on Traditional and Nontraditional Learners." *Proceedings of the 26th Adult Education Research Conference.* Laramie: University of Wyoming Press, 1987.

Coombs, N. "Using CMC to Overcome Physical Disabilities." In R. Mason and A. Kaye (eds.), *Mindweave.* Elmsford, N.Y.: Pergamon Press, 1989.

"The Correspondence University." In O. Mackenzie and E. Christensen (eds.), *The Changing World of Correspondence Study.* University Park: Pennsylvania State University Press, 1971. (First published in *Harper's Weekly*, Oct. 27, 1883, *27*, 676.)

Crane, V. "Student Uses of Annenberg/CPB Telecourses in the Fall

of 1984." Unpublished manuscript, Corporation for Public Broadcasting/Research Communications, 1985. (ED 264 822)

Cranton, P. *Planning Instruction for Adult Learners.* Toronto: Wall and Thompson, 1989.

Cross, K. P. *Adults as Learners: Increasing Participation and Facilitating Learning.* San Francisco: Jossey-Bass, 1981.

Curtis, F. A. "Demand and Supply Considerations for Evaluating a New Distance Education Program in Natural Resources Planning and Management in North America." *Environmentalist,* 1985, *5* (2), 129-135.

Curtis, F. A., and Bakshi, T. S., "Market Research for a Proposed Natural Resources Planning and Management Program by Home Study." *Distance Education,* 1984, *5* (1), 93-102.

Curzon, A. J. "Correspondence Education in England and in the Netherlands." *Comparative Education,* 1977, *13* (3), 249-261.

Cutright, P. J., and Edvalson, T. "Online Reference and Document Delivery Service Library Network." Salem: Oregon State Library, 1988. (ED 306 926)

Dahloff, U. *Reforming Higher Education and External Studies in Sweden and Australia.* Uppsala, Sweden: Acta Universitatis Upsaliensis/Almqvist & Wiksell International, 1977.

Dailey, J. M. "Forecasting Mass Communication." Paper presented at the annual meeting of the Central States Speech Association, Chicago, Apr. 12-14, 1984. (ED 255 853)

Daniel, J. S., Stroud, M. A., and Thompson, J. R. (eds.), *Learning at a Distance: A World Perspective.* Edmonton, Alberta: Athabasca University/International Council for Correspondence Education, 1982. (ED 222 635)

Danna, S. R. "Remember MPATI?" *E-ITV,* 1984, *16,* 96-99.

Deaton, R., and Clark, F. W. "Teleconferencing and Programmed Instruction in Rural Montana: A Case Example in Foster Care Education." *Human Services in the Rural Environment,* 1987, *10* (3), 14-17.

DeBloois, M. *Effectiveness of Interactive Videodisc Training: A Comprehensive Review.* Logan, Utah: Utah State University Press, 1983. (ED 278 370)

Denton, D. K. "A Study of the Motivational Orientation of Full-Time Military Students in a Technical Degree Program." Un-

published doctoral dissertation, Department of Educational Leadership, Southern Illinois University, 1982.

Dinsdale, W. A. "Inception and Development of Postal Tuition." *The Statist*, 1953, pp. 572-575.

Dodds, J. "The Credibility of Distance Education." Walton, England: Open University of the United Kingdom Press, 1981. (ED 222 150)

Donald, J. G. "Knowledge Structures: Methods for Exploring Course Content." *Journal of Higher Education*, 1983, 54 (1), 31-41.

Doyle, R. J. "The Results of Graduate External Degree Programs: Some Emerging Trends." *Alternative Higher Education*, 1979, *4* (1), 48.

Dunn, S. L. "The Changing University." *Futurist*, 1983, *17* (4), 55-60.

Ebner, D. G., and others. "Videodiscs Can Improve Instructional Effectiveness." *Instructional Innovator*, 1984, *29* (6), 26-29.

Edstrom, L. O. *Mass Education*. Stockholm: Almqvist and Wiksell, 1970.

Empire State College. *Empire State College. State University of New York 1986-1987 Bulletin*. Saratoga Springs, N.Y.: Empire State College, 1986.

Empire State College. *Empire State College. State University of New York 1987-1988 Bulletin*. Albany, N.Y.: Empire State College, 1987.

Encyclopaedia Britannica s.v. "correspondence education." Vol. 6, 1970, 544A-545A.

Engel, H. A. "WHA, Wisconsin's Pioneer." Unpublished manuscript, Wisconsin State Historical Society, 1936.

Escotet, M. A. *Tendencias de la educación superiór a distancia*. San Jose, Calif.: Editorial UNED, 1980.

Even, M. J. "Adapting Cognitive Style Theory in Practice." *Lifelong Learning*, 1982, *5* (5), 14-17, 27.

Eveslage, S. A. "Retooling for Tomorrow with Corporate Outreach Programs." *Educational Record*, 1986, *67* (2-3), 48-52.

Feasley, C. E. "Distance Education." In L. C. Deighton (ed.), *Encyclopedia of Education*. Vol. 3. New York: Macmillan, 1982.

Feasley, C. E. *Serving Learners at a Distance*. ASHE-ERIC Higher

Education Research Report, no. 5. Washington, D.C.: ASHE-ERIC, 1983.

Feasley, C. E., and others. *Independent Study Program Profiles 1987-88: Final Report.* Washington, D.C.: National University Continuing Education Association, 1989. (ED 304 502)

Federal Communications Commission. "Cable Television Report and Order." *Federal Register,* 1972, *37* (30), pt. 2, pp. 3252-3341.

Feldman, K. A., and Newcomb, T. M. *The Impact of College on Students.* San Francisco: Jossey-Bass, 1969.

Fields, C. M. "A Space-Age University Without Campus or Faculty Offers Its TV Courses Nationwide Via Satellite." *Chronicle of Higher Education,* 1987, *33* (44), 16-17.

Freedman, L. *Quality in Continuing Education: Principles, Practices, and Standards for Colleges and Universities.* San Francisco: Jossey-Bass, 1987.

Gage, N. (ed.). *Handbook of Research on Teaching.* Skokie, Ill.: Rand McNally, 1963.

Gallien, K. J. "For Adult Audiences Only." *Currents,* 1986, *12* (5), 16-20.

Garlinger, D. K., and Frank, B. M. "Teacher Student Cognitive Style and Academic Achievement: A Mini-Meta-Analysis." *Journal of Classroom Behavior,* 1988, *21* (2), 2-8.

Garrison, D. R. "Researching Dropout in Distance Education." *Distance Education,* 1987, *8* (1), 95-101.

Garrison, D. R. *Understanding Distance Education: A Framework for the Future.* Boston: Routledge & Kegan Paul, 1989.

Garrison, D. R., and Shale, D. "The Common Process as a Unifying Concept in Distance Education." Unpublished manuscript, University of Calgary, 1987.

George, M. D. "Assessing Program Quality." In R. F. Wilson (ed.), *Designing Academic Program Reviews.* New Directions for Higher Education, no. 37. San Francisco: Jossey-Bass, 1987.

Gilligan, C. "Women's Place in Man's Life Cycle." *Harvard Educational Review,* 1979, *49* (4), 431-446.

Ging, T. J., and Blackburn, R. T. "Individual and Contextual Correlates of Faculty Adoption of an Innovation." Paper presented at the annual conference of the American Educational Research Association, San Francisco, Apr. 1986.

Glatter, R., and Wedell, E. G. *Study by Correspondence.* London: Longmans, 1971.

Goodspeed, T. W. *William Rainey Harper.* Chicago: University of Chicago Press, 1928.

Gooler, D. "Evaluating Distance Education Programmes." *Canadian Journal of University Continuing Education,* 1979, *6* (1), 43–55.

Gooler, D. D. "Using Integrated Information Technologies for Out-Of-Class Learning." In J. A. Niemi and D. D. Gooler (eds.), *Technologies for Learning Outside the Classroom.* New Directions for Continuing Education, no. 34. San Francisco: Jossey-Bass, 1987.

Gorham, J. "Differences Between Teaching Adults and Teaching Pre-Adults: A Closer Look." *Adult Education Quarterly,* 1985, *35* (4), 194–209.

Grotelueschen, A. D. "Program Evaluation." In A. B. Knox and Associates (eds.), *Developing, Administering, and Evaluating Adult Education.* San Francisco: Jossey-Bass, 1980.

Guskey, T. R., and Gates, S. L. "A Synthesis of Research on Group Mastery Learning Programs." Paper presented at the annual meeting of the American Educational Research Association, Chicago, Mar. 31–Apr. 4, 1985. (ED 262 088)

Hailes, P. J. "An Analysis of Computer Conferences Supporting the Distance Learner." Paper presented at the 67th annual conference of the American Educational Research Association, San Francisco, Apr. 18, 1986. (ED 271 582)

Hales, R. L., and Felt, S. D. "Extending Graduate Level Education: A Management Model." Paper presented at the annual convention of the Association for Educational Communications and Technology, Las Vegas, Jan. 18–21, 1986. (ED 287 771)

Hall, J. W., and Hassenger, R. "Nontraditional Higher Education Programs." In H. E. Mitzel and others (eds.), *Encyclopedia of Educational Research.* (5th ed.) Vol. 3. New York: Free Press, 1982.

Hankin, J. N. "Where Were You Twelve Years Ago?" *Vital Speeches of the Day,* 1988, *54,* 300–306.

Harris, C. S. "The Information Age and the Growing Informal

Educational Environment." *Teacher Education and Practice,* 1986, *3* (1), 47–51.

Hart, A. M. *Calvert and Hillyer, 1897–1947.* Baltimore: Waverly Press, 1947.

Hartley, S. S. "Meta-Analysis of the Effects of Individually-Paced Instruction in Mathematics." Unpublished doctoral dissertation, University of Colorado, Boulder, 1978.

Hartnett, R. T., and others. *The British Open University in the United States.* Princeton, N.J.: Educational Technology Systems, 1974.

Heinich, R., Molenda, M., and Russell, J. D. *Instructional Media and the New Technologies of Instruction.* (2nd ed.) New York: Wiley, 1985.

Herrmann, A. "A Conceptual Framework for Understanding the Transitions in Perceptions of External Students." *Distance Education,* 1988, *9* (1), 5–26.

Hersey, P., and Blanchard, K. H. "So You Want to Know Your Leadership Style?" *Training and Development,* 1974, *28* (2), 22–27.

Hershfield, A. F. "Distance Education: The Promise and the Confusion!" Paper presented at the 12th Annual International Conference on Improving University Teaching, Heidelberg, Germany, July 15–18, 1986. (ED 278 186)

Holbrook, D. W. "Accreditation: A Workable Option." In J. S. Daniel and others, *Learning at a Distance: A World Perspective.* Edmonton, Canada: International Council on Correspondence Education, Athabasca University, 1982. (ED 222 635)

Holdampf, B. A. "Innovative Associate Degree Nursing Program—Remote Area." Unpublished manuscript, Department of Occupational Education and Technology, Texas Education Agency, 1983. (ED 248 402)

Holm, S. M. "Retention of Adult Learners in an Individualized Baccalaureate Degree Program." Unpublished manuscript, University of Minnesota, 1988. (ED 298 250)

Holmberg, B. *Status and Trends of Distance Education.* New York: Nichols, 1981.

Holmberg, B. *The Growth and Structure of Distance Education.* London: Croom Helm, 1986.

Holmberg, B. *Theory and Practice of Distance Education.* Boston: Routledge & Kegan Paul, 1989.

Houle, C. D. *The Inquiring Mind.* Madison, Wis.: University of Wisconsin Press, 1961.

Hugdahl, E. O. "Continuing Education for Private Piano Teachers: A Breakthrough for the '80s." Paper presented at the 2nd National Conference on Piano Pedagogy, Champaign, Ill., Oct. 24, 1980. (ED 198 811)

Hult, R. E. "The Effectiveness of University Television Instruction and Factors Influencing Student Attitudes." *College Student Journal,* 1980, *14,* 5-7.

Ice, J. Personal communication (letter), 1990.

Inglio, P. "Promoting Positive Learning Attitudes." Weipa, Australia: External Studies Unit, Brisbane College of Advanced Education, 1985. (ED 288 009)

International Correspondence Schools. Advertisement. *TV Guide,* Jan. 20-26, 1990.

Jacobs, R. L., and Gedeon, D. V. "The Social Behaviors of Field Dependent Students in a Personalized System of Instruction Course." *Interchange of Educational Policy,* 1982, *9* (2), 145-157.

Jellen, H. G., and Verduin, J. R., Jr. *Handbook for Differential Education of the Gifted: A Taxonomy of 32 Key Concepts.* Carbondale: Southern Illinois University Press, 1986.

Jellen, H. G., and Verduin, J. R., Jr. *Differentielle Erziehung Besonders Begabter: Ein Taxonomischer Ansatz* [Differential education of the highly gifted: a taxonomical assessment]. Frankfort, Germany: Deutsches Institut für Internationale Pedagogische Forschung, 1989.

Johnson, L. G. "Faculty Receptivity to an Innovation: A Study of Attitudes Toward External Degree Programs." *Journal of Higher Education,* 1984, *55* (4), 481-499.

Kasworm, C. E., and Anderson, C. A. "Perceptions of Decision Makers Concerning Microcomputers for Adult Learning." In D. G. Gueulette (ed.), *Microcomputers for Adult Learning: Potentials and Perils.* Chicago: Follett, 1982.

Kaunda, M. M. "Degree and Diploma Courses in Correspondence Education." In L. O. Edstrom, R. Erdos, and R. Prosser (eds.), *Mass Education.* Stockholm: Almqvist and Wiksell, 1970.

Kaye, A. "Distance Education: The State of the Art." *Prospects,* 1988, *18* (1), 43–54.

Kaye, A., and Harry, K. *Using the Media for Adult Basic Education.* London: Croom Helm, 1982.

Keegan, D. "On Defining Distance Education." *Distance Education,* 1980, *1* (1), 13–36.

Keegan, D. *The Foundations of Distance Education.* London: Croom Helm, 1986.

Keegan, D., and Rumble, G. "The DTUs: An Appraisal." In G. Rumble and K. Harry (eds.), *The Distance Teaching Universities.* London: Croom Helm, 1982.

Kember, D. A. "A Longitudinal-Process Model of Drop-Out from Distance Education." *Journal of Higher Education,* 1989, *60* (3), 278–290.

Kimmel, H. S., and Lucas, G. S. "Project GRADS." Harrisburg: Pennsylvania State Department of Education, 1984. (ED 254 676)

Kleinkauf, C., and Robinson, M. "Audio-Conferencing and Social Work Education in Alaska." *Human Services in the Rural Environment,* 1987, *10* (3), 29–31.

Knowles, M. S. *The Modern Practice of Adult Education.* (1st ed.) New York: Association Press, 1970.

Knowles, M. S. *The Modern Practice of Adult Education: Pedagogy vs. Andragogy.* (2nd ed.) Chicago: Association Press/Follett, 1980.

Knox, A. B. "Proficiency Theory of Adult Learning." *Contemporary Educational Psychology,* 1980, *5,* 378–404.

Knox, A. B. *Helping Adults Learn: A Guide to Planning, Implementing, and Conducting Programs.* San Francisco: Jossey-Bass, 1986.

Koenig, A. E., and Hill, R. B. *The Farther Vision: Educational Television Today.* Madison, Wis.: University of Wisconsin Press, 1967.

Kotler, P. *Marketing for Nonprofit Organizations.* (2nd ed.) Englewood Cliffs, N.J.: Prentice-Hall, 1982.

Krathwohl, D., Bloom, B. S., and Masia, B. B. *Taxonomy of Educational Goals. The Classification of Educational Goals, Handbook 2: Affective Domain.* New York: McKay, 1964.

Kuh, G. D. "The Case for Attendance." *Journal of College Admissions,* 1985, *107*, 3–8.

Kuh, G. D., Coomes, M. D., and Lundquist, I. A. "What Prospective Students Really Need to Know About Institutional Quality." *College and University,* 1984, *59*, 167–175.

Kulik, C.-L. C., and Kulik, J. A. "Effectiveness of Computer-Based Education in Colleges." Paper presented at the 69th annual meeting of the American Educational Research Association, Chicago, Mar. 31–Apr. 4, 1985. (ED 263 890)

Kulik, C.-L. C., and Kulik, J. A. "Mastery Testing and Student Learning: A Meta-Analysis." *Journal of Educational Technology Systems,* 1987, *15* (3), 325–345.

Kulik, C.-L. C., Kulik, J. A., and Schwalb, B. J. "The Effectiveness of Computer-Based Adult Education." Paper presented at the 69th annual meeting of the American Educational Research Association, Chicago, Mar. 31–Apr. 4, 1985. (ED 263 888)

Kulik, C.-L. C., Schwalb, B. J., and Kulik, J. A. "Programmed Instruction in Secondary Education: A Meta-Analysis of Evaluation Findings." *Journal of Educational Research,* 1982, *75* (3), 133–138.

Kulik, J. A. "Individualized Systems of Instruction." In H. E. Mitzel (ed.), *Encyclopedia of Education Research.* (5th ed.) Vol. 2. New York: Macmillan, 1983.

Kulik, J. A., Bangert, R. L., and Williams, G. W. "Effects of Computer-Based Teaching on Secondary School Students." *Journal of Educational Psychology,* 1983, *75* (1), 19–26.

Kulik, J. A., Cohen, P. A., and Ebeling, B. J. "Effectiveness of Programmed Instruction in Higher Education: A Meta-Analysis of Findings." *Educational Evaluation and Policy Analysis,* 1980, *2* (6), 51–64.

Kulik, J. A., Jaksa, P., and Kulik, C.-L. C. "Research on Component Features of Keller's Personalized System of Instruction." *Journal of Personalized System of Instruction, 3* (1), 2–14.

Kulik, J. A., Kulik, C.-L. C., and Bangert-Drowns, R. L. "The Importance of Outcome Studies: A Reply to Clark." *Educational Computing Systems,* 1985, *1* (4), 381–386.

Kulik, J. A., Kulik, C.-L. C., and Cohen, P. A. "Research on Audio-

Tutorial Instruction: A Meta-Analysis of Comparative Studies." *Research in Higher Education*, 1979, *11*, 321–341.

Kutscher, R. E. "Projections 2000: Overview and Implications." *Monthly Labor Review*, 1987, *110* (9), 3–9.

Lamy, T., and Henri, F. "Télé-Université: Ten Years of Distance Education in Quebec." *Programmed Learning and Educational Technology*, 1983, *20* (3), 197–201.

Laverty, J. R. "A Report on Some Continuing Education and Independent Study Programs in North America." Unpublished manuscript, Division of Independent Studies, Queensland University, Australia, 1984. (ED 283 969)

Lewis, L. H. "New Educational Technologies for the Future." In S. B. Merriam and P. M. Cunningham (eds.), *Handbook of Adult and Continuing Education*. San Francisco: Jossey-Bass, 1989.

Lewis, O. Personal communication (letter), 1990.

Lewis, R. J. *Meeting Learners' Needs Through Telecommunications*. Washington, D.C.: American Association for Higher Education, 1983.

Lewis, R. J. *Instructional Applications of Information Technologies: A Survey of Higher Education in the West*. Boulder, Colo.: Western Interstate Commission for Higher Education, 1985.

Lewis, R. J., and Wall, M. "Exploring Obstacles to Uses of Technology in Higher Education." Unpublished manuscript, Academy for Educational Development, 1988. (ED 304 073)

Lighty, W. H. "Correspondence Study Teaching." In O. MacKenzie, and E. C. Christensen (eds.), *The Changing World of Correspondence Study*. University Park: Pennsylvania State University Press, 1971. (Originally published in 1915.)

Lindeman, E. C. (title n.a.). In R. Gessner (ed.), *The Democratic Man: Selected Writings of Edward Lindeman*. Boston: Beacon Press, 1956. (Excerpt originally written by Lindeman in 1927.)

Lipsett, L., and Avakian, A. N. "Affective Development of Adult Students." *Alternative Higher Education*, 1979, *3* (4), 211–221.

Loewenthal, N. H., Blackwelder, J., and Broomall, J. K. "Correspondence Instruction and the Adult Student." In A. B. Knox (ed.), *Teaching Adults Effectively*. New Directions for Continuing Education, no. 6. San Francisco: Jossey-Bass, 1980.

Losty, B. P., and Gardiner, S. "Graduates of a Non-Traditional

Bachelor of Arts Degree Program: A Follow-Up." *Alternative Higher Education*, 1978, *2* (4), 266–274.

Ludlow, N. "Interview with Michael Lambert." *American Journal of Distance Education*, 1987, *1* (2), 67–71.

Lyness, A. L. "Performance and Norms of Time for Adult Learners Instructed in CPR by an Interactive Videodisc System." Paper presented at the 5th Annual Conference on Research in Nursing, San Francisco, Jan. 14–16, 1987. (ED 281 986)

Lysakowski, R. S., and Walberg, H. J. "Instructional Effects of Cues, Participation, and Corrective Feedback." *American Educational Research Journal*, 1982, *19* (4), 559–578.

Mace, J. "Mythology in the Making: Is the Open University Really Cost-Effective?" *Higher Education*, 1978, 7, 295–309.

McIntosh, N., and Rigg, M. "Employers and the Open University." Unpublished manuscript, Milton Keynes, England: Survey Research Department, Open University of the United Kingdom, 1979.

Macken, E. *Home-Based Education*. Washington, D.C.: U.S. Department of Health, Education, and Welfare, 1976.

Macken, E., Van den Heuval, R., Suppes, P., and Suppes, T. *Home-Based Education*. Stanford, Calif.: Stanford University Press, 1976.

Mackenzie, O., and Christensen, E. L. (eds.). *The Changing World of Correspondence Study*. University Park: Pennsylvania State University Press, 1971.

Maher, T. G. "Hands-On Verification of Mechanics Training." Pomona, Calif.: California State Polytechnic University Press, 1988. (ED 290 026)

Manburg, A. "Program Delivery in Distance Education—One Successful Strategy." Paper presented at the 2nd annual conference of the University Without Walls International Council, Toronto, June 11, 1983. (ED 235 884)

Mareth, P. "Television, Noncommercial." In B. S. Cayne (ed.), *Academic American Encyclopedia*. Vol. 19. Danbury, Conn.: Grolier 1986.

Mathieson, D. E. *Correspondence Study: A Summary Review of the Research and Development Literature*. Syracuse, N.Y.: Syracuse University Press, 1971. (ED 047 163)

Mays, M., and Lumsden, D. B. "NTU—A Technological University for the Technology-Based Society." *Tech Trends,* May/June 1988, pp. 18–22.

Medsker, L., and others. *Extending Opportunities for a College Degree.* Berkeley, Calif.: University of California Press, 1975.

Meinhold, R. W. "Determining the Educational Needs of AFL-CIO Union Members in Southeast Florida." Unpublished manuscript, Southeast Florida Educational Consortium, 1981.

Mellon, T. A. "More Effective ABE Instruction for Institutionalized Adult Alcoholics and Addicts Through the Cambridge [Kentucky] GED Video Series." Unpublished manuscript, Pennsylvania State Department of Education, 1983. (ED 245 078)

Merriam, S., and Mullins, L. "Havighurst's Developmental Tasks: A Study of Their Importance Relative to Income, Age, and Sex." *Adult Education Quarterly,* 1981, 31 (3), 123–141.

Middletown, T. "The Education Utility." *American Educator,* 1986, *10* (4), 18–25.

Miller, C. R. *Essential Guide to Interactive Videodisc Hardware Application.* Westport, Conn.: Meckler, 1987.

Moore, M. G. "Toward a Theory of Independent Learning and Teaching." *Journal of Higher Education,* 1973, *44* (9), 661–679.

Moore, M. G. "A Model of Independent Study." *Epistologidaktika,* 1977, *1,* 6–40.

Moore, M. G. "Independence and Autonomy." In R. D. Boyd and J. W. Apps (eds.), *Redefining the Discipline of Adult Education.* San Francisco: Jossey-Bass, 1980.

Moore, M. G. "Some Observations on Current Research in Distance Education." *Epistolodidaktika,* 1985, *1,* 35–66.

Moore, M. G. "Distance Learning in the United States: The Near Future." *Distance Education,* 1987a, 38–46.

Moore, M. G. "University Distance Education of Adults." *Tech-Trends,* Sept. 1987b, pp. 13–18.

Moore, M. G. "Recruiting and Retaining Adult Students in Distance Education." In P. S. Cookson (ed.), *Recruiting and Retaining Adult Students.* New Directions for Continuing Education, no. 41. San Francisco: Jossey-Bass, 1989.

Morrison, T. R. "Beyond Legitimacy." *International Journal of Lifelong Education,* 1989, *8* (1), 3–32.

Morstain, B. R., and Smart, J. C. "Reasons for Participation in Adult Education Courses: A Multivariate Analysis of Group Differences." *Adult Education*, 1974, *24*, 83–98.

Moss, G. D., and Brew, A. "The Contribution of the Open University to Innovation in Higher Education." *Higher Education*, 1981, *10*, 141–151.

Moulton, M. *National University Extension Association Conference, Madison, Wisconsin, 1915, Proceedings.* Washington, D.C., National University Extension Association, 1915.

Murgatroyd, S. "Student Learning Differences and the Role of Regional Support Services." *Institutional Research Review*, 1982, *1*, 81–100.

Murgatroyd, S., and Woudstra, A. "Issues in the Management of Distance Education." *American Journal of Distance Education*, 1989, *3* (2), 129–135.

National Center for Education Statistics. *Participation in Adult Education, May, 1984.* Washington, D.C.: U.S. Department of Education, 1986a. (ED 274 800)

National Center for Education Statistics. *Trends in Adult Education, 1969–1984.* Washington, D.C.: U.S. Department of Education, 1986b.

National Center for Education Statistics. *Digest of Education Statistics.* (24th ed.) Washington, D.C.: U.S. Department of Education, 1988a.

National Center for Education Statistics. *Projections of Education Statistics to 1997–98.* Washington, D.C.: U.S. Department of Education, 1988b.

National Home Study Council. *Predicting Distant Education to the Year 2000.* Washington, D.C.: National Home Study Council, 1982.

National Home Study Council. *1983 Home Study Survey.* Washington, D.C.: National Home Study Council, 1983 (ED 244 067)

New York Institute of Technology. *Catalog 1987/88 New York Institute of Technology.* Old Westbury: New York Institute of Technology, 1988.

New York State Education Department. *Recognition of Nontraditional Educational Experience.* Albany: Office for Policy Analysis, New York State Education Department, 1987. (ED 284 998)

Niemeyer, D. "Postsecondary Consortia and Distance Learning." In E. E. Miller and M. L. Mosley (eds.), *Educational Media and Technology Yearbook*. (11th ed.) Littleton, Colo.: Libraries Unlimited, 1985.

Niemiec, R., and Walberg, H. J. "Comparative Effects of Computer-Assisted Instruction: A Synthesis of Reviews." *Journal of Educational Computer Research*, 1987, *3* (1), 19–37.

Noffsinger, J. S. *Correspondence Schools, Lyceums, Chautauquas*. New York: Macmillan, 1926.

Nottingham Andragogy Group. "Towards a Developmental Theory of Andragogy." Unpublished manuscript, Department of Adult Education, University of Nottingham, England, 1983.

Nova University. *Nova University Center for Higher Education: Catalog 1985–86*. Fort Lauderdale, Fla.: Nova University, 1985.

Orlansky, S., and String, J. *Cost-Effectiveness of Computer-Based Education in Military Training*. IDA paper, p–1375. Arlington, Va.: Science, and Technical Divisions, Institute for Defense Analysis, 1979.

Paulet, R. "Counseling Distance Learners." *TechTrends*, Sept. 1987, pp. 26–28.

Peinovich, P. Personal communication (letter), 1990.

Peiper, W. J., Richardson, J. J., Harmon, K. R., and Keller, R. A. *Interactive Graphics Simulator*. Denver: Essex Corporation, 1984. (ED 247 495)

Perraton, H. *Alternative Routes to Formal Education*. Baltimore, Md.: Johns Hopkins University Press, 1982.

Perry, W. *The State of Distance Learning Worldwide*. Milton Keynes, England: Center for Distance Learning of the United Nations, 1984. (ED 254 201)

Peters, O. "New Perspectives in Correspondence Study in Europe." In O. MacKenzie and E. L. Christensen (eds.), *The Changing World of Correspondence Study*. University Park: Pennsylvania State University Press, 1968.

Peters, O. *Die Didaktische Struktur des Fernunterrichts*. [The didactic structure of distance teaching]. Weinheim and Basel: Beltz, 1973.

Peterson, D. A. *Facilitating Education for Older Learners*. San Francisco: Jossey-Bass, 1983.

Peterson, R. E., and Associates. *Lifelong Learning in America: An Overview of Current Practices, Available Resources, and Future Prospects.* San Francisco: Jossey-Bass, 1979.

Phillips, A. F., and Pease, P. S. "Computer Conferencing and Education: Complementary or Contradictory Concepts?" *American Journal of Distance Education,* 1987, *(2),* 44–52.

Phillips, D. L. "Videoconferencing at Penn State." *Technological Horizons in Education,* 1987, *14* (8), 52–54.

Phillips, G. M., and Santoro, G. M. "Teaching Group Discussions Via Computer-Mediated Communication." *Communication Education,* 1989, *38* (2), 151–161.

Pieotrowski, C. "Locus of Control, Field Dependence–Independence as Factors in Learning and Memory." Unpublished manuscript, University of West Florida, 1982. (ED 247 495)

Pinches, C. A. "The Technological Side of Teaching by Telephone." In L. A. Parker and B. Ricconini (eds.), *The Status of the Telephone in Education.* Madison, Wis.: University of Wisconsin-Extension, 1975.

Pratt, D. D. "Andragogy as a Relational Construct." *Adult Education Quarterly,* 1988, *38* (3), 160–181.

Public Broadcasting Service. *PBS Adult Learning Satellite Service.* Alexandria, Va.: Public Broadcasting Service, 1989.

Purdy, L. "Telecourse Students: How Well Do They Learn?" Unpublished manuscript, University of California, San Diego, 1978. (ED 154 851)

Rachal, J. R. "The Computer in the ABE and GED Classroom: A Review of the Literature." *Adult Education Quarterly,* 1984, *35* (4), 86–95.

Regents College Degrees 1986–1987. Albany, N.Y.: Regents College Degrees, University of the State of New York, 1986.

Regents External Degrees (and) College Proficiency Examinations. Albany, N.Y.: New York State Education Department, Regents External Degree Programs, 1982.

Reid, F.G.M., and Champness, B. G. "Wisconsin Educational Telephone Network." *British Journal of Educational Technology,* 1983, *16* (2), 85–101.

Richards, A. J. "After the Associate Degree: Distance Education via Computer Conferencing." In Sullins, W. R., Hoerner, J. L., and

Whisnant, W. T. (eds.), *Increasing Rural Adults' Participation in Collegial Programs.* Blacksburg: Virginia Polytechnic Institute and State University, Department of Education, 1987.

Rigas, A. L. *Video Outreach Graduate Program.* Battle Creek, Mich.: Kellogg Foundation, 1982. (ED 221 113)

Rio Salada Community College. "GED Preparation Via the Sundial Network." Unpublished manuscript, Arizona State Department of Education, 1985. (ED 260 283)

Roberts, L. "The Electronic Seminar: Distance Education by Computer Conferencing." Paper presented at the 5th Annual Conference on Non-Traditional and Interdisciplinary Programs, Fairfax, Va., May 1987. (ED 291 358)

Robins, K., and Hepworth, M. "Electronic Spaces: New Technologies and the Futures of Cities." *Futures,* 1988, *21* (2), 155-175.

Roeder, S. D. "Evaluation of Teleconferencing for Continuing Pharmaceutical Education." *American Journal of Pharmaceutical Education,* 1983, *47* (2), 116-119.

Rowntree, D. "Two Styles of Communication and Their Implications for Learning." In J. Baggaly, H. Jamieson, and H. Marchant (eds.), *Aspects of Educational Technology.* Vol. 7: *Communication and Learning.* London: Pitman, 1975.

Rumble, G. *The Planning and Management of Distance Education.* London: Croom Helm, 1986.

Rumble, G., and Harry, K. *The Distance Teaching Universities.* New York: St. Martin's Press, 1982.

Saba, F. "Integrated Telecommunications Systems and Instructional Communication." In M. G. Moore and G. C. Clark (eds.), *Reading in the Principles of Distance Education.* University Park: Pennsylvania State University Press, 1989.

Sachs, L. A., and others. "A Comparison of Medical Students' Performances in Independent Student and Traditional Programs." *Journal of Medical Education,* 1985, *60* (8), 602-609.

Schrader, M. A. "An Analysis of the Students Enrolled in the Correspondence Study Course, 'Medical Terminology.'" Unpublished manuscript, Nova University, 1987. (ED 281 595)

Scott, J. A. "Integration of Non-Traditional Programs into the Mainstream of Academic Institutions." *Innovative Higher Education,* 1985, *9,* 81-91.

Scriven, M. *The Logic of Evaluation*. Inverness, Calif.: Edgepress, 1980.

Sculley, J. "The Relationship Between Business and Higher Education: A Perspective on the Twenty-First Century." *EDUCOM Bulletin*, 1988, *23* (1), 20–25.

Sebermer, J. "Attitude Formation and Attitude Change in Nursing Education." *Educational Communication and Technology Journal*, 1988, *36* (4), 187–210.

Sewart, D. "Distance Teaching: A Contradiction in Terms?" *Teaching at a Distance*, 1981, *19*, 8–18.

Shale, D. "A Study of Course Completion Rates." *Institutional Studies Report*, Vol. 6. Edmonton, Canada: Athabasca University, 1984, p. 27.

Sharp, L. M., and Sosdian, C. P. "External Degrees: How Well Do They Serve Their Holders?" *Journal of Higher Education*, 1979, *50* (5), 615–649.

Silvestri, G. T., and Lukasiewicz, L. M. "Projections 2000: A Look at Occupational Employment Trends to the Year 2000." *Monthly Labor Review*, 1987, *110* (9), 46–63.

Simerly, R. G. "Integrating Marketing into Strategic Planning." In R. G. Simerly and Associates, *Handbook of Marketing for Continuing Education*. San Francisco: Jossey-Bass, 1989.

Simonson, M. R. "Media and Persuasive Messages." *Instructional Innovator*, 1984, *29* (2), 23–24.

Simpson, E. J. "The Classification of Educational Objectives in the Psychomotor Domain." In F. Urbach (ed.), *The Psychomotor Domain*. Washington, D.C.: Gryphon House, 1972.

Skinner, B. F. *The Technology of Teaching*, East Norwalk, Conn.: Appleton-Century-Crofts, 1968.

Slatta, R. W. "Scholarnet: The Beginning of a World Academic Community." *Futurist*, 1987, *21* (2), 17–19.

Slotnick, R. S. "Original Courseware for Introductory Psychology: Implementation and Evaluation." *Collegiate Microcomputer*, 1988, *6* (4), 349–360.

Smith, K. C. *External Studies of New England: A Silver Jubilee Review*. Armidale, Australia: University of New England, 1975.

Smith, R. C. "Developing Distance Learning Systems. The UKOU

Experiment: Some Lessons." In G. R. Reddy (ed.), *Open University: The Ivory Towers Thrown Open*. New Delhi: Sterling, 1988.

Smith, R. M. *Learning How to Learn—Applied Theory for Adults*. Chicago: Follett, 1982.

Smith, S. G., Jones, L. L., and Waugh, M. L. "Production and Evaluation of Interactive Lessons in Laboratory Instruction." *Journal of Computer-Based Instruction*, 1986, *13* (4), 117–121, 1987.

Sosdian, C. P., and Sharp, L. M. "The External Degree as a Credential." Washington D.C.: National Institute of Education, 1978.

Sparkes, J. J. "The Problem of Creating a Discipline of Distance Education." *Distance Education*, 1983, *4* (2), 179–186.

Sparkes, J. J. "On the Design of Effective Distance Teaching Courses." Paper presented at the 13th annual conference of the International Council on Distance Education, Melbourne, Australia, Aug. 1985. (ED 275 285)

Spear, G. E., and Mocker, D. W. "The Organizing Circumstance: Environmental Determinants in Self-Directed Learning." *Adult Education Quarterly*, 1981, *35* (1), 1–10.

Sroufe, G. E. *The National Ed.D. Program for Educational Leaders*. Fort Lauderdale, Fla.: Nova University Press, 1982. (ED 226 436)

Stanley-Muchow, J. L., and Poe, D. Y. "Teleconferencing: An Avenue for College Coursework in Nursing Home Settings." *International Journal of Aging and Human Development*, 1988, *26* (3), 201–210.

Stern, C. "Teaching the Distance Learner." *Programmed Language and Educational Technology*, 1987, *23* (4), 358–364.

Stetson, K. W. *University Without Walls: A Comparison of Student, Faculty, and Staff Perceptions at Selected Institutions*. Chicago: Universitas, 1979.

Stevens, S. M. "Surrogate Laboratory Experiments." Unpublished doctoral dissertation, University of Nebraska, Lincoln, 1984.

Subramanian, S. "Education by Correspondence in Sweden, Russia, and Poland: Report of a Visit Made by S. Subramanian." In R. Glatter and E. G. Wedell, *Study by Correspondence*. London: Longmans, 1971.

Sullins, W. R., and others. "Increasing Rural Adults' Participation in Collegial Programs." Unpublished manuscript, Virginia Polytechnic Institute and State University, 1987.

Sullivan, E. *External Degree Programs*. New York: American Council on Education, 1984.

Takemoto, P. A. "Exploring the Educational Potential of Audio." In J. A. Niemi and D. D. Gooler (eds.), *Technologies for Learning Outside the Classroom*. New Directions for Continuing Education, no. 34. San Francisco: Jossey-Bass, 1987.

Taylor, E., and Kaye, T. "Andragogy by Design." *Programmed Learning and Educational Technology*, 1986, *23* (1), 62–69.

Taylor, J. C., and others. "Student Persistence in Distance Education: A Cross-Cultural Multi-Institutional Perspective." *Distance Education*, 1986, *7* (1), 68–91.

Thomas A. Edison State College. *Thomas A. Edison State College: 1989–91 Catalog*. Trenton, N.J.: Thomas A. Edison State College, 1989.

Thompson, G., and Knox, A. B. "Designing for Diversity: Are Field-Dependent Learners Less Suited to Distance Education Programs of Instruction?" *Contemporary Educational Psychology*, 1987, *12* (1), 17–29.

Thornton, R., and Mitchell, I. *Counseling the Distance Learner: A Survey of Trends and Literature*. Adelaide, Australia: Adelaide University Press, 1978.

Thorpe, M. *Evaluating Open and Distance Learning*. London: Longmans, 1988.

Tomlinson, R. "Local Media Resource Centers." In A. W. Bates (ed.), *The Role of Technology in Distance Education*. London: Croom Helm, 1984.

Turner, J. A. "Private Company to Offer 170 Courses by Computer in 'Electronic University.'" *Chronicle of Higher Education*, 1983, *27* (4), 18.

"USAFI: The Worldwide Campus." *USAF Instructor's Journal, 4* (2), 1966.

U.S. Bureau of the Census. *Statistical Abstracts of the United States*. (109th ed.) Washington, D.C.: U.S. Bureau of the Census, U.S. Department of Commerce, 1989.

U.S. Department of Defense. *Education Programs for the Depart-*

ment of Defense. Pensacola, Fla.: Defense Activity for Educational Delivery Systems, U.S. Department of Defense, 1987.

U.S. Department of Education. *Digest of Education Statistics.* Washington, D.C.: U.S. Department of Education, 1989.

U.S. Department of the Navy. *Educational Opportunities* (16-pp. pamphlet). Washington, D.C.: U.S. Department of the Navy, 1985.

U.S. Navy. *Educational Opportunities.* No. D201.2: ED8. Washington, D.C.: U.S. Government Printing Office, 1985.

Valiga, M. J. "Structuring the Perceived Outcomes of Higher Education." Paper presented at the 22nd annual forum of the Association for Institutional Research, Denver, May 16-19, 1982. (ED 220 024)

Valore, L. "TEL TEST: Immediate Feedback on Correspondence Exams." In L. Campbell-Thrane (ed.), *Correspondence Education Moves to the Year 2000.* Columbus, Ohio: National Center for Research in Vocational Education, 1984.

Van Enckevort, G., Harry, K., Morin, P., and Schutze, H. G. (eds.). *Distance Higher Education and the Adult Learner.* Herrien, the Netherlands: Dutch Open University Press, 1987.

Verduin, J. R., Jr. *Conceptual Models in Teacher Education.* Washington, D.C.: AACTE, 1967a.

Verduin, J. R., Jr. *Cooperative Curriculum Improvement.* Englewood Cliffs, N.J.: Prentice-Hall, 1967b.

Verduin, J. R., Jr. *Curriculum Building for Adult Learning.* Carbondale, Ill.: Southern Illinois University Press, 1980.

Verduin, J. R., Jr., and Heinz, C. *Pre-student Teaching Laboratory Experiences.* Dubuque, Iowa: Kendall-Hunt, 1970.

Verduin, J. R., Jr., Miller, H. G., and Greer, C. E. *Adults Teaching Adults: Principles and Strategies.* Austin, Tex.: Learning Concepts, 1977.

Verduin, J. R., Jr., Miller, H. G., and Greer, C. E. *The Lifelong Learning Experience: An Introduction.* Springfield, Ill.: Thomas, 1986.

Verduin, J. R., Jr., and others. *Project Follow Through.* Springfield, Ill.: OSPI, 1971.

Wagner, L. "The Economics of the Open University Revisited." *Higher Education,* 1977, *6* (3), 369-381.

Wakatama, M. A. *Correspondence Education in Central Africa.* New York: University Press of America, 1983.

Walters, L., and Sieben, G. "Cognitive Style and Learning Science in Elementary Schools." *Science Education,* 1982, *58* (1), 65–74.

Watkins, B. T. "Enrollment Up in Universities' Home Studies Courses." *Chronicle of Higher Education,* 1984, *23,* 1–4.

Watson, J. A., Calvert, S. L., and Collins, R. "An Information Technologies Workstation for Schools and Homes: Proximate, Border Zone, and Distant Educational Possibilities for the Future." *Educational Technologies,* 1987, *27* (11), 14–19.

Wedemeyer, C. A. *Learning at the Back Door.* Madison, Wis.: University of Wisconsin Press, 1983.

Weidman, J. C. "Undergraduate Socialization." Paper presented at the annual meeting of the Association for the Student of Higher Education, Baltimore, Md., Nov. 21–24, 1987. (ED 292 392)

Weisner, P. "Some Observations on Telecourse Resource and Practice." *Adult Education Quarterly,* 1983, *33* (4), 215–221.

Weisner, P. "Utilizing Television." In J. A. Niemi and D. D. Gooler (eds.), *Technologies for Learning Outside the Classroom.* New Directions for Continuing Education, no. 34. San Francisco: Jossey-Bass, 1987.

Wertheim, J. B. "The Medium Is . . .: Nontraditional Approaches to Counseling Adult Learners." In F. R. DiSilvestro (ed.), *Advising and Counseling Adult Learners.* New Directions for Continuing Education, no. 10. San Francisco: Jossey-Bass, 1981.

West, D. C. "Providing Quality Education for the 1980s." *Liberal Education,* 1984, *70* (2), 153–157.

Whitney, D. R., and Malizio, A. G. *Guide to Educational Credit by Examination.* (2nd ed.) New York: American Council on Education/Macmillan, 1987.

Whittington, N. "Is Instructional Television Educationally Effective? A Research Review." *American Journal of Distance Education,* 1987, *1* (1), 47–57.

Willen, B. *Distance Education at Swedish Universities.* Stockholm: Almqvist and Wiksell, 1981.

Willett, J. B., Yamashita, J. M., and Anderson, R. D. "A Meta-Analysis of Instructional Systems Applied in Science Teaching." *Journal of Research in Science Teaching,* 1983, *20* (5), 405–417.

Witkins, H. A., Moore, C. A., Goodenough, D. R., and Cox, P. W. "Educational Implications of Cognitive Styles." *Review of Educational Research,* 1977, *47* (1), 1–64.

Woodley, A., and Parlett, M. "Student Dropout." *Teaching at a Distance,* 1983, *24,* 3–23.

Woolfe, R., Murgatroyd, S., and Rhys, S. *Guidance and Counseling in Adult and Continuing Education.* Milton Keynes, England: Open University of the United Kingdom Press, 1987.

Worth, V. "Empire State College/State University of New York Center for Distance Learning. A Case Study." Unpublished manuscript, Open University of the United Kingdom, 1982. (ED 235 772)

Young, K. E. "Correspondence Education: From the Back of the Bus to the Driver's Seat." In L. Campbell-Thrane (ed.), *Correspondence Education Moves to the Year 2000.* Columbus, Ohio: National Center for Research in Vocational Education, 1984.

Yule, R. M. "The Problem of Pacing a Student Learning at Home." *Programmed Learning and Educational Technology,* 1983, *22* (1), 315.

Zigerell, J. *Distance Education: An Information Age Approach to Adult Education.* Columbus, Ohio: ERIC Clearinghouse on Adult, Career, and Vocational Education, 1984.

Name Index

Subject Index

A

Administration of distance education: communication in, 179–183; consortia, 175–179; and counseling learners, 177–179; mixed-mode, 174–175; organizational aspects of, 166–173; and organizational philosophy, 171–173; sole responsibility model, 173–174

Adult education: adult basic education (ABE), 6, 75; career education, 6–7; forms of, 5–8; general equivalency degree (GED), 69, 75; leisure and enrichment education, 7–8

Adult learners: characteristics of, 21–23, 28–29; distance students, 23–24; entering behavior of, assessment of, 156–158; learning styles, 29–31; motivation of, 24–28; proficiencies of, 25

Adult learning; assessing outcomes, 88–103; learning behavior, 147–155; proficiency, 25, 147; styles of, 29–31; theories of, 134–136

Affective domain, 25, 150–152

Affective skills, 88, 150–152; development in distance education, 99–101; evaluation of, 154–155

American College Testing/Proficiency Examination Program (ACT/PEP), 36

American Open University, New York Institute of Technology, 77

Andragogy, 131–136; differences between adults and children, 28–29, 133–134; and teaching styles, 131–132

Annenberg/CPB Foundation, 23–24, 27, 60, 116

Athabasca University, 55–56, 111

Audiocassettes: advantages and disadvantages of, 60–61; in counseling, 178; uses of, 59–60, 84

B

Board of Governors of State Colleges and Universities, 113

Brigham Young University, 48, 50–51

British Broadcasting Company (BBC), 70, 113

Bureau of Labor Statistics, United States, 197-198

C

Calvert School, 17

Carnegie Commission, 68

Centres de Tele-Enseignement Universitaire (CTU), 235

Characteristics of Adults as Learners (CAL), 28

Chautauqua movement, 16–17

Chicago TV College, 92